SHAKESPEARE'S FAVORITE NOVEL

A Study of The Golden Asse As Prime Source

J.J.M. Tobin

UNIVERSITY PRESS OF AMERICA

LANHAM • NEW YORK • LONDON

PR
2955
.A68
T6
1984

Copyright © 1984 by

University Press of America,™ Inc.

4720 Boston Way
Lanham, MD 20706

3 Henrietta Street
London WC2E 8LU England

All rights reserved
Printed in the United States of America

Library of Congress Cataloging in Publication Data

Tobin, J. J. M.
  Shakespeare's favorite novel.

  Includes index.
  1. Shakespeare, William, 1564-1616—Sources.
  2. Apuleius. Metamorphoses. I. Title.
  PR2955.A68T6 1984   822.3'3   84-5135
  ISBN 0-8191-3896-7 (alk. paper)
  ISBN 0-8191-3897-5 (pbk. : alk. paper)

All University Press of America books are produced on acid-free
paper which exceeds the minimum standards set by the National
Historical Publications and Records Commission.

TO ROSEMARY

Acknowledgements

Parts of this book have appeared in the following journals: <u>Archiv für das Studium der neueren Sprachen und Literaturen</u>, <u>Cahiers élisabéthains</u>, <u>The Classical Bulletin</u>, <u>English Studies</u>, <u>Essays in Criticism</u>, <u>Hamlet Studies</u>, <u>Notes and Queries</u>, <u>Renaissance and Renascences in Western Literature</u>, <u>Shakespeare Survey</u> and <u>Studia Neophilologica</u>. I am grateful to the editors for permission to use this material.

Extracts from D.T. Starnes' article are reprinted by permission of the Modern Language Association of America from "Shakespeare and Apuleius," <u>PMLA</u>, 60(1945), 1021-1050. The extract from John Dover Wilson's <u>Shakespeare's Happy Comedies</u> is reprinted by permission of Northwestern University Press.

I wish to thank the Faculty Development Committee of the College of Liberal Arts at the University of Massachusetts-Boston for funds to defray the cost of typing.

TABLE OF CONTENTS

Acknowledgements		v
Preface		ix
Introduction		xi
Chapter One:	THE EARLY PLAYS AND <u>VENUS AND ADONIS</u>	1
Chapter Two:	ROMANTIC PLAYS OF THE MID-1590's AND SONNETS	25
Chapter Three:	THE FALSTAFF PLAYS -- AND DOGBERRY	51
Chapter Four:	THE GREAT TRAGEDIES (1)	71
Chapter Five:	THE PROBLEM PLAYS	97
Chapter Six:	THE GREAT TRAGEDIES (2)	117
Chapter Seven:	THE ROMANCES	141
Conclusion		161
Appendix A:	Chapter Headings of <u>The Golden Asse</u>	167
Appendix B:	<u>Othello</u> and the <u>Apologia</u> of Apuleius	173
Index of characters (Shakespearean)		183
Index of characters (Apuleian)		185
Index of names		187

Preface

A number of people are responsible for encouraging me in the belief that this introduction to Apuleius and Shakespeare is of value.

First and foremost is my wife Rosemary Barton Tobin whose learning, judgment, and cheerful and cheering patience have been my salvation fully as much as were those other special roses without which Lucius would have been forever lost in asininity.

I am grateful to the late Geoffrey Bullough with whom many years ago I had the great good fortune to study as a Fulbright scholar, especially for his critical encouragement and his view that the age of source study had not ended with his magnum opus. I owe thanks to the late J.C. Maxwell for publishing the first of my Apuleian observations and for his insistence that I "get it right." Kenneth Muir generously answered queries; Harold Jenkins has been particularly kind, even when flatly disagreeing; and Stephen Greenblatt very helpfully told me of Harsnett's knowledge of Apuleius.

I owe a special debt of gratitude to Richard S. Tyrell for his very many acts of personal kindness and professional support, and to my colleague V.F. Petronella for both his friendship and the force of his scholarly example. John L. Mahoney, teacher and friend, took time from his own work to read the manuscript and to offer encouragement. I wish also to acknowledge the aid of R.A. Greene who patiently distinguished the just from the merely ingenious. My admirable father-in-law John E. Barton is responsible for my first reading Apuleius and for much else otherwise impossible without him.

My students, quite captivated by the tale of Cupid and Psyche, have been quick to see patterns of Apuleian material in the canon and been remarkably wise in their discussions of the blindness of true love. I am particularly grateful to them and to the three scholars who have contributed most to this modest work: P.A. Duhamel, first and best of teachers, John Velz, Shakespearean keeper of the classical flame, and Gwynne Evans, gifted editor and the archetype of critical kindness.

None is responsible for any errors which I may have committed, nor is Ms. V.R. Macy, to whom I am grateful for her skill and care in both deciphering and typing.

J.J.M Tobin
University of Massachusetts/Boston

Belmont, Massachusetts
February 2, 1984

x

INTRODUCTION

Mention of Apuleius today in the context of Shakespearean studies is likely to elicit among knowledgeable students a discerning nod towards A Midsummer Night's Dream and the assification of Bottom, and not very much more. Even the best one volume study of Shakespeare's sources, Kenneth Muir's The Sources of Shakespeare's Plays (1977),[1] has but a single mention of Apuleius, and Geoffrey Bullough's magisterial eight volume Narrative and Dramatic Sources (1957-75)[2] has only two citations. However, Apuleius was in fact a source of quite considerable importance to Shakespeare, and it is the purpose of this study to demonstrate the prevalence of Apuleian elements throughout the canon and to indicate something of the significance such elements have for our increased understanding of aspects of Shakespeare's plots, characters, themes, and diction.

It is not that hitherto we have had a complete conspiracy of silence on the issue of Apuleius and Shakespeare, for the more recent Arden editions[3] show an appreciation of Shakespeare's use of the Apuleian Metamorphoses in Adlington's 1566 version, The Golden Asse, and John Velz in his very valuable Shakespeare and the Classical Tradition (1968)[4] discriminates amongst the arguments, chiefly, but not exclusively over Apuleian presence or absence in A Midsummer Night's Dream, made by English, German and American scholars. Yet a combination of the varying degrees of cogency in these partial briefs and the natural time-lag in such matters before general acceptance by the most orthodox and rightly conservative authorities has suppressed the truth of Apuleius' importance to Shakespeare, an importance, I suggest, scarcely surpassed by Holinshed, Ovid, and Plutarch.

To begin with it is important to remind ourselves of just who and what Apuleius was both in actuality and in the eyes of Shakespeare and his contemporaries. In brief, Apuleius was a rhetorician and neo-Platonic philosopher of the second century A.D. who wrote among other works the declamation De Deo Socratis (on the daimon of Socrates) and the Apologia (a defense of himself against the charge of witchcraft), the excerpts from a declamation called the Florida, and the 'novel,' Metamorphoses, known in English as The Golden Asse, involving the varied adventures of Lucius, a man transformed into a donkey as the result of excessive curiosity, and the work for which Apuleius was chiefly known in Shakespeare's day and is in ours.

Although Apuleius' baroque Latin excludes him from syllabi of accepted Latin authors, he has in fact never been far from the attention of scholars, critics, and co-opting creative writers. While there are signs that both Lactantius and Ausonius knew Apuleius well,[5] the medieval tradition of which Shakespeare may have had some dim awareness began with St. Augustine, a "writer of immense prestige in Shakespeare's time and (whose) works were readily available in both Latin and English."[6] Augustine in both the City of God and in his letters,[7] worries over the possibility that his fellow North African had indeed been transformed into an ass and expostulates against the practice of considering Apuleius as a greater wonder-worker than Christ. Martianus Capella, yet another North African, in his enormously influential encyclopedia of the fifth century borrowed for his marriage of Philologia and Mercury from the story of Cupid and Psyche, which is the central episode (Bks. IV-VI) of the eleven book Metamorphoses, and in the next century Fulgentius Planciades, the mythographer, first allegorized the story of Cupid and Psyche as a tale of the soul and heavenly desire.[8] Among later medieval works both the Historia regum Britanniae of Geoffrey of Monmouth (a writer known to Shakespeare on evidence from King Lear)[9] and Huon de Bordeaux (a source for Oberon in A Midsummer Night's Dream)[10] show signs of Apuleian influence. However, most interesting to students of Shakespeare who know of his use of Boccaccio in All's Well That Ends Well and Cymbeline is Boccaccio's enthusiasm for Apuleius, an enthusiasm shown not only in his copying the Metamorphoses in his own hand, or telling the story of Cupid and Psyche with allegorization in the Genealogy of the Gods, but his retelling of three Apuleian adventures in the Decameron, Day five, story ten, Day seven, story two, and Day eight, story eight. In addition, Shakespeare's greatest English predecessor, Chaucer, whose works we know that he read most carefully,[11] is now increasingly thought to have known The Golden Ass as part of the Menippean satiric tradition he himself belonged to and as an analogue to his Canterbury Tales "which exhibits the same diverse collocations of styles and stories."[12]

    Whatever Shakespeare's implicit awareness of the importance of Apuleius in the Middle Ages, he had in his own time quite explicit references to Apuleius and creative incorporations of Apuleian material, for the Renaissance in theory and practice found value in the style and matter of the author of the Metamorphoses, the Apologia, and the Florida. The Christian Humanists of the sixteenth century, such as Erasmus and Vives urged the study of Apuleius for content as well as style[13] and in the case of Erasmus and his friend Sir Thomas More, enthusiasts of the Lucianic tradition of comic irony to which Apuleius belongs,[14] elements of Apuleian diction and/or allusions to Apuleian episodes recur in their works, including Utopia, De Tristitia Christi, De Copia, etc.[15] Writers of the English Renaissance may thus have learned of Apuleius in their grammar school studies, but from 1566 onwards they could have read the Metamorphoses in William Adlington's translation, The Golden Asse, a work which went through five editions by the end of 1600. Almost every one of the major English writers of the period, dramatic and non-dramatic, made use of The Golden Asse, sometimes along with the Latin original.

In An Apology for Poetry Sir Philip Sidney cites Apuleius with appropriate neo-classical discrimination between what is legitimate in pure tragic drama, as opposed to what is proper for fictional narrative:

> But besides these gross absurdities, how all their plays be neither right tragedies, nor right comedies, mingling kings and clowns, not because the matter so carrieth it, but thrust in the clown by head and shoulders to play a part in magestical matters with neither decency nor discretion, so as neither the admiration and commiseration, nor the right sportfulness, is by their mongrel tragi-comedy obtained, I know Apuleius did somewhat so, but that is a thing recounted with space oftime, not represented in one moment, . . .[16]

Sidney in the Arcadia would incorporate from The Golden Asse the names Aristomenes and Charite, a direct allusion to Psyche, the theme of 'love's transforming power,'[17] and in the Countess of Pembroke's Arcadia the tragi-comic plot device of a seeming poisoning.[18] This last element of poison-love-death-like trance derives from the episode in Book X of The Golden Asse in which a passionate step-mother intends a poisoning but is instead provided with a sleeping-draught. What Sidney found for Gynecia's plot would prove just as valuable for Elizabethan and Jacobean dramatists, including not only writers like Dekker, but Shakespeare himself (as we shall see below) who were without Sydney's scruples about the need to avoid on the stage too gross an appearance of improbability. That the torment of Gynecia,

Phèdre-like in its intensity, is among the most memorable aspects of the Arcadia, and that the Arcadia itself is the most significant piece of creative prose in the Elizabethan period suggests something not only of the availability but the potency of Apuleius' The Golden Asse as source material.

As in prose so in poetry, for Spenser in The Faerie Queene repeated Sidney's tactic of Apuleian borrowing, and if anything increased the incorporating of materials from The Golden Asse. Even as he was working on the epic Spenser made use of The Golden Asse in his minor poem, Muiopotmos, or The Fate of the Butterflie (1591), a 'mock-heroic jeu d'esprit'[19] to some, to others a didactic work on the self-destructive nature of human happiness. Indeed, considering the use of the myth of Cupid and Psyche in the poem, a myth which we know and Spenser knew can be read as 'an allegory of the rational soul bound in marriage to Divine love but disturbed in its Marital duties by the lower levels of the mind,'[20] we can read the poem on the more sober level of the traditional war between reason and appetite.

Spenser's positive gift for embodying philosophic concepts in verse without quite completely defining his terms led him to make considerable use of episodes of The Golden Asse in The Faerie Queene. In fact three of the most crucial scenes of the poem are fundamentally Apuleian, the garden of Adonis (III.vi), and Isis Church (V.ii), and, even, The Cave of Mammon (II.vii). The explicit introduction of Cupid and Psyche into comparison with Adonis and Venus is interpreted as the stage in generation beyond that produced by the union of form and matter for it is "the creation of the soul through the action of Love."[21] The rearing of Amoret by Psyche along with her infant daughter Pleasure is a guarantee that Amoret will attain the height of "goodly womanhead," even as her otherwise reared sister, Belphoebe, will reach the perfection of "maidenhead."

When in Book V Britomart visits Isis Church Spenser was recalling among much material derived from Plutarch and Diodorus the dominant role of Isis in The Golden Asse and the vision granted to Lucius (Book XI) but even more importantly he based the dream of Britomart and the impregnating serpent (amphibian) lover upon the experience of Psyche whose initially invisible husband she thought to be a monstrous serpent. That the crocodile in Britomart's dream should represent her true love even as Osiris is the true love of Isis is in keeping with the ultimately sacramentalized marriage of Cupid and Psyche, a Grecian pair of immortal lovers who are an elegantly refracted image of Osiris and Isis.

Within the text itself no episode continues to cause such vigorous scholarly-critical debate as does the Cave of Mammon (II.vii). The chief differing interpretations of the temptation undergone by Guyon suggest that it involves lust, pride and curiosity, or avarice, or gluttony, vainglory and avarice. These divergent interpretations are not always mutually exclusive, and it is agreed that Natale Comes whose Mythologiae is a pervasive influence upon the poem does associate greed and curiosity. A clear contributing source for the description of Guyon's descent into the house of Mammon, the garden of Proserpina, and his subsequent faint upon return is Psyche's descent in The Golden Asse of Apuleius (Adlington translation) into "the desolate house of Pluto," past "the gate of Proserpina" where after refusing Proserpina's offer of "delicate meat and drink" she succumbs to the temptation to open the mysterious box in which she finds "only an infernal and deadly sleep, which immediately invaded all her members . . . she . . . lay . . . as a sleeping corpse." However, the immortal Cupid descends from the chamber in which he has been enclosed in order to save her, not without an indictment that she had "nigh perished again with . . . overmuch curiosity." Spenser was at some pains not to conceal his source, for he describes the salvific angel who demonstrates in the opening of the eighth canto that there is care in heaven, "Like as Cupido on Idaean hill" (II.viii.6.1). Those who champion the idea that Guyon's temptation is fundamentally that of avarice may note that the advice given to Psyche preparatory to her descent involves her bribing Charon who, along with Pluto, will do nothing without reward. The lesson is: "hereby you may see that avarice reigneth even amongst the dead." Further, the outstretched hands of Tantalus and Pilate, seemingly symbols of curiosity, are suggested by the example foretold to Psyche of "an old man swimming on the top of the river holding up his deadly hands." It might be added that the linking of Pilate and Tantalus, the origin of which the distinguished Spenserian A.C. Hamilton states is unknown, may derive not from any supposed but now lost tradition of their conjunction, but rather from a simple process of association in the mind of the habitually punning Spenser as he read Psyche's remark in Apuleius when she rhetorically asks why she should not take a little of the beauty from the box given by Proserpina: "'Ecce' . . . inepta ego divinae formositatis gerula, quae nec tantillum quidem indidem mihi delibo, . . ." But for the medial vowel and terminal consonant we have "Tantalus," and as for "Ecce" itself, it cries out in Pilate's notorious 'Ecce homo' of John 19.6 (Vulgate). For both the proponents of the interpretation of Guyon's temptation as one of avarice, and more profoundly, those who see it as ultimately a temptation of intemperate curiosity, Apuleius is significantly present in a third central episode in the poem.[23]

In addition to these motifs and episodes drawn from the story of Cupid and Psyche, Spenser made use of a number of other Apuleian elements in the course of the composition of The Faerie Queene. Among these is the description of the wounding of Amoret (III.xii.20-21) which carries some of the diction used in Adlington's version of the mutilating of Socrates by the witch (not sorcerer) Meroe, to whom he had been in sexual thrall. Spenser has here recalled both the theme of sexual dependence and the preternatural power of the mutilator, and then has reversed the roles of the genders--male victim becomes female in The Faerie Queene and witch becomes sorcerer. In this tactic of gender reversal Spenser anticipated Shakespeare who, for example, in Othello V.ii.1-22 gives to the Moor the role and speech of the would-be murderous Psyche and to Desdemona that of the innocent and sleeping Cupid.

Spenser also made use of the frame tale which surrounds the story of Cupid and Psyche, the narrative of Charite who, among other adventures, was kidnapped by robbers and brought to a cave only to escape riding on an ass by means of the imaginative heroism of her lover. In particular Spenser has anticipated again, by a very little time, Shakespeare's strategy in A Midsummer Night's Dream of redeploying a number of the elements in the story of Psyche itself into a new design. Spenser re-used different strands or, rather, different sections of the mosaic that is Charite's Apuleian life. Specifically, Mirabella's riding upon an asse (VI.vii.27) and Pastorella's Charite-like audience of cowherds and shepherds, and even the name of the Blatant Beast itself have been affected by elements in the story of Charite. Indeed, if the Blatant Beast represents not only the false speech of slander, but also the obverse falsity of flattery, then the address to Charite by the thievish kidnappers provided another part of the constellation of elements separated into the discrete but related tesserae of Book VI. Anxious to quiet the distraught Charite, the thieves assure her they mean no harm: "his et his similibus blateratis nequicquam dolor sedatur puellae"--with such and like flattering words they endeavored to appease the gentlewoman."

These instances are perhaps sufficient to indicate how widespread was Spenser's use of Apuleius. Some instances clearly show the poet's interest in allegorical significance, others in narrative motifs, and still others in the beauty of the Apuleian/Adlingtonian descriptions. Of course, the issue of allusion versus echo remains crucial and constantly problematic, but whether true allusion or simple echo each of these instances is Apuleian.[24]

Motifs and thematic patterns worthy of imitation are naturally enough to be found in the extended narratives of Sidney and Spenser, but even the shorter narrative of Marlowe's unfinished Hero and Leander makes use of descriptive materials from The Golden Asse. Chapman who used Apuleius in his drama did not incorporate such material into his continuation. Both the description of the crowd which admires the beautiful Hero and that of the temple of Venus to which Hero moves are borrowed in part from Adlington's descriptions of Psyche admired by the throngs formerly devoted to Venus and of the palace of Cupid to which Psyche moves.[25]

This brief sketch of the prevalence of Apuleian materials in the work of the major non-dramatic writers of the English Renaissance could be extended past the time of Shakespeare to include even the "last Elizabethan," Milton himself, for there is evidence that the poet who had made use of the fairy tale of Cupid and Psyche near the end of the Comus of 1645 and specifically referred to Psyche in the middle of Areopagitica, incorporated elements of the Metamorphoses, a narrative which has as its central theme that of the sin, suffering, and redemption, into Paradise Lost, a narrative poem with the same theme. Moreover, the conclusion of Paradise Regained shows further evidence not only of theme from the Metamorphoses, but also of diction absorbed from Adlington's version.[26]

These instances are perhaps sufficient to indicate just how widespread was the use of Apuleius amongst the most important non-dramatic writers of Shakespeare's day. Some instances clearly show the writer's interest in thematic, often allegorical significance, others in surprising turns of plot, and still others in the beauty of Apuleian/Adlingtonian description. When the relatively more leisured non-dramatic artists drew so frequently upon The Golden Asse, it is not very surprising to find that those workers in the highly pressurized world of the Elizabethan theatre, where new material to satisfy Henslowe or one's fellow shareholders was always needed, turned again and again to The Golden Asse.

The locus classicus describing this state of affairs is Gosson's observation in 1582:

> I may boldly say it because I have seen it that the Palace of Pleasure, The Golden Ass, The Ethiopian History, Annals of France, The Round Table, bawdy comedies in Latin, French, Italian and Spanish have been thoroughly ransacked to furnish the Playe houses in London.[27]

Whatever the relative frequency of borrowings from these other sources, The Golden Asse itself was 'ransacked,' after Gosson's observation at least, by George Chapman, Thomas Dekker, Thomas Heywood, Ben Jonson, and John Marston. In addition there was the now lost collaborative play by Dekker, Chettle, and Day, commissioned by Henslowe in 1600, The Golden Asse or Cupid and Psyche. Because the Metamorphoses, ultimately a comic novel of bestial transformation ending in a religious conversion, is so episodic and because these episodes are often 'Milesian tales,' that is, "mannered (stories) of bizarre adventure or sexual adventure"[28] the Elizabethan-Jacobean dramatist had available to him just the romantic, bizarre, sometimes even grotesque material he was looking for. A number of these episodes deal with witches, unfaithful wives, murder, revenge, frustrated lust, and magical practices. And if these narrative opportunities were not enough to capture the eye of the insatiably matter-hungry dramatist, there is within the novel the beautiful fairy tale of Cupid and Psyche.

We do not know the titles of the pre-1582 plays which Gosson thought of as incorporating material from The Golden Asse. The earliest example of a play containing an Apuleian element, apart from Shakespeare's early and middle work, is Dekker's Satiromastix[29] of 1601 (published 1602), that strange mixture of anti-Jonsonian lampooning and romantic tragi-comedy. Dekker in Act V has returned to the same episode in Book X, Chapter 44 of The Golden Asse in which an intended victim of poisoning turns out to have been saved by a sleeping potion which Sidney had used for Gynecia's plot in Arcadia. An older, married woman's lust is replaced in a reversal of gender relationships frequent in Apuleian borrowings by the lust of King William Rufus for the newly married Celestine whose death is no death at all. What was good enough for Sidney and Dekker will turn out to be good enough for Shakespeare not only in the obvious instance of the plot of the wicked queen in Cymbeline, but elsewhere in plays written at the time of Satiromastix and just after. Marston's The Wonder of Women or The Tragedy of Sophonisba (1606) is the first of these plays to make use of an element from the story of Cupid and Psyche, an element which Shakespeare had already made very much his own by repeated use. Perhaps Marston had learned from Dekker, his anti-Jonsonian co-partner, the advantages of recourse to The Golden Asse of Apuleius. Certainly both Marston and Dekker had learned the advantages of using Nashe,"little Apuleius" as Gabriel Harvey had called him,[30] and the habits of borrowing and co-opting one another's tactics were common amongst the small group of busy playwrights of the day.

In general, as George Geckle has shown, Sophonisba is like Psyche, "a type of the faithful woman who displays fortitude under the most trying conditions," with Sophonisba's concluding drink of poisoned wine which allows her to maintain her "glory" analogous to the "pot of immortalitie" prepared for Psyche by Jupiter.[31] Of particular interest is the reversal of gender roles in the Erictho episode in which the lustful Syphax is warned (like Psyche in Apuleius) not to attempt to see the face of the invisible lover. When he violates the prohibition only to discover the loathesome body of the witch Erictho, he makes a discovery which is an absolute reversal of Psyche's view of the handsome god of love when she was expecting a monster. To complete the inverted parallel Marston has established an infernal punishment for Syphax who has impregnated a demon, while his source provides Psyche with a celestial reward and impregnation by a deity. Marston may have noted in the life of Apuleius with which Adlington prefaced his translation that Apuleius was "born in Madaura . . . under the jurisdiction of Syphax" and from this small hint gone on to create an unhistorical character based on the fate of men who, as Adlington explains, are "drowned in the sensual lusts of the flesh."[32] Adlington's reference to Syphax occurs in the same sentence in which we learn that Apuleius' father was "called Theseus," a fact of some supporting interest when we consider Shakespeare's use of The Golden Asse in A Midsummer Night's Dream.

In the case of George Chapman there are clear signs that in both The Shadow of Night (1594) and Hero and

Leander (1598) this learned and often difficult poet was working within the tradition of morally interpreted metamorphoses within which Adlington's The Golden Asse is a prime example.[33] By the time of the mature comedy, The Widow's Tears (1606) Chapman as dramatist, although still clearly interested in the ethical bases of his sources, combined that ethical concern with one directed toward plot construction. It is well known that the main plot of the comedy, that of the "dead" husband Lysander and his testing of his tearful "widow" Cynthia is based upon the most celebrated episode in The Satyricon of Petronius, the novella called "The Widow of Ephesus." It is also known that Apuleius had some knowledge of Petronius' work which is the only other surviving romance of a length comparable to the Metamorphoses.[34] Sometimes too much has been made of Apuleius' borrowing from Petronius, but there is no doubt that there are some echoes of language and that certain situations in the later work are modelled upon The Satyricon. What is most interesting for our interest in Chapman's play is that Apuleius seems deliberately to have rewritten the basic situation of "The Widow of Ephesus" with a complete reversal of Petronius' jaded view of wifely loyalty in the story of Charite and Thrasyllus in Book VIII of The Metamorphoses. The idealism of the widow Charite confronted by the aggressive wooer Thrasyllus, "a combination of Sextus Tarquinius and Catiline,"[35] is a clear and calculated contrast to the all-too-human behavior of the widow in The Satyricon. We now know, thanks to the discovery of Joel Kaplan, that Chapman turned to this Apuleian version of "The Widow of Ephesus" story which he was making use of in the Lysander-Cynthia plot for the sub-plot in which Tharsalio (etymologically, as in Apuleius, "bold" or "overbold") pursues and conquers the widow Eudora.[36] It is quite possible that the classically learned Chapman understood that Apuleius had rewritten the tale of Petronius, but even if he had not, the situational parallelism with thematic reversal would have been sufficiently obvious for him to think in Apuleian terms once he had begun with Petronius. Professor Kaplan points out that Chapman improved upon

> the tombside seduction of the widow of Ephesus . . . by having the husband, Lysander, stage his own funeral and return in disguise to test Cynthia's vows. When his wooing proves all too successful, Chapman has the disillusioned Lysander confess to his own murder in a vain attempt to prevent Cynthia from capitulating. Thrasyllus' actual crime is thus trans-

formed into Lysander's false self-accusation increasing the comic discomfiture Lysander must suffer when he realizes that Cynthia is no Charite.[37]

Indeed, Cynthia is more like Queen Gertrude of Denmark, a character otherwise influenced by Apuleian material, in her frailty.

The Widow's Tears is a play about the inconstancy of women, a theme prominent throughout the Elizabethan and Jacobean periods and no less prominent in the work of Shakespeare. It is also a play in which characters, apart from Tharsalio "undergo a kind of metamorphosis,"[38] and in which the major characters again, apart from Tharsalio, are described at one time or another in the imagery of animal transformation. Not only has the name of Tharsalio been borrowed from The Metamorphoses and so also has the motif of the lustfully aggressive suitor of a lamenting widow, but the theme of the Apuleian episode has been suppressed in favor of its original, cynical model of wifely fidelity as found in Petronius. Marston could reverse the role of genders in the Apuleian episode of Cupid and Psyche and Chapman could and did invert the theme of another episode in Apuleius. The lesson to be drawn from these tactics on the part of the dramatists is that comparable situations of plot need not imply tonal and/or thematic similarity. One has the perception that English Renaissance playwrights have the same kind of interpretive independence as had medieval and Renaissance mythographers who could find in the same myth lessons of equal and opposite moral significance.

If the veterans of one side in the war of the theatres, Dekker and Marston, could make use of Apuleius, so could Jonson on the other. And if his sometime collaborator, one of only two other men who Jonson thought "could make a mask," had borrowed from The Golden Asse how much the more likely could Jonson, even if he had not been able in the course of his working relationship to notice what Shakespeare had been doing with the same text. We know that in his private collection of extracts, Timber or Discoveries, a kind of commonplace book which he intended to revise for publication, there is a reference to Apuleius' Metamorphoses Book I where Socrates warns Lucius not to rail against the witch Meroe,[39] and another to his De Magia. In The Underwood there is what looks to be a version of Apuleius' "togati vulturii"[40] in Metamorphoses X, 33, where Lucius, condemned soon to copulate with a woman prisoner, watches

a pageant of the judgment of Paris. However, it is in
The Masque of Queenes (1609) that Jonson's use of Apuleian material is most extensive, and, for students of
Shakespeare's similar practice in Macbeth of three
years earlier, the most interesting. In The Masque of
Queenes Jonson's marginalia direct attention first to
the fact, apropos the disturbing of the universe, that
'these powers of troubling nature are frequently ascrib'd to Witches'[41] and cites, among other references,
Apuleius' description in Book I of the witch Meroe and
that in Book II by Byrrhena to Lucius of the witch Pamphile. The marginalia continue with a note on the "use
of gathering flesh, bones and sculls" which has been
drawn from the episode in Book III of the "asino aureo,"
where Pamphile transforms bits and pieces of human bodies and, unknown to herself, three goat-skins into
three seeming men. This graphically described process
of mixing such entrails had as we know been adopted by
Shakespeare in Macbeth IV.i, but the episode of the
goat-skins turned men itself had still earlier found its
way into Much Ado About Nothing. The final reference to
Apuleius in the marginalia of The Masque of Queenes
glosses the practice of "pronouncing of wordes, & pouring out of liquors, on the earth." Jonson cites Cornelius Agrippa's description of such a technique, a description which, Jonson goes on to state, Agrippa derived from Apuleius in "lib.iii.de Asin. aur." where in
the stage immediately following the mixing of the entrails Pamphile recites certain charms and dips the
gruesome ingredients into water, milk, honey, and mead.

  The Masque of Queenes by its genre may seem not so
immediately proximate an analogue to the plays of Shakespeare, apart from the witch-laden Macbeth, but Shakespeare, who as we know was affected by the changing
trends and fashions of his day, has in The Tempest a
masque with anti-masque which also shows signs of Apuleian matter. Jonson did as others did and one of the
others was Shakespeare. And if we may correctly assume
that Jonson went directly to Apuleius' Latin, whatever
his knowledge of Adlington's English version, we may
note that Shakespeare, he of the "small Latine" gives
several clear indications of also having read Apuleius
in the original.

  Twenty years after the death of Shakespeare, Thomas
Heywood, a practiced borrower from his predecessors,
Shakespeare most especially, wrote near the end of his
own lengthy career Love's Mistress, or The Queen's Masque (1636), a dramatized version of the Cupid and Psyche

narrative staged by Inigo Jones. Heywood states in his preface 'To the Reader,' that

> The argument is taken from Apuleius, an excellent Morrall, if truly understood, and may be called a golden Truth, contained in a leaden fable, which though it bee not altogether conspicuous to the vulgar, yet to those of learning and judgment, no lesse apprehended in the Paraphrase, then approved in the Original.[42]

However, there is other evidence that Heywood who had been an actor at the Rose may have acted in the now lost play of "the gowlden asse or cuped & siches" by Dekker, Chettle, and Day in 1600 and may have "cribbed years afterwards from the manuscript of his part,"[43] or recalled lines from his memory. There are passages attributed to Dekker in R. Allot's England's Parnassus (1600) which reappear in Love's Mistress and seem to have come from the lost play on the same subject on Cupid and Psyche.[44] Such a use of Apuleius/Adlington and somebody else's use of the same material is a form of creative source contamination characteristic of writers of the period, not excluding Shakespeare.

There are three levels to the play: the critical dialogue between Apuleius (Heywood himself) and the ignorant Midas, the narrative of the adventures of Cupid and Psyche, and the pastoral episodes of Shepherds. The element most interesting to students of Apuleius and The Golden Asse as embodied on the English stage is the explicit heightening by Heywood of the Neo-platonic allegory of the tale in such a way that what might not be "altogether conspicuous to the vulgar" would be clear enough to the Masque's court audience. So Heywood has Apuleius instruct Midas,

> Misunderstanding fool, thus much conceive:
> Psyche is Anima, Psyche is the Soul;
> The Soul, a virgin, longs to be a bride;
> The Soul's immortal, whom then can she woo
> But Heaven? whom wed but immortality?
> (I.vi.56-60)[45]

Although there is a current tendency to underrate Heywood and criticize writers of masques as morally deficient for their frequent displays of sycophancy, Heywood is often a talented cratsman and Love's Mistress is particularly successful in interweaving Apuleian material and thematic concerns with dance and spectacle.

Later even Milton would make use of Cupid and Psyche in his masque of <u>Comus</u> (1645), where following not only Spenser but Boccaccio in the allegorical version of the Apuleian story he doubles the off-spring of Cupid and Psyche, turning the daughter 'Pleasure' of the tale into the twins 'Youth and Joy.' Indeed, Milton would continue reworking the tale of Cupid and Psyche later in his career, as is clear from elements of theme and diction in both epics <u>Paradise Lost</u> and <u>Paradise Regained</u>.[46]

This survey of Apuleian material in the dramatists contemporary with Shakespeare reveals that the playwrights of the day were as enthusiastic in borrowing from <u>The Golden Asse</u> as were those pre-1582 authors cited by Gosson. Names, episodes, characters, themes, and even allegorizations were taken over without blush by the writers, minor and major, of the period, for they all realized just how productively malleable such material could be. Moreover, the frequency with which parts of <u>The Golden Asse</u> were reworked doubtless produced in the minds of the great frequenters of playhouses and those who had read the novel on its own, the sweet double pleasure of recognition of the familiar now varied in surprising ways.

Shakespeare began, developed, and concluded his career in the midst of such Apuleian borrowings, and to think that he would note the practice of others and transcendingly imitate their tactics in his own work is but to recognize an obvious and important truth.

INTRODUCTION

[1] Kenneth Muir, The Sources of Shakespeare's Plays (London: Methuen, 1977), 68.

[2] Geoffrey Bullough, ed., Narrative and Dramatic Sources of Shakespeare (London: Routledge & Kegan Paul, 1957-75), I, 372, VIII, 16.

[3] See especially A Midsummer Night's Dream, ed. Harold Brooks, and Richard III, ed. Antony Hammond.

[4] John Velz, Shakespeare and the Classical Tradition, A Critical Guide to Commentary, 1660-1960 (Minneapolis: University of Minnesota Press, 1968).

[5] See Elizabeth H. Haight, Apuleius and His Influence (New York: Longmans, Green, 1927), 92-3.

[6] Roland Mushat Frye, Shakespeare and Christian Doctrine (Princeton: Princeton University Press, 1963), 11.

[7] See P.G. Walsh, The Roman Novel (Cambridge: Cambridge University Press, 1970), 229.

[8] Haight, 101.

[9] Haight, 102.

[10] Muir, The Sources of Shakespeare's Plays, 67, and Haight, 105.

[11] See Ann Thompson, Shakespeare's Chaucer, A Study in Literary Origins (Liverpool: Liverpool University Press, 1978).

[12] F. Anne Payne, Chaucer and Menippean Satire (Madison: The University of Wisconsin Press, 1981), 25.

[13] See T.W. Baldwin, William Shakesper's Small Latine and Lesse Greeke (Urbana: University of Illinois Press), I, 190; II, 26, 185, 247.

[14] See, for example, Douglas Duncan, Ben Jonson and the Lucianic Tradition (Cambridge: Cambridge University Press, 1978).

[15] See, for example, Letter 61 in *The Correspondence of Erasmus, Letters 1 to 141, 1484 to 1500*, translated by Mynors and Thomson, anotated by Ferguson (Toronto: The University of Toronto Press, 1974), 128, and *Utopia*, edited Surtz and Hexter in *The Complete Works of St. Thomas More* (New Haven and London: Yale University Press, 1965), IV, 580, and *De Tristitia Christi*, ed. and trans. Clarence H. Miller in *The Complete Works of St. Thomas More* (New Haven and London: Yale University Press) XIV, pt. 1 197.

[16] Sir Philip Sidney, *An Apology for Poetry*, ed. Geoffrey Shepherd (Manchester: Manchester University Press), 135.

[17] Dorothy Connell, *Sir Philip Sidney, The Makers Mind* (Oxford: Clarendon Press, 1977), 25.

[18] Sir Philip Sidney, *The Countess of Pembroke's Arcadia (The Old Arcadia)*, ed. Jean Robertson (Oxford: Clarendon Press, 1973), xxiii.

[19] Millar Maclure, "Spenser," *English Poetry and Prose, 1540-1674*, ed. Christopher Ricks (London: Barrie & Jenkins), 70-71.

[20] Don Cameron Allen, *Image and Meaning* (Baltimore: The Johns Hopkins Press, 1960), 29.

[21] Thomas P. Roche, Jr., *The Kindly Flame*: A Study of the *Faerie Queene* III and IV (Princeton: Princeton University Press, 1964), 126.

[22] See Jane Aptekar, *Icons of Justice*: Iconography and Thematic Imagery in the *Faerie Queene* V (New York: Columbia University Press, 1969), 105.

[23] See "Spenserian Parallels," *Essays in Criticism* (Oxford), xxix, 268.

[24] For other Apuleian elements, see my "On Apuleius and Spenser," in *Spenser at Kalamazoo 1982*, ed., Russell J. Meyer (Clarion State College, 1982), esp., 6-8.

[25] L.C. Martin, *Marlowe's Poems* (London: Methuen, 1931), 34-5.

[26] See "Milton and Apuleius," *Res Publica Litterarum* (forthcoming).

[27] Used as an epigraph by Geoffrey Bullough, Narrative and Dramatic Sources of Shakespeare.

[28] P.G. Walsh, The Roman Novel (Cambridge: Cambridge University Press, 1970), 15.

[29] Wilhelm Creizenach, The English Drama in the Age of Shakespeare, trans. Cecile Hugon (Philadelphia: J.B. Lippincott, 1916), 223.

[30] See especially The Poems of John Marston, ed. Arnold Davenport (Liverpool: Liverpool University Press, 1961), 30.

[31] George L. Geckle, John Marston's Drama (London and Toronto: Associated University Presses, 1980), 188.

[32] Quoted by Geckle, 187.

[33] See Raymond B. Waddington, The Mind's Empire, Myth and Form in George Chapman's Narrative Poems (Baltimore and London: The Johns Hopkins Press, 1974), esp. 60-61, 178.

[34] Walsh, The Roman Novel, 163.

[35] Ibid.

[36] Joel H. Kaplan, "Apuleius as a Chapman Source," Notes and Queries, ccxx (1975), 252.

[37] Ibid.

[38] The Widow's Tears, ed., Ethel M. Smeak (Lincoln: University of Nebraska Press, 1966), xx.

[39] Ben Jonson, ed., C.H. Herford and P. and E. Simpson (Oxford: Clarendon Press, 1925-52) XI, 225.

[40] Jonson, op. cit., 65.

[41] Jonson, VII, 289.

[42] Thomas Heywood, The Dramatic Works of Thomas Heywood, ed. R.H. Shepherd (London: John Pearson, 1974) V, 85.

[43] E.K. Chambers, according to W.L. Halstead, "Dekker's Cupid and Psyche and Thomas Heywood," ELH, XI (1944), 185.

[44] Halstead, 184-85.

[45] Line numbering as in *Love's Mistress, or The Queen's Masque*, ed. Raymond C. Shady (Salzburg: Inst. of Engl. Sprache und Literatur, 1977).

[46] "Milton and Apuleius," *Res Publica Litterarum* (forthcoming).

CHAPTER ONE

THE EARLY PLAYS AND VENUS AND ADONIS

Shakespeare was not slow to adopt the practice of using Apuleian material in the composition of his works for there is considerable evidence of such adoption in the History plays, The Second Part of Henry the Sixth and Richard the Third, The Comedy of Errors, The Tragedy of Titus Andronicus, and even the Ovidian erotic poem Venus and Adonis. This material has been reshaped primarily for use in the development of plot and the revealing of character, but it also contributes to the diction, atmosphere and, ultimately, the themes of both the plays and the narrative poem. An examination of the materials in the source and in the works brings us as close as we can get at this distance in time to both the heart of Shakespeare's creative imagination and, sometimes, to meanings in the works otherwise less easily discernible.

If we accept for the purposes of argument the standard chronology of Shakespeare's works provided by J.G. McManaway, then the first play in which the young dramatist turned to The Golden Asse is The Second Part of Henry the Sixth.[1] In particular there are some striking parallels in the famous scene of the hunger and death of Jack Cade (IV.x) and in two sequential episodes at the end of Chapter 17 and the beginning of Chapter 18 devoted to the career of Lucius, newly transformed into an ass, the protagonist of the novel.[2] Both the rebel and the asinine Lucius are forced by hunger to enter another's garden during the heat of the day in quest of an unfamiliar vegetable diet only to be confronted by the gardener or owner of the garden who kills (Shakespeare) or tries to kill (Apuleius) the hardly refreshed intruder. Each is viewed as a wretched thief. Diction common to both texts[3] includes "hungry," "sallet"/"sallets," "hear(e)s,"[4] "truncheon," "sword," "meat," "thief"/ "theefe," "climbing," "wretch," and "slain"/"slaine." In addition, the dismemberment and dunghill burial of Cade's body which is described at the end of the scene may have been suggested by a combination of the fate of Lucius' brother ass and the dung used by Lucius at the conclusion of his difficulties with the gardner and his associates.

Some further indication that Shakespeare was recalling this section of The Golden Asse during the composition of 2 Henry VI is provided by the "ban-dogs"

1

(I.i.78),[5] a term unique in the canon and apparently echoing the 'Bandogs' which pursue Lucius just after his battle with the gardener.

   Further indication that Shakespeare was recalling other sections of The Golden Asse in other scenes of the history play is provided not necessarily by the witch Margery Jourdain who can raise spirits in the manner of the Apuleian witches Meroe and Pamphile, but by such rare phrasings in the canon as that at the arrest of Gloucester (III.i) 'condign punishment' (III.i.130) which echoes Adlington's 'condigne and worthy punishment' (68) both in a context of arrest and trial, as does also the Cardinal's earlier aside to Gloucester, 'This news, I think, hath turn'd your weapon's edge' (II.i.176) which recalls the phrasing from another reversal in the context of yet another murderous plot, '. . . tooke the razor . . . and the razor turned his edge' (112-13), and equally York's comparison of the relationship between himself and the three realms with the fate of Meleager, "As did the fatal brand Althaea burnt/Unto the Prince's heart of Calydon" (I.i.234-35), an analogy which Apuleius had used to describe the narrow escape of the asinine Lucius at the end of Book Seven: "So I enforced the queane to leave off, otherwise I had died as Meleager did by the sticke, which his mad mother Althea cast into the fire." (155)

   Among the difficulties in determining Shakespeare's source material is the fact that a phrase in Shakespeare's consciousness which allowed the linking of two passages may itself be absent from his work.[6] Such seems to be the case with Cade and Lucius. Fortunately, the missing link is provided by Grafton in his A Chronicle at Large, a work known to have been read by Shakespeare, where it is stated that Cade went into Sussex ". . . in habit disguysed . . . but all his Metamorphosis or transfiguration little prevalyed . . . till one Alexander Iden . . . found him in a garden . . ."[7] Adlington had pointed out in the opening of his translation that many would prefer that his work not be called The Golden Asse, but " . . . Metamorphosis, that is to say, A transfiguration or transformation . . ." (13). This hint provided by Grafton, coupled with the partial similarity of theme (Cade for his presumption is punished by a bestial hunger and death, while Lucius for his presumption and curiosity is condemned for a term to a beast's existence), seems to have led Shakespeare to think of his Kentish rebel in terms of Lucius' predicament.

In the interpretation of the character of Jack Cade it is customarily pointed out that his moral and social inferiority is indicated by his speaking in prose while other characters, including his conqueror, speak in verse. Perhaps, but the use of terms from Lucius' asininity need not add to a further denigration of Cade. Apuleius is at pains to point out that for all of Lucius' bestial appearance he never loses his human sensibility. Shakespeare who throughout his works gives a decent send-off to figures of opposition, may have recalled Lucius' humanity when he gave Cade a courageous end. As it is, Cade's earlier attempts at metamorphosis into John Mortimer and, by wearing his armor, into Sir Humphrey Stafford failed miserably. His ultimate transformation into hungry beast has something of the condign about it.

At the end of his first tetralogy Shakespeare returned to The Golden Asse and its story of Cupid and Psyche (Chapter 22) for Tyrrel's description of the murder of the princes in Richard III, IV.iii.1-22. The model for this murder is the near-murder of the innocent Cupid by the hesitant Psyche as described by Apuleius and by Adlington, for Shakespeare seems to have read both the original Latin and the English version. Although terms describing the innocence of the victims in Richard III are present in the singular in Apuleius, e.g., "child" for "children" and "babe" for "babes," there is little doubt that Shakespeare could have found these plurals in his known sources, especially Hall. However, Shakespeare did reduce the plural 'pillowes' as in Hall to a singular as is the case in Apuleius (112).

It is the hesitation at the moment of execution which is especially noteworthy here. Shakespeare could have recalled it from the True Tragedy of Richard III,[8] but also from Apuleius. The description of Psyche's balking at the murder is parallel in diction to the murderer Forrest's " . . . almost changed my mind" (IV.iii. 15, my italics). Apuleius says of Psyche " . . . she changed her mind" (112). The murderers in Richard III are moved by the very special sweetness of the victims' nature: "The most replenished sweet work of Nature" (IV.iii.18). This superlative sweetness echoes that of Cupid as Psyche hesitates before "the most meeke and sweetest beast of all beasts" (112). The "beauty" (112) of the sleeping Cupid and his being "kissed" by Psyche (113) seems to have produced the "beauty kiss'd" of IV. iii.13. The principle of hesitation and the elements of diction common to the two passages suggest that

Shakespeare had recalled or reread Adlington's version of the scene from Apuleius of the anticipated murder of one innocent youth as he composed the description of the murder of the innocent pair of boys in Richard III.

The most striking image in Tyrrel's speech, the lips of the boys as red roses on a stalk, has no source in Adlington. The closest suggested source is the ballad of The Babes in the Wood where young victims of a cruel uncle have lips which are smeared with blackberries and who die in one another's arms.[9] The red-rosed lips of the white rose Yorkist princes is, of course, a particularly elegant stroke by Shakespeare suggestive of the common humanity of all victims in the wars of York and Lancaster. I suggest that Shakespeare was led to the rosy lips from the same section of Psyche's hesitation in the novel, but from Apuleius' Latin rather than from Adlington's English. Adlington does not describe the exact color of the blood shed by Psyche when she accidentally pricks her finger on one of Cupid's arrows. The key phrase is ". . . parvulae sanguinis rosei guttae."[10] From his historical sources Shakespeare knew that the murder of the princes had to be bloodless. What he did was to transfer the rosy-colored blood in Apuleius to the color of the lips of the innocent boys, a pair of Cupids.

There is still a mystery in this murder description of Richard III, IV.iii: how does the hesitant, male murderer Forrest derive so readily in spite of his gender from hesitant female Psyche. Here again Apuleius' original wording and Shakespeare's more than small Latin provide the answer. Adlington tells us that "Psyches (somewhat feeble in body and mind, yet mooved by cruelty of fate) received boldness and brought forth the lampe, and tooke the razor, so by her audacity she changed her mind" (112). But Adlington made his translation, as Charles Whibley has shown, by the aid of an intermediate French version with the result that he missed completely the specific and tellingly powerful phrase of Apuleius, "sexum audacia mutatur," that is, "by her boldness she changed her gender," i.e., to male,[11] not "changed her mind." Shakespeare seems to have had both the original and the translation before him in memory or upon his desk, rather as we know he did with the other Metamorphoses of Ovid and Golding's version,[12] for he has kept "changed" and "mind" for Forrest and given him a newly transformed "male" model for his murder. As we see within the Metamorphoses people are transformed not only into animals but, equally unnaturally, to yet other human selves.

In <u>Venus and Adonis</u>, a narrative with animal models for human behavior, the story of a would-be transformation of boy into man, Shakespeare made use of the <u>Metamorphoses</u> of Ovid and the <u>Metamorphoses</u> of Apuleius. The conflation by Shakespeare of the story of Venus and Adonis from Book X of Ovid's poem with those of Narcissus in Book III and Salmacis-Hermaphroditus in Book IV is well known. However, less well understood is Shakespeare's use of Apuleius even though a clear analysis of the relationship amongst the Ovidian, Apuleian, and Shakespearean materials was made by D.T. Starnes back in 1945.[13] The core of the problem of determining the sources of the poem lies in the fact that Apuleius, the author of the <u>Metamorphoses</u>, was a close reader of the <u>Metamorphoses</u> of Ovid, and that Shakespeare was a close reader of both <u>Metamorphoses</u>. The layers of this palimpsest have been separated correctly by Starnes in the following way. The hunting scene in <u>The Golden Asse</u>, Book VIII, Chapter 32, in which Lepolemus, victimized by the treachery of his lustful 'friend' Thrasyllus (for Chapman's use of the continuation of this episode in <u>The Widow's Tears</u>, see <u>supra</u>), is killed by a fearsome boar, provided Shakespeare with the natural and destructive boar (however extended by critics into a symbol of death) for his poem, while Ovid with his Calydonian boar, a creature of supernatural force, in Book VIII did not. Some lines in the poem which seem to derive from Golding's version of the <u>Metamorphoses</u> of Ovid in fact are closer to the diction in Adlington's English version of the Apuleian text. A comparison of the apposite passages[14] makes clear Shakespeare's reliance upon <u>The Golden Asse</u>:

> His eyes like glow-worms shine when he doth fret,
> . . . .
> Being mov'd, he strikes, what e'er is in his way,
> And whom he strikes his crooked tushes slay.
>
> His brawny sides, with hairy bristles armed,
> Are better proof than thy spear's point can enter;
> His short thick neck cannot be easily harmed;
> Being ireful, on the lion he will venter,

> The thorny brambles and embracing bushes,
> As fearful of him, part, through whom he rushes.
>
> (Venus and Adonis, 621,623-30)

and

> His eies did glister blud and fire: right dreadfull was to see
> His brawned necke, right dredful was his hair which grew as thicke
> With pricking points as one of them could well by other sticke.
> And like a front of armed Pikes set close in battell ray
> The sturdie bristles on his back stoode staring up alway.
>
> (Golding's Ovid, Metamorphoses, VIII, 376-80)

and

> When they were come within the chase to a great thicket fortressed about with bryers and thornes, they compassed round with their Dogs and beset every place with nets: by and by warning was given to let loose. The Dogs rushed in with such a cry, that all the Forrest rang againe with the noyse, but behold there leaped out no Goat, nor Deere, nor gentle Hinde, but an horrible and dangerous wild Boare, hard and thick skinned, bristled terribly with thornes, foming at the mouth, grinding his teeth, and looking direfully with fiery eyes. The Dogs that first set upon him, he tore and rent with his tushes, and then he ranne quite through the nets, and escaped away.
>
> (Adlington, 160-61)

Ovid/Golding's "bristles" have clearly influenced the "hairy bristles" (625) of the poem. Apuleius/Adlington's description of the wood "fortressed about with the bryers and thornes," details absent from Ovid's poem, have affected the "thorny brambles and embracing bushes" (629). Shakespeare seems to have incorporated in the same passage details from both Ovid and Apuleius.

However, there are several instances of his use of details from Apuleius not present in Ovid. Starnes provided a brief table of clearly Apuleian influences.[15]

(1) In Shakespeare and in Apuleius, but not in Ovid, we hear the baying of the hounds before we see the animal or hear results of the chase.
(Venus and Adonis, ll. 868-69; Golden Asse, VIII, 161)

(2) In the poem as in the story we learn soon after hearing the baying of the hounds that it is no gentle beast at bay. "For now she knows it is no gentle chase" (V. and A., l. 883). "There leaped out no Goat, nor Deere, nor gentle Hinde . . ."
(G.A., p. 161)

(3) In the poem as in the story the boar breaks through the barriers and escapes for a period, though he is later pursued. The Calydonian boar in Ovid, once roused, fights savagely the dogs and the hunters. At the end of her imaginative description Venus (V. and A., l. 629) concludes "The thorny brambles and embracing bushes, As fearful of him, through whom he rushes." "Then he ranne," writes Apuleius, "quite through the nets and escaped away."
(G.A., p. 161)

(4) In the poem as in the novel the woman (goddess) runs towards the chase to seek her lover, who the reader knows, has been slain by the boar. (In Ovid Meta. X, 843-47) Venus sees from her chariot in the sky her dead Adonis, and descends).

(5) In Shakespeare and Apuleius the woman (goddess) is almost frantic as she runs to the chase. A second fear "Madly hurries her (Venus) she knows not whither, this way she runs, and now she will no further, But back retires . . . She treads the path that she untreads again" (ll. 904-8).[16] Charite "as a mad and raging woman ran up and down the streets

and country fields, crying and howling lamentably."

(G.A., 162)

(6) In both the poem and the story, when the woman has found her dead lover, she throws herself weeping down by (upon) his body. "With this she (Venus) falleth in the place she stood, And stains her face with his congealed blood" (V. and A., ll. 1121-22). "Charite threw herselfe upon him weeping and lamenting grievously for his death." (162) For this action of falling down, there is no parallel in Ovid's account (cf. Met. Golding's trans., X. ll. 843ff.).

So much of Shakespeare's borrowing is a matter not of either/or, but both/and. Such is the case in Venus and Adonis where the two Metamorphoses, Ovid's and Apuleius', each in English translation, have been combined to provide circumstantial detail for the narrative, with the Apuleian material adding not only to the texture of the poem but providing the motif of a final embrace. That Shakespeare who had been using The Golden Asse in his early dramas, as we have seen, should have turned again to the novel for the composition of his non-dramatic narrative poem is understandable not only from the perspective of the Elizabethan casualness about genre distinction, but also from the presence in the novel of references to Venus and Adonis, references which may be presumed to have established links in the poet's creative imagination with Ovid's poem which he had read as far back as his grammar school days. Apuleius refers to "the proud young man Adonis who was torne by a Bore" (II.56-7) and later in Book VIII, Chapter 36, to "Venus, with Adonis" (173). We have already seen in our discussion of 2 Henry VI that Apuleius refers to the story of Meleager which is inextricably bound with the narrative of the Calydonian boar, a creature which he and Shakespeare after him reduce to a mere animal without obvious supernatural features.

In addition, Shakespeare seems to have incorporated diction from yet another section of The Golden Asse in Venus' lamentation in her apostrophe to Jove:

"O Jove," quoth she, how much a fool was I,
To be of such a weak and silly mind,

> To wail his death who lives, and must not die
> Till mutual overthrow of mortal kind!
> For he being dead, with him is beauty slain,
> And beauty dead, black chaos comes again.
> (1015-21)

In Book II, Chapter 8 ("How Apuleius fortuned to meet with his Cousin Byrrhena"), Apuleius receives a warning from his aunt Byrrhena to avoid the wiles of "Pamphiles who is the wife of Milo" (44) his host (and a miser who has a house full of "treasure," shortly to be robbed by "theeves" -- compare Venus' next two lines, "Fie, fie, fond love, thou are as full of fear/As one with treasure laden, hemm'd with thieves," (1021-22). Pamphiles is not only a lustful matron with an eye for young men, "for as soone as shee espieth any comely yong man, shee is forthwith stricken with his love, and presently setteth her whole minde and affection on him. Shee soweth her seed of flattery, shee invades his spirit and intangleth him with continuall snares of unmeasurable love" (44), but "the most chiefe and principall Magitian and Enchantresse living, who . . . can throw down all the powers of the heavens into the deepe bottoms of hell and reduce all the whole world againe to the old Chaos" (44). Venus, a lustful matron with an eye for the special young man Adonis, having done all that she could to bewitch the object of her love, now laments his loss with scarcely held skepticism of his actual death in terms which recall her appetitive Apuleian model. This same "chaos" will recur in the heavily Apuleian-influenced tragedy of Othello, but its presence here serves to remind the student of Shakespeare's creative process that the use of the most obvious element in a source, e.g., the boar hunt in Chapter 32, far from exhausting the value of that source in general actually invites further scrutiny for, as here, matters of theme and diction. Adonis is transformed into a purple flower, not a hairy ass, but the desire Venus had to transform the young man into a mature sexual partner parallels and is in part drawn from the passion of Pamphile for analogously attractive young men, men as youthful as Lucius who after his transformation will listen to the fatal boar hunt of Book VIII, Chapter 32.

The Golden Asse, for all its many episodes of violence and death, is not only pervasively humorous, but its plot is with the restoration of Lucius to his full humanity ultimately comedic. Whatever the ease with which Shakespeare could borrow from appropriately violent and threatening sequences in the novel for his historical tragedies and erotic narrative poem, it was matched by the skill he shows in incorporating Apuleian matter in his comedies, beginning with his very first effort in the genre, The Comedy of Errors (1593).

The atmosphere of Ephesus as perceived by Antipholus and Dromio of Syracuse has no correspondence with the ambience of Plautus' Menaechmi, the chief source for The Comedy of Errors.[17] Starnes argued that Shakespeare, "unconsciously perhaps,"[18] recalled the witch-filled novel of Apuleius which he had been reading for the first time early in his career. Shortly after his arrival in Ephesus Antipholus of Syracuse comments

> They say this town is full of cozenage:
> As nimble jugglers[19] that deceive the eye,
> Dark working sorcerers that change the mind,
> Soul-killing witches that deform the body
> (I.ii.97-100)

Such sorcerers and witches who deform bodies are absent from Plautus as is any reference to a sorceress, the epithet Antipholus later applies to the Courtesan:

> Avoid them, friend, what tell'st thou me of supping?
> Thou art, as you all are, a sorceress
> . . . .
> . . . .
> Avaunt, thou witch!
> (IV.iii.65-66,79)

In the midst of his master's diatribe, Dromio of Syracuse cites some specifics of conjuring, specifics like those Ben Jonson would employ in The Masque of Queenes and from the same Apuleian source:

> Some devils ask but the pairings of one's nails,
> A rush, a hair, a drop of blood, a pin,
> A nut, a cherry-stone;
> (IV.iii.71-73)

Dromio had earlier expressed anxiety over the attentions of Nell:

> I, amaz'd, ran from her as a witch.
> And I think, if my breast had not been made of faith,

and my heart of steel,
She had transform'd me to a curtal dog, and made me
turn i' th' wheel.
(III.ii.143-46)

The prevalence of witches, their enthusiasm for both physical and spiritual deformations with bits and pieces of human bodies, and their power of transformation, are striking features of The Golden Asse is as clear from such episodes as those of Meroe, Pamphile, and of Thelyphron, the mutilated victim of witches in Book II, Chapter II, who is asked by Byrrhena to describe the loss of his ears and nose after Lucius had commented that witches take dead bodies which "are digged out of their graves, and the bones of them that are burnt be stollen away, and the toes and fingers of such as are slaine be cut off, and afflict and torment such as live" (53).

It is extremely difficult to interpret Shakespeare's use of any source as 'unconscious' and in the case of The Comedy of Errors the argument that the Apuleian-derived material on witches is the result of subconscious recall is made more difficult to sustain by the second Apuleian feature in the play, which Starnes himself noted, the repeated statements by Dromio of Syracuse that he has been transformed into an ass and the echoing of this theme by Antipholus and Dromio of Ephesus.

The women Adriana and Luciana are the first to introduce the theme of asininity into the play when they discuss the putative mastery of Adriana's husband, Antipholus of Syracuse: "O know he is the bridle of your will./There's none but asses will be bridled so" (II.i. 13-14). In the next scene Dromio of Syracuse and his master Antipholus respond to Luciana's abuse with

S. Dro. I am transformed, master, am not I

S. Ant. I think thou art in mind and so am I.

S. Dro. Nay, master, both in mind and in my shape.

S. Ant. Thou hast thine own form.

S. Dro. No, I am an ape.

Luc.   If thou art chang'd to aught, 'tis to an ass.

> S. Dro. 'Tis true she rides me and I long
> for grass.
> 'Tis so, I am an ass, else it could
> never be
> But I should know her as well as she
> knows me.
> (II.ii.195-202)

The collective response of the Syracusan master and servant, with the addition of the master's puzzled "Am I in earth, in heaven, or in hell?/Sleeping or waking, mad or well-advised" (II.ii.212-13) is in Ephesus a proleptic version of the transformation, changed appetite, and puzzled and puzzling dream experience of Bottom in the wood of Athens, a known Apuleian-derived episode. Asininity is rampant in The Comedy of Errors for Antipholus of Ephesus berates his servant Dromio and he responds:

> E. Ant. I think thou art an ass.
>
> E. Dromio Marry, so it doth appear
> By the wrongs I suffer and the blows
> I bear.
> I should kick, being kick'd, and
> being at that pass,
> You would keep from my heels, and
> beware of an ass.
> (III.i.15-18)

and

> If thou hadst been Dromio today in my place,
> Thou wouldst have chang'd thy face for a
> name, or thy name for an ass.
> (III.i.46-47)

Dromio of Syracuse returns to this theme in the next scene of antiphonal asininity: "I am an ass, I am a woman's man, and besides myself" (III.ii.77-78). Four scenes later the Ephesian pair exchange the following:

> E. Ant. Thou art sensible in nothing but
> blows and so is an ass.
>
> E. Dro. I am an ass indeed; you may prove it
> by my long ears. I have serv'd him
> from the hour of my nativity to this
> instant, and have nothing at his
> hands for my service but blows.
> (IV.iv.27-32)

Asinine transformation, punishment by beating, and
forced servitude are, of course, features of the career
of Lucius in The Golden Asse and metamorphosis is fundamentally involved with the problem of identity. So
clearly is it the case that Shakespeare in his early
farce with multiple confusions of identity was naturally
enough drawn to the story of Lucius who acquires a true
self only when his role in life is determined by religious vocation. In The Comedy of Errors religious vocation turns out to be only an extended temporary role
for Aemilia as in the end she turns from abbess to wife
when everyone knows himself for what he is.

There are other hints that Shakespeare had Apuleius' novel in mind during the composition of The Comedy of Errors including the references to the "nimble
jugglers" (I.ii.98) and Punch as a "threadbare juggler"
(V.i.240), which may derive from the athletic "Iugler"
(I, chapter 2) whom Apuleius saw in Athens. There are
the frequent references to hunger and at III.i.27 a niggardly host, exactly the nature of the host of Lucius
when he visits the miserly Milo, husband of the witch
Pamphile. There is the comparison made by Dromio of
Syracuse, "As from a bear a man would run for life,/So
fly I from her that would be my wife," which may have
been prompted by the predicament of Lucius who met a
"marvailous great Beare" and ran "to the intent I would
escape from the terrible Beare, but especially from the
boy that was worse than the Beare" (VII, Chapter 30,
152). The Comedy of Errors, in spite of the thinness of
its verse and the natural absence of character development in a farce, shows not only Shakespeare's high level
of scenic artistry at this early stage of his career,
but also his growing awareness that The Golden Asse was
indeed a treasury of material for atmospheric details
and thematic analogies, not the least of which was that
of metamorphosis as a vehicle for the development of
identity.

Titus Andronicus, like the other 'classical' works
of the early period, Venus and Adonis and The Comedy of
Errors, draws upon Apuleius. In particular, Shakespeare
has looked carefully at two scenes of punishment and
death in the novel for incorporation into his most violent play. "Any writer of tragedies is likely to repeat to some extent in death scenes"[20] and Shakespeare
as we have observed in both 2 Henry VI and Richard III
went to The Golden Asse for its useful scenes of near-death and in Titus he drew from two scenes of actual

demise for the deaths of both the villain Aaron and the villainess Tamora in the final scene of the play.

Lucius commands the Apuleian form of Aaron's death:

> Set him breast-deep in earth and famish him,
> There let him stand and rave and cry for food.
> If any one relieves or pities him,
> For the offense he dies. This is our doom.
> Some stay to see him fast'ned in the earth.
> (V.iii.179-83)

This appears to be a somewhat shortened version of the gruesome end of the Moor in the prose tale 'source' of Shakespeare's earliest tragedy.[21] The horrible death in the tale is very close to that of the luxurious servant depicted by Apuleius in Book VIII, Chapter 35:

> The Master taking in evil part the death of these twaine, tooke his servant which was the cause of this murther by his luxurie, and first after he had put off all his apparell, he annointed his body with honey, and then bound him sure to a fig-tree, where in a rotten stocke a great number of Pismares had builded their neasts, the Pismares after they had felt the sweetnesse of the honey came upon his body, and by little and little in continuance of time devoured all his flesh, in such sort, that there remained on the tree but his bare bones. (171)

It may well be that Shakespeare modified the description of the torment of Aaron because earlier in the play Tamora had been allowed use of the more painful aspects of the Apuleian version in her directive to Chiron and Demetrius as they prepared to rape Lavinia, "But when ye have the honey we desire,/Let not this wasp outlive us both to sting" (II.iii.131-32).

Whether or not the use of this aspect of the tortured servant-episode in The Golden Asse necessitated a reduction of details in Aaron's death, Shakespeare turned to the death of Psyche's sister in The Golden Asse for his description of the disposition of the body of Tamora herself. The final lines of the play echo the passage in Apuleius devoted to the demise of the first of Psyche's two evil sisters:

> As for that ravenous tiger Tamora,
> No funeral rite, not man <u>in</u> <u>mourning</u> <u>weed</u>,
> No mournful bell shall ring her burial,
> But throw her forth to <u>beasts</u> and <u>birds</u> to
>   <u>prey</u>:
> Her life was <u>beastly</u> and devoid of pity
> And being <u>dead</u>, let <u>birds</u> on her take pity.
>   (V.iii.195-200)

Apuleius in Adlington's version, describes the death of Psyche's sister in the following manner:

> . . . and so she cast her selfe <u>headlong</u> from the mountaine: but shee fell not into the valley neither alive nor <u>dead</u>, for all the members and parts of her <u>body</u> were torne amongst the rockes, wherby she was made <u>a</u> <u>prey</u> unto the <u>birds</u> and wild <u>beasts</u>, as <u>she</u> worthily deserved (115).

The striking aspect of the parallels in diction which describe the violent ends of these villainous women is reinforced by the thematic similarity. It is important to recall both that the death and dishonoring of Tamora is an act of revenge by the Andronici and that the death of the sister is an act of revenge by Psyche, elsewhere in the story the model of patience and passivity. The theme of condign punishment is common to both passages. In addition, we should note that the sisters of Psyche had been at great pains to remind her of the oracle of Apollo which had forecast a serpent-husband for her, and that the opening of Apollo's verse prophecy with its diction, iussive subjunctive, and prepositional phrase has been conflated with the description of the sister who had thought that she was on her way to a new husband. The oracle began, "<u>Let</u> Psyches corps be clad <u>in</u> <u>mourning</u> <u>weed</u>" (111).

The "<u>headlong</u>" fall of this sister may have found its way into the earlier part of this same scene of the tragedy when Marcus offers the Romans the death of the entire Andronici family:

> The poor remainder of the Andronici
> Will hand in hand all <u>headlong</u> hurl ourselves,
> And on the ragged stones beat forth our souls,
>   (V.iii.131-33)

The reference to "hand in hand" is doubtless designed to remind the audience subtly of the earlier manual mutilations done to Titus and Lavinia, but the offered "headlong" fall of the surviving Andronici is particularly Apuleian for not only does Psyche's sister descend that way, but so also is it the motion of the distraught wife of the Aaron-like luxurious servant, who "cast her selfe headlong into a deepe pit" (171).

There are other aspects of the tragedy which betray a close reading of The Golden Asse by its author -- and at this late date no one will believe that author to be other than Shakespeare. Indeed, the use of Apuleian material in the play adds to the powerful arguments of contemporary attribution, e.g., that of Francis Meres, and internal evidence of structural sophistication. Among these aspects are the fragments of the Risus festival and rare or unique words or phrases.

Most intriguing is the presence of bits and pieces of Chapter Three of The Golden Asse in which Lucius is sportingly victimized at the festival of Risus, an annual celebration of laughter, which in the case of Lucius involves a mock trial, an indictment for murder, and the mutilation of "corpses." Aaron's boastful confession to Lucius Andronicus includes the Moor's description of his glee at the sight of Titus' discovery of the heads of his sons where he "almost broke my heart with extreme laughter" (V.i.113) and his citing of his gruesomely playful practice of grave-robbing, "Oft have I digg'd up dead men from their graves,/And set them upright at their dear friends' door" (V.i.135-6). These lines first echo both the response of Lucius' dinner table companions who hear his being warned of witches, "all the people laughed heartily" (53) and that of the entire population as he is led to prison for 'murder,' "there was not one but laughed exceedingly" (64). They then echo Lucius' expression of fear of "the blind inevitable trenches of witches, for they say that the dead bodies are digged out of their graves" (53), and his description of his 'murder' of the three 'theeves,' "when I had slaine them all, I knocked sweating and breathing at the doore til Fotis let me in" (63).

Indeed, Aaron's telling of Tamora of "this sport" (V.i.118), of these "heinous deeds" (V.i.123) recalls the wording in Lucius' discovery of "three blown bladders mangled" (68), which discovery caused laughter "at this passing sport" (69) for the event was not truly a "heynous offense" (65). And the bodies turned bladders "mangled" reminds one that Aaron's 'sport' has involved

Titus' "mangled daughter" (III.i.255) whose fate elicits the bizarre laughter of her father, "Ha, ha, ha!" (III.i.264).

Some diction in the conclusion of the Risus episode has been recalled in the description of the trauma suffered by Titus (III.i.233ff.) as "their stomachs . . . sport . . . sorrow" (69) recur in "their stomachs" (III.i.233), "their sports" (III.i.238), and "sorrow" (III.i.245). And from the preparation to the Risus episode, in the same sentence which affected Aaron's boasting speech in V.i., the "trenches" carved by the witches so dreaded by Lucius appear in the visage of Titus. In the confrontation between Titus and Tamora as she personifies Revenge, the old man speaks of his appearance with "these trenches made by grief and care" (V.ii.23), a description which recalls Lucius' anxiety over "the blind inevitable trenches of witches" (53).

Two other episodes from The Golden Asse have affected the final act of the play in Titus' dealings with Tamora, and a third has affected the opening scene of the play. Titus, amazed at the reversal of Saturninus in regard to Lavinia, exclaims "These words are razors to my wounded heart" (I.i.314). Psyche, astonished at the reversal of her expectation in the midst of her would-be murder of her 'serpent' husband, was "amazed in mind, with a pale countenance all trembling fel on her knees and thought to hide the razor, yea verily in her own heart" (113). In the play there follows Saturninus' proposal to Tamora with wording that reflects some of the diction in the narrative of Charite's dream just before she is calmed by the telling of the tale of Cupid and Psyche:

> And tapers burn so bright, and every thing
> In readiness for Hymenaeus stand,
> I will not re-salute the streets of Rome,
> Or climb my palace, till from forth this place
> I lead espoused my bride along with me.
> . . . .
> . . . .
> . . . .
>   Prince Saturnine,
> Whose wisdom hath her fortune conquered.
> There shall we consummate our spousal rites.
>   (I.i.324-28, 335-37)

Compare Charite's description of part of her soon-to-be-interrupted marriage ceremony, "torches were set in every place in the honour of Hymeneus, my espouse was accompanied with his parents . . . my unhappy mother . . . decked me like a bride" (97) and her learning of the marriage of Psyche with "the melody of Hymeneus" (101), a marriage which has "a perfect consummation" with her "Spouse" (104). "Hymeneus" is unique in the canon and "consummate" occurs in the canon for the first time here in Titus Andronicus. Shakespeare seems again to have been looking at the Apuleian original for he follows properly the sequence of vowels which Adlington had abbreviated, 'hymenaeum' (4.26.17) and 'hymenaei' (4.33.17).

In the final act the unique 'hell-hounds' of Titus' aside, "A pair of cursed hell-hounds and their dame" (V.ii.145) recalls the description of the fate of the thief Thrasileon who, as Lucius overhears, " . . . valiantly resisted the gaping and ravenous mouths of the hell hounds" (93), with 'ravenous' appearing later in the description of Tamora as "a ravenous tiger" (V.iii.5,195).

Tamora, in an aside, speaks of "our determined jest" (V.ii.139) and much of the laughter and cruel game at the expense of Titus has a parallel in the laughter and the slightly less gory sport at the expense of Lucius, but Titus has his own determined jest which has an important Apuleian ingredient. Titus' announcement that Chiron and Demetrius are the flesh upon which "their mother daintily hath fed" (V.iii.61) echoes the "feeding daintily" of Adlington (223). There is another 'daintily' in the canon later in Antony and Cleopatra, but there is no other combination of 'fed' and 'daintily.' What is so interesting about this echo is that it is perfectly understandable, for Lucius observes a pageant of the Judgment of Paris in which personified abstractions appear, "Two young men" arrive, "whereof one (was) named Terror, and the other Feare" (224-25). It will be remembered that Chiron and Demetrius, two young men armed, are the half-personified ministers of Tamora/Revenge called Rape and Murder.[22] The rarity of such personifications in both The Golden Asse and Shakespeare's plays adds to the likelihood that the description in the former was recalled during the composition of this earliest tragedy amongst the latter.

Of supporting interest is the fact that Lucius arrives at the pageant after escaping enforced sexual intercourse with a murderess who had killed not only her husband, but her daughter, "whereupon she prepared a dinner with her owne hands, and empoysoned both the wife of the Physitian and her owne daughter" (222). Such dinner-time domestic slaughter and the manually-focused violence of Lucius' initial response of suicide which was frustrated because "I lacked hands and was not able to hold a knife" (223), may have drawn Shakespeare's attention to these very pages in The Golden Asse.

In addition, Shakespeare's punningly associative imagination may have been especially stimulated by the happy conjunction of the ethnic background of Chiron, Demetrius, and Tamora -- they are Goths -- and of the kind of animals who are, like Tamora, Queen of the Goths, "feeding daintily" when Lucius arrives at the scene of the pageant -- they are goats, "as in many young and tender Goates, plucking and feeding daintily" (223). The Goths/Goats association was doubtless an easy one, for later in As You Like It the pun is made explicit in Touchstone's "I am here with thee and thy goats as the most capricious poet Ovid, was among the Goths" (III.iii.7-9).

Such a series of parallels with domestic murder, personified abstractions, unique diction, and punning association, all in so few consecutive pages of The Golden Asse makes highly probable Shakespeare's use of the novel in the beginning of the final scene of the play even as he would use it for the death of Aaron and the disposition of the body of Tamora at the end of the play.

One final observation on the name "Lucius" is required -- not only is it particularly appropriate that it be Lucius, eldest son of Titus, who orders Aaron to be set breast-deep in the earth and famished and who orders that Tamora's body be thrown to the beasts and birds of prey because both endings are derived from episodes in Apuleius' novel of the adventures of Lucius; not only is young Lucius, the grandson of Titus, a dramatic cousin of the Yorkist princes who meet an Apuleian end, as noted above; but it is a fact that beginning with Titus Andronicus all of the plays in the canon which include a Lucius, Titus Andronicus, Julius Caesar, Timon of Athens, Antony and Cleopatra, and Cymbeline, whatever the other classical influences, have Apuleian material woven into their textures.

By the end of this early period of his work Shakespeare had learned that he could use Apuleius' novel in a number of ways. First, he had seen that the Latin original offered hints which the valuable Adlington version for all its primary importance did not. He clearly had appreciated the variety of materials which this most episodic novel afforded, as the use of elements from the beginning of the work to its penultimate book readily shows. He already had seen that a single episode could be reused in differing ways and the evidence shows that the story of Cupid and Psyche had so many intriguingly reworkable aspects for him that it was to be the most frequent in appearance, and ultimately most important in significance, of the borrowed material. He had naturally enough perceived that circumstantial details could be drawn from the novel to add to the atmosphere of his plays. Particularly valuable were the details pertaining to witches and witchcraft -- and the linking of witchery and asininity was a thematic conjunction to which Shakespeare would return in his maturity (e.g., Othello).

He had focused on death scenes or scenes of near-death in Apuleius for the passing of several characters, Jack Cade, the Yorkist princes, Adonis, Aaron, and Tamora, and would return to such Apuleian scenes of fatality later in the canon. He had learned to shift gender, change number, and alter the result of these scenes without ruling out a subsequent return to the same scenes with their proper gender, number, and denouement. He had acquired a skill in interweaving materials from replicating sources, not only Apuleian, but Ovidian, with the result that the Shakespearean work is sometimes a palimpsest with each layer contributing particular diction and shaded elements of meaning.

Most importantly, he had realized that metamorphosis is a matter of role and identity -- and that the quest for self-knowledge, the theme of nosce teipsum which is at the heart of both the comedy and tragedy of Shakespeare, is concretely emphasized by the success and failure of metamorphosed characters. Various interpretations of the early works have noted not only the principle of metamorphosis, even when they have not included an awareness of its Apuleian origin, but also have observed the distance between the action, however violent and/or grotesque, and the response of the audience, whether in the theatre or the study. At times it is as if our feelings had been anesthetized to the horrible acts displayed or described. I believe that there are two good and ample reasons for this coolness or absence of emotional response. First, when the event displayed or described is grotesque, as, say, the mutilations described by Aaron or the dismemberment performed by Titus, there follows a response of double effect which reciprocally cancels the release of feelings normally belonging to either of the single effects. That is, "this unsettling technique, which drags the reader's feelings in opposite directions at once, is the most conspicuous effect of the grotesque," As Neil Rhodes adds in his most valuable study of Thomas Nashe, "frivolity and the macabre or, more generally laughter and revulsion, are the twin polarities of the grotesque."[23] The equal and opposite pull of laughter and revulsion produces an emotional stasis.

The grotesque is a feature of the Apuleian novel, and it has been argued that Titus Andronicus in its mood of "mature sophistication" or the "hardboiled mood"[24] produces the same kind of emotional neutrality as do such near-contemporary works as Cambyses and Tamburlaine. This sophisticated mood has as "its essence . . . an attitude of disillusioned amusement or 'artistic' detachment in the portrayal of man's comic or tragic destiny."[25] I suggest that the chief cause of this mood of detachment lies in the principle of metamorphosis itself. Although we usually see in modern examples of metamorphosis, a kind of punishment, e.g., Kafka as a bug, as we judge, rightly, that Lucius' metamorphosis into an ass is punishment for his curiosity and sensuality, it is important to recognize that the new form, however grotesquely degrading in externals, is often a protective guise, one which allows the protagonist to continue his existence, enrich his experience, and finally to learn about the world and his relation to it. It is not an antic disposition alone that is a safety device, but transmogrifications which provide a kind of security and a freedom, often a license, to observe people and acts otherwise denied to normal humanity in civilized society.[26] Detachment is an obvious corollary to this change of shape. It is a feature of other disguised lovers in the picaresque tradition of the novel which descends from The Golden Asse,[27] and it is a feature of those early plays of Shakespeare which stress metamorphosis or borrow from the Metamorphoses.[28]

CHAPTER ONE

[1] J.G. McManaway, "Recent Studies in Shakespeare's Chronology," Shakespeare Survey, III (1950), 22-33.

[2] Throughout I have used Adlington's translations as edited by Charles Whibley in The Tudor Translations, ed., W.E. Henley (London: David Nutt, 1893), IV.

[3] In Chapter 17 Lucius enters a stable, in Chapter 18 the garden behind the stable. Shakespeare has conflated the similar passages.

[4] Current scholarly opinion holds that the stage directions in 2 Henry VI are authorial.

[5] Line numberings as in The Riverside Shakespeare, ed. G. Blakemore Evans, et al. (Boston: Houghton Mifflin, 1974).

[6] See Kenneth Muir, The Sources of Shakespeare's Plays (London: Methuen, 1977), 11.

[7] Quoted by Dover Wilson in his edition of 2 Henry VI (Cambridge University Press, 1968 repr.), 191-92.

[8] Lines 1295-1301. See Geoffrey Bullough, ed., Narrative and Dramatic Sources of Shakespeare (London: Routledge & Kegan Paul, 1957-75) III, 328.

[9] Bullough, 245.

[10] See the Loeb edition of The Golden Ass, ed., S. Gaselee (London: Heinemann, 1915), 232, where "rosei" is still untranslated.

[11] Metamorphoses, 5.22.4.

[12] See Muir, Sources (1977), 3-4.

[13] D.T. Starnes, "Shakespeare and Apuleius," PMLA, LX (1945), 1021-50.

[14] These are Starnes' distinctions, 1028.

[15] Starnes (with pagination changed to that of Tudor Translation edition, 1893), 1029.

[16] Starnes, 1029, footnote 19.

[17] T.W. Baldwin in On the Compositional Genetics of The Comedy of Errors (Urbana: University of Illinois Press), 222ff. draws attention to arguments that the witchcraft references come from Plautus' Amphitruo.

[18] Starnes, 1022.

[19] Lucius sees a "Jugler" in Athens, The Golden Asse, 21.

[20] W.B.C. Watkins, Shakespeare and Spenser (Princeton: Princeton University Press, 1950), 311.

[21] Bullough, Narrative and Dramatic Sources, VIII, 16.

[22] For an illuminating discussion of Chiron and Demetrius as Rape and Murder, see the appendix of H.F. Brooks to Titus Andronicus, ed. J.C. Maxwell (London: Methuen, 1966), 131-32. For Shakespeare's use of Nashe's Christ's Tears over Jerusalem in this passage, see my article in Notes and Queries, April, 1984.

[23] Neil Rhodes, Elizabethan Grotesque (London: Routledge & Kegan Paul, 1980), 10.

[24] William T. Hastings, "The Hardboiled Shakspere," Shakespeare Association Bulletin, XVII (1942), 119.

[25] Ibid., 121.

[26] Irving Massey, The Gaping Pig, Literature and Metamorphosis (Berkeley: University of California Press, 1976).

[27] P.G. Walsh, The Roman Novel, 234ff.

[28] In the matter of dating, I have now come to accept the argument that The Taming of the Shrew is earlier than The Comedy of Errors. See Brian Morris' New Arden edition of The Taming of the Shrew (London: Methuen, 1981), 50-65.

CHAPTER TWO

ROMANTIC PLAYS OF THE MID-1590'S AND SONNETS

Putting aside considerations of history plays for the moment, we can say that Romantic comedy, and Romantic tragedy in the case of Romeo and Juliet, occupied the attention of Shakespeare in the middle nineties. And it is in these plays that we come closer to the quintessentially Shakespearean response to life, one generally characterized by kindness, humor, sympathy, and compassion. It might be assumed that, accordingly, the 'hard-boiled' Apuleius might disappear as a source, but this is not the case. There are many moods in Apuleius, and even if there had not been such variety, Shakespeare had already demonstrated a willingness to change or reverse the mood of his source when he saw fit. Accordingly, Apuleian elements appear in this next group of works, sometimes even as one would most obviously expect, at other times in the most surprising and pervasive of ways.

The two most important sources for The Two Gentlemen of Verona are Diana Enamorada of Montemayor and Have with you to Saffron-walden of Nashe.[1] The use of Nashe's work provided some salt to balance the artificial sweetness of the play's Lylyean quality, but it also may have led Shakespeare to move easily from the thought of little Apuleius to Apuleius himself, if indeed the process were not the reverse, for Valentine and the Robin Hood-like outlaws of the forest (IV.i, V.iii, V.iv) derive in part from an episode in The Golden Asse, Book VII. Starnes argued correctly that there are close correspondences in scene, characters, and plotting, and that these larger correspondences were made yet more discernible by the close parallels in the smaller details of phrasing.[2] Starnes, along with many other scholars, thought incorrectly that The Two Gentlemen of Verona is quite early, c. 1592, a view which added force to Starnes' equally incorrect theory that Shakespeare had read The Golden Asse during the beginning of his playwrighting career, ignored the text throughout the middle of his creative life and then returned to The Golden Asse late in his career, around the time of the composition of Macbeth. However much Starnes erred in missing the very many instances of Apuleian material in the plays between A Midsummer Night's Dream and Macbeth, he was quite right about the existence of a relationship between The Two Gentlemen of Verona and The Golden Asse.

The situation of Valentine and the outlaws in The Two Gentlemen of Verona has the banished Valentine arriving in the forest where surrounded by outlaws he is elected their "general," "captain,""commander," and "king" on the bases of his "goodly shape" and linguistic ability. He accepts the offer "Provided that you do no outrages/On silly women or poor passengers" (IV. i.69-70). Thus when his beloved Silvia is captured by the outlaws he is able to rescue her, and forgive them so completely that he finds employment for them with the Duke. In Book VII, Chap. 24-6 Lepolemus, the strong handsome fiancé of Charite, to whom the calming tale of Cupid and Psyche has been told, comes to the cave of her robber captives, is chosen their captain on the bases of his appearance and alleged experience as the thief Haemus (his alias), prevents the death of Charite and brings about her escape. He kills the outlaws. Starnes provided a table of parallels in the following way:

(1) Valentine, like Lepolemus, appears before the thieves in ragged clothes. "My riches," says Valentine, "are those poor habitments" (IV.i.13). Lepolemus "was poorly appareled, insomuch that you might see all his belly naked" (VII,140).[3]

(2) When Valentine meets the outlaws, he addresses them as "my friends" (IV.i.7). Likewise, Lepolemus first speaking to the thieves calls them "my faithful companions" (p. 140).

(3) The outlaws of the play have their quarters in a forest on the frontiers of Mantua; the thieves' den in the novel is a cave in a mountain, concealed by a dense forest.

(4) In the play, one of the outlaws brings Silvia "to our captain's cave" (V.iii. 12). In the story the thieves bring Charite into a cave (Bk. IV,95; VII, 137).

(5) The hero in the play, as in the story, deceives the bandits by lying to them; Valentine lies that he is banished for murder; Lepolemus falsely represents himself as the renowned thief Haemus,

formerly captain of a great company of thieves.

(6) In the play (IV.i.73-74), as in the story (VII,145) attention is given to the treasure of the thieves.[4]

The Two Gentlemen of Verona is a romantic comedy in which one does not expect much depth of characterization, and indeed there is none. The Apuleian material affects primarily the setting of the incident which allows Valentine to display some degree of creative enterprise. When Shakespeare needed a model for Valentine as savior in the midst of his band of admittedly not all that dangerous thieves, he found it in the episode of Lepolemus saving Charite from the murderous thieves of The Golden Asse. The improbability of the events in the source made easy the connection with the equally improbable episode of Valentine in the forest. One other connecting element which may have helped Shakespeare to think of Valentine in terms of Lepolemus is the subsequent adventure of the fatal hunt in which Lepolemus falls victim to the treachery of his "friend" Thrasillus, who has been overcome by his love for Lepolemus' wife Charite. Such a conflict between the claims of friendship and the demands of love lies at the heart of The Two Gentlemen of Verona, with Proteus behaving as an ineffective Thrasillus. The metamorphosed Lucius is both participant and auditor of these episodes and Thrasillus is turned from frustrated lover to murderer. The love for Charite has transformed Thrasillus, even as initially Proteus claims that he has been 'metamorphis'd' by Julia. The reversal of the outcome in the novel is only another example of Shakespeare's willingness to borrow material without respect to its tonal or story-line integrity.

Love and friendship are themes of Love's Labor's Lost but without the tragi-comic collision of The Two Gentlemen of Verona. The long final scene of the play shows two signs of Apuleian influence, the simile of Boyet at V.ii.257 and the concluding song which begins with reference to flowers culled from Gerard's Herbal and ends with an owl and a serving girl who in conjunction with one another recall Lucius' experience with both.

Love's Labor's Lost is a play with some few references to Cupid and an even larger number of comments on light, particularly on the theme that "by light we lose light" (V.ii.376), or as Berowne had earlier expressed it, "Light seeking light, doth light of light beguile" (I.i.77). Accordingly, it is not surprising to find Boyet echoing some of the diction in the manifestly reworkable scene of Psyche's mistaken use of light to extinguish the light of Cupid. Boyet, commenting on the critical asides of the ladies, says:

> The tongues of mocking wenches are as keen
> As is the <u>razor's edge</u> invisible,
> Cutting a <u>smaller hair</u> than may be seen;
> (V.ii.256-58)

This recalls the familiar "<u>razor</u>" which "turned its <u>edge</u>" (113) when Psyche sought to kill the hitherto "invisible" Cupid upon the advice of the critical sisters. The context of both passages in play and novel provide other details of note. The ladies are hidden by their masks from the sight of the amorous Lords of Navarre even as Cupid is hidden from the sight of Psyche. The Lords of Navarre are guilty of breach of faith and broken promise by virtue of their amorous activities, even as Cupid perceives that on the part of Psyche "promise and faith was broken" (113). The initial punishment of the King by Rosaline is his "<u>absence</u> only" (V.ii.223), just as Cupid tells Psyche that she will "be sufficiently punished by my <u>absence</u>" (114), with the effect that Psyche is <u>weeping</u> and <u>lamenting</u> pitteously" (114). Rosaline describes the Lords and King of Navarre as "They were all in <u>lamentable</u> cases!/The King was <u>weeping</u>-ripe for a good <u>word</u>" (V.ii.273-74).

Most suggestive of influence are the parallel references to excessive or even dark-creating light. Light by light beguiled, so clearly a theme of <u>Love's Labor's Lost</u>, recalls not simply Psyche's statement to Cupid, "I little esteeme to see your visage and figure, little doe I regard the night and darknesse thereof, for you are my only light" (109) or her description of her invisible husband to her sisters, "one that loveth not the light of day" (111), but also both, "at whose sight the very lamp encreased his light for joy," (part of the sentence which goes on immediately to "and the razor turned its edge" 113), and "the brightness whereof did darken the light of the lamp" (113). The fact that Psyche is a strikingly clear case of the truth of Berowne's "By light we lose light" (V.ii.376) recalls how <u>Love's Labor's Lost</u>, influenced by the tale of Cupid and Psyche, belongs for all its lightness of tone to the tradition of Renaissance works which concern themselves with the theme of the blindness of love.

There are obviously examples of the Petrarchan tradition of the blinding force of female beauty, as in

> What peremptory eagle-sighted eye
> Dares look upon the heaven of her brow,
> That is not blinded by her majesty.
> (IV.iii.222-24)

But we have here together with the reference to sight, light and darkness the sequence of broken pledge, curiosity (as to who is behind the vizards), punishment, and (the promise of) reward. Wind summarizes the Neo-Platonic reading of Cupid and Psyche thus:

> When Psyche succumbs, in the story of Apuleius, to the desire to see Amor with her eyes, she learns that this causes the God to vanish; and it is only after she has atoned for her curiosity, and produced the vessel of beauty from the realm of death, that she is allowed to regain the transcendent Amor . . .[5]

Some refraction of this reading shines through the comedy, with the realm of death surfacing to complete the rhythm in the news brought by Marcade that the Princess' father, the King of France, is dead -- and that as a consequence the lovers will have to prove themselves in a twelve month period of trial. Love is more powerful than the intellect, and all that the lovers of Navarre had learned from the rhetoric handbooks of courtly behavior is laughed to scorn in the light of reality. The artificial behavior of the King and his lords at the opening of the play in establishing their little Academy is exposed for what it is by the nature of reality. The pride of intellect which created such a neatly bounded world of either/or gives way to a recognition that love, with its embracing of contradictions in a world of both/and, is a superior vehicle for understanding.[6] The lessons of clarity become the lessons of truth taught, as Psyche learned to her temporary cost and ultimate benefit, in the school of night, and as Berowne and his colleagues learn when they are lightly tortured by those who might inspire them.[7]

Apuleian material is found most often at the conclusion of Shakespeare's plays, chiefly because the end of a play includes the death, deaths, or escapes from death of various characters -- and the episodes in <u>The Golden Asse</u> are replete with deaths. But it is not only death that comes at the end of Shakespeare's plays, and the life force of sexuality which appears in the final song of <u>Love's Labor's Lost</u> is equally and particularly Apuleian. I suggest that the conjunction of the staring owl and greasy Joan has been prompted by juxtaposition in <u>The Golden Asse</u> of the witch's owl and the serving maid Fotis, and that the Apuleian origin adds weight to the sexual significance of the line "while greasy Joan doth keel the pot" (V.ii.920,929).

It will be remembered that Fotis, now the "love" of Lucius, brings him to observe the transformation of her mistress into "an Owle" (79), the bird Lucius wishes to become in order to satisfy his curiosity about metamorphoses and witches. The sexual relationship of Fotis and Lucius had begun a little before when Lucius had returned to Milo's house after dinner at Byrrhena's home. He is impressed by both the shape and movement of Fotis as she prepares supper:

> When I was within the house I found my deare and sweet love Fotis mincing of meat and making pottage for her master and mistresse, the Cupboard was all set with wines, and I thought I smelled the savor of some dainty meats: she had about her middle a white and clean apron, and shee was girdled about her body under the paps with a swathell of red silke, and she stirred <u>the pot</u> and turned the meat with her faire and white hands, in such sort that with stirring and turning the same, her loynes and hips did likewise move and shake, which was in my mind a comely sight to see.
> These things when I saw I was halfe amazed, and stood musing with my selfe, and my courage came then upon mee, which before was scant. And I spake unto Fotis <u>merrily</u> and sayd, O Fotis, how trimmely you can stirre <u>the pot</u>, and how finely, with shaking your buttockes, you can make pottage. O happy and twice happy is hee to whom you give leave and licence but to touch you there. Then shee being likewise merrily disposed made answer, Depart I say, Miser from me, depart from my fire, for if the flame thereof doe never so little blaze forth it will burne thee extreamly, and none can extinguish the heate thereof but I alone, who in stirring <u>the pot</u> and making the bed can so finely shake my self. (45-46)

The parallel of sexual movement and the cooking process is clear. So too is the parallel between greasy Joan and Fotis in so far as they are both cooks who paradoxically cool by stirring, as "keel" signifies and as Fotis states ("and none can extinguish the heate thereof but I alone, in stirring the pot"). In addition, there is the parallel mood of cheerfulness -- the owl sings with "A merry note" (V.ii.919, 928) and Lucius speaks "merrily" (45) to Fotis who is "merrily disposed" (45). Further, the adjective used to describe Joan, "greasy" is of itself suggestive of sexuality as we know not only from the gloss on the word in a book like Partridge's Shakespeare's Bawdy as "obscene,"[8] but also from the use of a variant, "greasily" in the same sense earlier in Love's Labor's Lost when Maria criticizes Costard and Boyet, "Come, come, you talk greasily, your lips grow foul" (IV.i.137).

It may be objected that while the parallelisms of sexual scouring maids and the cooling process of sexual stirring are present and that while the possibility is there that Shakespeare was recalling Fotis when he wrote Joan, the fact remains that Adlington does not use "greasy" to describe Fotis or her actions. However, there is a poem about Apuleius and Fotis by George Gascoigne in which Fotis is said to have

> . . . greazde this quest (i.e., Lucius) with
>   sauce of Sorcerie
> And fedde his minde with knacks both quaint
>   and strange:
> Lo here the treazon and the treacherie
> Of gadding girles, when they delight to range.
> For Lucius thinking to become a foule
> Became a foole, yea more than that an Asse,
> A bobbing blocke, a beating stocke an owle,
> Etc.

The resonance of "greazde" and "quaint" underscores the sexuality of Fotis and even if Gascoigne has confused the story somewhat by having Lucius become both owl and ass. His poem provides the link in Shakespeare's mind between Fotis and Joan, a link forged by "greazed"/ "greasy." As to the question of whether or not Shakespeare knew this poem by Gascoigne, we may note that Gascoigne clearly advertizes the poem in his collection called The Posies (1575), in the section "Weedes," with the preamble:

31

David's salutacions to Berzabe wherein are
three sonets in sequence, written uppon this
occation. The deviser hereof amongst other
friendes had named a gentlewoman his Berzabe,
and she was content to call him hir David.
The man presented his Lady with a booke of
The Golden Asse, written by Lucius Apuleius,
and in the beginning of the booke wrote this
sequence. You must conferre it with the
Historye of Apuleius, for else it will have
small grace.

The Posies itself featured first among the "Herbes"
Gascoigne's "Comedie called Supposes," an adaptation of
Aristo's comedy I Suppositi and first published in 1566.
We know that Shakespeare read the Supposes for it provided the Bianca plot in The Taming of the Shrew.[11] If
he had read the comedy in the edition of 1575 he may
have read other works in the same edition including the
poem about Fotis who "greazde" her guest. That he did
indeed read this edition seems likely for its epigraph,
which is repeated on the title pages of both sections,
"Hearbes" and "Weedes," is "Tam Marti quam Mercurio,"
a tag which has affected the very last lines of the
play when Don Armado, who earlier in the pageant of the
nine worthies had as Hector referred to "armi-potent
Mars" (V.ii.644,651), judges that "The words of Mercury
are harsh after the songs of Apollo" (V.ii.930-31).

Shakespeare sometimes ended his comedies on a
clearly raw sexual note, e.g., The Merchant of Venice
and Nerissa's ring, and he has done so here in Love's
Labor's Lost with the aid of Apuleius and George Gascoigne.

Of all the plays in the canon A Midsummer Night's
Dream is the one most readily accepted as Apuleian in
source. Not that every scholar has been willing to
accept Bottom's translation as derived from The Golden
Asse for objections have been raised on the grounds
that the assification of Bottom is either explained
completely by other sources, e.g., Reginald Scot's Discovery of Witchcraft (1584), or is not explained by
Apuleius for the assification of Bottom is of his head
alone and it is done to him, while Lucius is completely
transformed and he has done it to himself.[12] Such arguments are careful to focus upon Bottom only and ignore other aspects of the play which have been affected
by the novel. They also ignore the fact that Shakespeare's use of sources is seldom a case of either/or,

but of both/and as in the case of Scot's Discovery of Witchcraft which refers to Apuleius' novel. The disinterested reader need not be impressed alone by the authority of Bullough and Muir, as well as others of near equal eminence, who argue that Bottom's translation is Apuleian, but can consider the case for himself.

Starnes pointed out that the novel and the comedy share two uncommon features: (1) an asinine transformation and (2) the man so transformed is loved and embraced by a woman much taken by his external form. Starnes summarizes the parallel actions of III.i.103ff. and IV.i.1-45 and the episodes in the novel thus:

> By Puck, Bottom is partially transformed into an ass. Titania, also under the spell of Puck, awakens and falls in love with Bottom the Ass. She speaks to him in terms of endearment, gives him four fairies to attend him. They lead him to Titania's bower. There Titania dismisses the attendant fairies, and she and Bottom retire together for the night, Titania saying, "I will wind thee in my arms."

> Lucius, in The Golden Ass, using ointment stolen from the sorceress Pamphile, is inadvertently metamophosed into an ass, retaining, like Bottom, the understanding of a man. After many unhappy adventures, he is beloved by a fine matron of Corinth. For a consideration, she is permitted to bring the ass to her home for the night. She kisses him and uses terms of endearment. She has four eunuchs prepare a bed for her and her beloved beast. She then dismisses the eunuchs, and the lady and the ass spend the night together -- She "oftimes embraced my body round about," relates Lucius the ass![13]

These parallels of situation are reinforced by parallels in wording, as in the following passages:

> Titania. And thy fair virtue's force (perforce) doth move me
> On the first view to say, to swear, I love thee.
>   (III.i.140-41)
> . . . .

> Thou art as wise as thou art beautiful
> (III.i.148)
> . . . .
> The summer still doth tend upon my state
> And I do love thee; therefore go with me
> (III.i.155-56)
> . . . .
> While I thy amiable cheeks do coy,
> . . . .
> And kiss thy fair large ears, my gentle joy.
> (IV.i.2,4)

and from the novel:

> She kissed me . . . with great affection
> casting out these and like loving words:
> "Thou art he whom I love, thou art he whom
> I only desire, without thee, I cannot live"
> (218).

Titania goes on to say:

> Sleep thou, and I will wind thee in my arms.
> . . . .
> So doth the woodbine the sweet honeysuckle
> Gently entwist; the female ivy so
> Enrings the barking fingers of the elm.
> O, how I love thee! how I dote on thee.
> (<u>They</u> <u>sleep</u>.)
> (IV.i.40,42-45)

While Lucius describes his experience with the amorous matron:

> But <u>in</u> the meane season she kissed me, and
> she looked in my mouth with burning eyes,
> saying: "I hold thee my cunny, I hold thee
> my nops, my sparrow," and therewithall she
> eftsoones imbraced my body round about, and
> had her pleasure with me (218-19).

Starnes did not point out a feature noted by Sister M. Generosa in the same year as his pioneering article: namely, that Puck as agent in the vengeful Oberon's plot to lead Titania into love with an ugly creature mirrors Cupid as agent in the vengeful Venus' unsuccessful plot against Psyche:

> And by and by she called her winged sonne
> Cupid . . . and brought him to the city,

and shewed him Psyches (for so the maid was
called), and having told the cause of her
anger, not without great rage, I pray thee
(quoth she) my dear childe . . . revenge the
injury which is done to thy mother by the
false and disobedient beauty of a mortall
maiden, and I pray thee, that without delay
shee may fall in love with the most miser-
ablest creature living, the most poore, the
most crooked, and the most vile, that there
may bee none found in all the world of like
wretchedness (99-100).[14]

Neither Starnes nor Generosa noted the importance of flowers, especially roses, in the play and the novel,[15] and neither observed that in the life of Apuleius "briefly described" before Adlington's translation of the novel itself we are told that he had a "father called Theseus (who) had passed all offices of dignity in his countrey with much honour" -- this from the same paragraph in which Marston would learn that Madaura, the country of Apuleius, was "under the jurisdiction of Syphax."

Quite independently of the work of Starnes and Generosa, J. Dover Wilson three years later saw a number of parallels between the play and the novel, especially in the story of Cupid and Psyche. Dover Wilson assumed that Shakespeare had rewritten a now lost comedy which was still closer to Apuleius' fairy tale, and he read The Golden Asse in S. Gaselee's corrected (in terms of a right translation) version in the Loeb Classics volume. There is no need to postulate a lost play and the use of Gaselee's more exact version leads to the loss of some tell-tale parallels. However, Dover Wilson is right to point out that Puck himself explicitly draws attention to Cupid in "Cupid is a knavish lad,/Thus to make poor females mad" (III.ii.440-41), that Venus anti-cipates the role of Oberon and Psyche that of Titania, and that there are seven parallels of significance:

> (1) Puck is introduced at the opening of Act II with an account of his Warwickshire mischief-making; Cupid is likewise intro-duced by Apuleius as the mischief-maker of Greek city life, "who by his evil man-ners, contemning all publique justice and law, armed with fire and arrowes, running up and downe in the nights from house to house, and corrupting the

lawfull marriages of every person, doth nothing but that which is evill . . ." (99-100).

(2) As the jealous Oberon summons Puck to help in his punishment of Titania, so the jealous Venus summons Cupid to help her to punish Psyche.

(3) The jealous anger of Oberon is the cause of disastrous seasons in the countryside which we see as a reflection of the rain and storms of 1594 and for which we found a possible source in Huon of Bordeaux.[16] But the jealousy of Venus brings disaster to the sea-faring Greeks, for, as a 'wordy and curious gull' relates, she "her self lasciviously use to ryot in the sea; wherby they say that they are now become no more gratious, pleasant, nor gentle, but incivile, monstrous and horrible" (116).

(4) Psyche is wafted by Zephyrus "into a deep valley," where she is sweetly couched amongst the soft and tender herbs, as in a bed of dewy grass and fragrant flowers, which looks like a direct suggestion for Titania's bower and the "bank where the wild thyme grows"[17] (II.i.249).

(5) As Titania is sung to by tiny attendant sprites, who feed her love with delicate fruits, so Psyche is waited upon by invisible spirits who serve her with "all sorts of wines like nectar" and "plentiful dishes of divers meats," furnishing her too with "the harmony of a large concourse" which "did so greatly thrill her ears that though there were no manner of person, yet seemed she in the midst of a great quire." (103-04)

(6) Oberon and Venus prescribe the same punishment for the victim. (Dover Wilson then cites part of the passage we have already quoted from Adlington, 99-100).

(7) Lastly, and perhaps most interesting parallel of all, Oberon's well-known lines at II.i,148ff., which begin

> Thou rememb'rest
> Since once I sat upon a promontory,
> And heard a mermaid on a dolphin's back
> Uttering such dulcet and harmonious breath
> That the rude sea grew civil at her song,

and continue a little later with the great tribute to the Maiden Queen, though undoubtedly, as we have seen above, a reference as it stands to the royal 'entertainment' presented to Elizabeth by Leicester in 1575, are discovered to be almost a distillation of Apuleius' scarcely less lovely description of Venus taking to her native element:

> When she had spoken these words she embraced and kissed her sonne, and took her voyage towards the sea.
> When she came upon the sea she began to cal the gods and goddesses, who were obedient at her voyce. For incontinent came the daughters of Nereus, singing with tunes melodiously: Portunus with his bristled and rough beard, Salita with her bosome full of fish, Palemon the driver of the Dolphine, the Trumpetters of Tryton, leaping hither and thither, and blowing with heavenly noyse: such was the company which followed Venus, marching towards the ocean sea (100).[18]

Whether or not one accepts each of these parallels as just, the list itself is persuasive so that we agree with Wilson's overall position that the myth of Cupid and Psyche has become part of the texture of <u>A Midsummer Night's Dream</u>. Some twenty-four years after <u>Dover Wilson</u>'s argument, and, independent of it, James A.S. McPeek described with a memorable simile, what had happened in the movement from novel to play:

> In effect, it may be argued that the fundamental pattern of the myth and the patterns of the main stories in the play are similar in several interlocking ways, and that if Shakespeare did not consciously recall the Psyche tale as he wrote, he nevertheless had in mind many of its archetypal features, so that the <u>Dream</u> in part becomes yet another example of what Northrup Frye designates as displaced myth. The general impression is not that of an ordering of the play to correspond

to the structure of the myth, but rather as
if the mosaic of the myth had been shattered
into its original tesserae, which Shakespeare
has picked up and arranged to suit his own
design.[19]

The tactic of picking tesserae to rework a design Shakespeare had already tried in Titus Andronicus with certain pieces from the Risus festival episode of The Golden Asse fitting into the grotesque lines of the tragedy. And later in Hamlet two large sections from the novel would be reshaped without losing the outline of their original form. Yet, tactics aside, the question arises what significance is to be read into so explicit a use of metamorphosis and asininity.

One can argue that Cupid and Psyche, like Pyramus and Thisbe, had been allegorized as the story of the soul's search for Christ and that the presence of both myths in the comedy, implicitly and explicitly, indicates that all this funny business about error, love, and blindness might be more serious than audiences in the theatre and the study usually view it. But we correctly think of Shakespeare as being unlike his contemporaries in his avoidance of allegorized myth.[21] Nevertheless, A Midsummer Night's Dream is a special play and an explicit asinine transformation is a most special occurrence on the stage. Accordingly, there have been interpretations of the play which suggest that a philosophical meaning is clearly present in the comedy. The two most intriguing of such interpretations are those of Omerod and Kermode.

David Omerod in the course of an essay arguing for the richness of the image of the labyrinthine wanderings of the lovers (with Bottom as a parodic Minotaur) points out that there were two seemingly contradictory traditions of the ass motif in the Renaissance. One tradition allowed for the appropriateness of Lucius' transformation: it is a fitting punishment for his lust and curiosity. The other, the tradition of the ass bearing the image of the goddess Isis, allowed for the ass as an image of vanity, falsely thinking that he is the recipient of the veneration directed to the icon he carries. Lucius actually carries such icons, and is, of course, ultimately restored to his humanity by the goddess Isis herself. As Omerod states the binary traditions in the novel:

> Apuleius' work, therefore, contains a graphic
> and debauched description of the depths of
> bestial love, together with an impassioned
> (indeed, almost mystical) description of a
> higher state of spiritual consciousness. The
> entire novel is, in a real sense, the story
> of an initiation.[22]

In the play Bottom, although eminently culpable on the grounds of vanity and unbridled self-aggrandizing enthusiasm, is transformed more from Puck's sportiveness than anything else, but it is very clear that he undergoes an experience which is ineffably illuminating. Just what this experience signifies in terms of the play as a whole is made clear by Frank Kermode who believes that "it is scarcely conceivable, though the point is disputed, that the love-affair between Titania and Bottom is not an allusion to The Golden Asse."[23]

If indeed the love affair of Bottom and Titania is an allusion, not an echo, an overt gesture by Shakespeare which would increase the pleasure of the better read members of his audience, then Kermode's argument has added force. He suggests that the neo-Platonic and Christian allegorical readings of the Cupid and Psyche story and of the vision of Isis granted to Lucius at the end of the novel are to be read into the texture of the play, especially the awakening of Bottom:

> I have had a most rare vision. I have had a
> dream, past the wit of man to say what dream
> it was. Man is but an ass, if he go about
> t'expound this dream. The eye of man hath
> not heard, the ear of man hath not seen,
> man's hand is not able to taste, his tongue
> to conceive, nor his heart to report, what
> my dream was. (IV.i.204,211-13)

This passage is not only a parody of 1 Corinthians 2.9ff., but is also a reminder that Apuleius/Lucius, following his restoration to human form, could not reveal the nature of his initiation into the Isiac religion, but was granted a direct vision of Isis herself. The author of Corinthians had, of course, also undergone a radical and religious conversion. "What they have in common is transformation, and an experience of divine love. Bottom has known the love of the triple goddess in a vision"[24] -- Titania in Ovid is the name for Diana (whose "bud," IV.i.73, is the source of the antidote Oberon uses to waken his love), and Diana is also Hecate the triple headed goddess, but Ovid also uses Titania as a name for Latona and Circe. The multiple names and rôles in the constellation around "Titania" parallel those attendant upon "Isis" who is "the mother of Gods" called variously "Minerva," "Venus," "Diana," "Proserpina," "Ceres," "Juno," "Bellona," and "Hecate" (233). Bottom's dream is of the kind called "oneiros or somnium," which is to say, however puzzling it is profoundly significant. The prohibition on articulating the nature of the new religion and the ineffability of the vision itself is attached to the truth that the love of God, Christian or Isiac, is a creatively blind love, an adumbration of which theme we have seen in Love's Labor's Lost. "Bottom is there to tell us that the blindness of love, the dominance of the mind over the eye, can be interpreted as a means to grace as well as to irrational animalism; that the two aspects are, perhaps, inseparable."[25]

The critical focus upon both the asinine transformation of Lucius and the tale of Cupid and Psyche in the interpretations of A Midsummer Night's Dream is a natural one based on an appreciation of the thematic interrelationship between the tale and the novel as a whole for "the adventures of Psyche are deliberately shaped to stress the connection between the maiden's error, suffering, and redemption, and the similar experiences of Lucius,"[26] as well as upon a perception that both aspects are present in the comedy. Just how allegorical a reading one wishes to elicit from the play in light of the allegorical tradition of the tale and the ambivalent ass-motif as understood in the Renaissance will depend upon one's willingness to accept A Midsummer Night's Dream as a special case within a canon of non-allegorical plays. It is a special case, and we should, like Lucius, be sufficiently curious to take a chance, for whatever the initial humiliating experience the ultimate reward is very great indeed.

Bottom and his colleagues put on the play of Pyramus and Thisbe, a work which shows in the midst of its uproariously funny performance and atrocious diction that love affairs can turn out disastrously. Romeo and Juliet, a tragic companion play to A Midsummer Night's Dream, is a serious version of Pyramus and Thisbe. As a companion play, Romeo and Juliet on the face of it should have some Apuleian material, if not necessarily so much as does the comedy. Indeed, all the other tragedies have an Apuleian element so that it would be surprising if Romeo and Juliet only had escaped scot free from the influence of the novel. A close study of the tragedy shows that there is a parallel episode just where one would expect to find it, at the end of the play, and on the theme most frequent at the conclusion, death.

When Romeo gazes upon the form of the apparently dead Juliet, he speaks of Juliet as the bride of death:

> Shall I believe
> That unsubstantial Death is amorous,
> And that the lean abhorred monster keeps
> Thee here in dark to be his paramour?
> For fear of that, I still will stay with thee
> And never from this (palace) of dim night
> Depart again. (V.iii.102-08)

This passage has been affected by some lines at the conclusion of Samuel Daniel's Complaint of Rosamund, but as is so often the case in Shakespeare's coalescent imagination two or more elements have been combined to create a new entity. It will be remembered that not only does Cupid, alleged by Psyche's evil sisters to be a devouring monster, conduct his relationship with his bride completely in the dark, but the wedding of Psyche was originally ordained with a "Serpent dire." Psyche is brought "not to her marriage, but to her final end and buriall" (101). In the event she is wafted by Zephyrus to the "Palace" (103)[27] of Cupid where the marriage is consummated in perfect darkness. Following this event invisible servants "presented to her such things as were necessary for her defloration" (104). Juliet's father under the impression that his daughter is dead explains to Paris that Death has slept with Juliet:

> There she lies,
> Flower as she was, deflowered by him.
> Death is my son-in-law. (IV.v.36-38)

This parallel of situation marked by funereal marriages with Death as the groom is made more likely when one notes that Friar Lawrence uses diction from Adlington's version when he discovers the body of Romeo just as Juliet is about to rise from her drugged sleep. He notes the blood "which stains/The stony entrance of this sepulchre . . . The lady stirs" (V.iii.140-41,147) and the stage direction is "Juliet rises"). The wording here echoes that in the story of the "ancient Physitian" who only pretended to supply a poison, but instead substituted a sleeping potion, the episode that Dekker and others were to find so malleable:

> . . . but if it be so that the child hath received the drinke and I tempered it with mine owne hands, he is yet alive and doth but sleepe, and after his sleepe, he shall returne to life againe, but if he be dead indeed, then may you further enquire of the causes of his death. The opinion of this ancient Physitian was found good, and every man had a desire to goe to the Sepulchre where the child was layd . . . Amongst them all the father of the child remooved with his owne hands the stone of the Sepulchre, and found his Sonne rising up after his dead and soporiferous sleepe, . . . (212).

Friar Lawrence combines the roles of potion-bringing physician and surrogate and benignant father, but Shakespeare has not only changed the gender of the child, but turned the outcome from comic to tragic. Such reversals he had practiced before and would practice again. Further evidence that this particular episode was influential upon the tragedy exists in the denouement where Friar Lawrence defends himself with some of the words of the Apuleian physician. Among such tell-tale words are "stopped her breath" (V.iii.211), "Seal up the mouth" (V.iii.216), and "condemned" (V.iii.227). Compare "stopped the mouth" (210), "the seale . . . sealed the purse" (211), and "condemned" (210,211). One notes that before the happy ending the "unhappy father was stroken with double dolour of the death of his two children" (208) and that there is double grief for the two warring families and for the Prince who, standing as a father in the state, has "lost a brace of kinsmen" (V.iii.295).

Romeo and Juliet lacks the pervasive use of Apuleian material found in A Midsummer Night's Dream, but there is the important adoption of the motifs of a bridal with death and a clarifying summation by a well-intentioned elder who provides a sleeping potion not a poison, both in the final scene of the play, the place where Apuleius is most frequently discovered in Shakespeare's works.

In Romeo and Juliet Shakespeare carried forward the treatment of love and love poetry begun in The Taming of the Shrew, The Two Gentlemen of Verona, Love's Labor's

Lost,[28] and A Midsummer Night's Dream.[29] The pretense
and sincerity of various lovers is analogous to the
themes of the sonnets and sonnet sequences of the nineties. Indeed, in Romeo and Juliet Shakespeare may be
said to have crossed the boundary separating lyric from
dramatic by incorporating "the sonnet mode into the art
of the play."[30] Shakespeare's sonnets themselves, by
general agreement works of the nineties, presumably
were affected by the poet's reading of The Golden Asse,
even as the plays of the same period so clearly were influenced by theme, diction, and incident from the novel.
We have already seen how the long narrative poem Venus
and Adonis incorporates elements from The Golden Asse.
In addition, we know the extraordinary use Shakespeare
made of themes and diction from the Metamorphoses of
Ovid, especially in Golding's translation,[31] so that it
would not be surprising to find that the Metamorphoses
of Apuleius, a work with the same theme of transformation and often appearing in conjunction with Ovid's poem
in various of the plays, had also contributed to the
themes and phrasing of the sonnets. However, this is
not the case, or at least not the case with the single
exception of the cluster composed of sonnets 53, 54,
and 55.

53

What is your substance, whereof are you made,
That millions of strange shadows on you tend?
Since every one hath, every one, one shade,
And you, but one, can every shadow lend:
Describe Adonis, and the counterfeit
Is poorly imitated after you;
On Helen's cheek all art of beauty set,
And you in Grecian tires are painted new;
Speak of the spring and foison of the year,
The one doth shadow of your beauty show,
The other as your bounty doth appear,
And you in every blessed shape we know.
 In all external grace you have some part,
 But you like none, none you, for constant
   heart.

54

O how much more doth beauty beauteous seem
By that sweet ornament which truth doth give!
The rose looks fair, but fairer we it deem
For that sweet odor which doth in it live.
The canker-blooms have full as deep a dye

As the perfumed tincture of the roses,
Hang on such thorns, and play as wantonly,
When summer's breath their masked <u>buds</u> discloses;
But for their virtue only is their show,
They live <u>unwoo'd</u>, and unrespected fade,
Die to <u>themselves</u>. Sweet roses do not so,
Of their sweet deaths are sweetest odors made:
   And so of you, beauteous and lovely youth,
   When that shall vade, by verse distills your truth.

55

Not marble nor the gilded [monuments]
Of princes shall outlive this pow'rful rhyme,
But you shall shine more bright in these contents
Than <u>unswept</u> stone, besmear'd with sluttish time.
When wasteful war shall <u>statues</u> overturn,
And broils root out the <u>work of</u> masonry,
Nor Mars his sword nor war's quick <u>fire</u> shall burn
The living record of your memory.
'Gainst death and all-oblivious enmity
Shall you pace forth; your <u>praise</u> shall still find room,
Even in the eyes of all posterity
That wear this world out to the ending doom.
   So till the <u>judgment</u> that yourself arise,
   You live in this, and dwell in lovers' eyes.

Sonnet 55 is usually viewed as among those addressed to the young man who is to be made immortal by his appearance in Shakespeare's poems.[32] The two basic sources for the poem and its particular theme of the pen's power to provide immortality are the last lines of Ovid's <u>Metamorphoses</u> and the opening of Horace's thirtieth ode from Book III. In the latter, the poet himself boasts that "part of me shall escape the death-goddess."[33] The conjunction of immortal fame and destructive goddess may have been the stimulating agent for Shakespeare's recollection of the opening of the story of Cupid and Psyche in which Venus' fame is dimmed, and consequently her powers of destructive vengeance are aroused. Psyche more lovely than her two sisters who deserve "<u>praise</u>" (98) is so beautiful that people begin to think that a new Venus has been born, "after the fame was spread into the next cities and bordering regions" (98).

> By occasion whereof such a contempt grew towards the goddesse Venus, that no person travelled unto the Towne Paphos, nor to the Isle Gyndos, nor to Cythera to worship her. Her ornaments were throwne out, her temples defaced, her pillowes and cushions torne, her ceremonies neglected, her images and <u>Statues</u> uncrowned, and her bare altars <u>unswept</u>, and fowl with the ashes of old burnt sacrifice. For why, every person honoured and worshipped this maiden in stead of Venus, . . . (99).

Venus reacts by commissioning her son Cupid, who is "armed with <u>fire</u> and arrowes" (99), to make Psyche fall in love with a vile creature. In the course of her indignant rage Venus points out that Jupiter had agreed with Paris' "just <u>judgement</u>" (99) of her primacy among all beauties, mortal and immortal. In Sonnet 55 Shakespeare has taken the theme of praise by poetry and contrasted it with the kind of praise which is dependent upon architectural and sculpted forms, the vehicles which prove so vulnerable for Venus' continued celebrity. Further, he has incorporated some of Adlington's diction into the sonnet with the "<u>unswept</u> stone" (1.4), the "<u>Statues</u>" (1.5),[34] "<u>fire</u>" (.7), "<u>praise</u>" (1.10), and "<u>judgment</u>" (1.13). The loss of fame suffered by Venus, even Venus, will not be experienced by the fortunate recipient of Shakespeare's poetic attention.

There is little likelihood that Shakespeare intended an allusion to Venus' predicament, even with the reference to her lover Mars (1.7), but there is some supporting evidence in Sonnets 53 and 54, poems which lead into Sonnet 55,[35] that this diction is at least an echo of <u>The Golden Asse</u>. In Sonnet 54 the idea is that posthumous praise is the perfume distilled by poetry from the flower of life. Less fair than the flower turned to scent are those which, when their masked <u>buds</u> are revealed, live only to themselves "unwoo'd and unrespected fade" (1.10). When in <u>The Golden Asse</u> Venus appeals to Cupid for aid against her supplanter, the initial result is that

> In the meane season Psyches with all her beauty received no <u>fruit</u> of honor. She was wondred at of all, she was praised of all,

> but she perceived that no King nor Prince,
> nor any of the superior sort did repaire
> to wooe her. (100).

The unwooed and now unhonored Psyche figures also in Sonnet 53. It will be remembered that Venus "the originall parent" (99) had protested over allowing any image of herself to be worshipped:

> If I shall suffer any mortall creature to
> present my Majesty on earth, or that any
> shall beare about a false surmised shape
> of my person, then in vain did Paris . . .
> preferre me . . . (99).

and that Psyche is described in the midst of her romantic isolation as having people marvel "at her divine beauty, as it were some image well painted and set out" (100). Her father in desperation seeks help from the oracle of Apollo who responds in Latin even though he is a "Grecian" (101). Sonnet 53 is devoted to the theme of shadow and substance, with the lover as unique in spite of counterfeit images. Some of the diction from the description of Venus' difficulty with Psyche as her image occurs in "beauty set" (1.7), "Grecian" (1.8), "painted" (1.8), and "shape" (1.12). Ingram and Redpath point out in their edition that "shadows" in line two (and "shadow" in line four) refers to "presumably not umbrae, in which colour, texture and detail are absent, but imagines, as the examples in lines 5 ff. show, though the phrase 'on you tend' would more naturally apply to umbrae."[36] In Apuleius' Latin the key words of Venus are "numinis" and "imaginem," and the descriptive term for Psyche is "simulacrum."

Although all three of these related Sonnets 53, 54, and 55 with their increasingly explicit stress upon the eternizing power of the poet reflect diction from the episode with the related theme of Venus' transitory fame, with Psyche as an ultimately imperfect and unwooed imitation, it is Sonnet 55 which is based not only upon a reversal of the source of the subject's gender but also a reversal of the source of the tale's plot. The young man, if indeed it is the young man, is guaranteed the immortality of poetry, free from rivals and the weaknesses of seemingly more substantial monuments.

In these romantic plays of the mid-1590's Shakespeare absorbed themes, motifs, and diction from The Golden Asse, sometimes quite directly, sometimes by way of considerable diffraction. Of particular interest in the matter of Shakespeare's borrowings at this time is his use of more than one episode from the novel in a single play. It is true that three related sonnets, 53, 54, 55 draw their Apuleian diction from only the tale of Cupid and Psyche with its themes of imitative beauty and transitory fame. However, in the plays we see evidence not only of the central fairy tale, but in A Midsummer Night's Dream also of the assification of Lucius itself and the passion of the Corinthian matron, in The Two Gentlemen of Verona of the outlaw election of a new captain and the tension between Thrasillus and Lepolemus, in Love's Labor's Lost, of the sexual and culinary powers of Fotis, and in Romeo and Juliet, of the well-intentioned physician who substitutes potion for poison. These multiple borrowings are the obverse of the truth that the presence of a source in any one play of Shakespeare is a near guarantee that the source will reappear in at least one other of his plays. Here we have in single plays not one but more than one element from an episodic single source.

The themes drawn from the novel, that love is blind, that friendship and love can collide, and that time is the destroyer of even the dignity of a goddess are transformed tonally in the comedies. Shakespeare's attitude toward the events in these plays allows him to metamorphose the effect of the themes which are presented in darker tones in The Golden Asse. In Romeo and Juliet he takes what is tragi-comic, the bridal death of Psyche and the physician's substitution of potion for poison, and removes the comic resolution.

In all these Apuleian incorporations Shakespeare shows himself willing to invert, reverse, and in general metamorphose in tone and structure the plot and theme of the source episode.

CHAPTER TWO

[1] See "Nashe and The Two Gentlemen of Verona," Notes and Queries, ccxxvi (1981), 122-23.

[2] Starnes, "Shakespeare and Apuleius," 1024.

[3] Changes have been made in spelling and line numbering to 1893 edition of The Golden Asse and the Riverside Shakespeare.

[4] Starnes, 1024-25.

[5] Edgar Wind, Pagan Mysteries in the Renaissance (London: Peregrine Books, 1967), 59.

[6] Wind, op. cit., 6.

[7] Wind, op. cit., 175.

[8] Eric Partridge, Shakespeare's Bawdy, A Literary & Psychological Essay and a Comprehensive Glossary (London: Routledge & Kegan Paul, 1955), 123.

[9] "David saluteth Bersabe" in The Poesies, ed., John W. Cunliffe (Cambridge: Cambridge University Press, 1907), 463-64.

[10] George Gascoigne, The Poesies, ed., John W. Cunliffe, (Cambridge: Cambridge University Press, 1907), 463.

[11] Muir, Sources, (1977), 19.

[12] So John R. Moore, as cited in Velz, Shakespeare and the Classical Tradition, 149.

[13] Starnes, 1030.

[14] Sister M. Generosa, "Apuleius and A Midsummer Night's Dream: Analogue or Source, Which?", Studies in Philology, XLII (1945), 198-204.

[15] But Hermann Reich did in his "Der Mann mit dein Eselkopf: Ein Mimodrama von klassischen Altertum verfolgt bis auf Shakespeare," Shakspeare Jahrbuch, XL (1904), 108-128, noted by Velz, Shakespeare and the Classical Tradition, 154-55.

[16] But see evidence that A Midsummer Night's Dream is dependent for certain names upon Nashe's Have with You to Saffron-Walden (1596) in "The Irony of 'Hermia' and 'Helena,'" American Notes and Queries 17 (1979), 154-56.

[17] The correct reading should be, malgré Wilson, "blows," not "grows."

[18] J. Dover Wilson, Shakespeare's Happy Comedies (Evanston: Northwestern University Press, 1963), esp. 217-19.

[19] James A.S. McPeek, "The Psyche Myth and A Midsummer Night's Dream," Shakespeare Quarterly, xxiii (1972), 69.

[20] Creative Imitation and Latin Literature, ed., David West and Tony Woodman, (Cambridge: Cambridge University Press, 1980), 239.

[21] Douglas Bush, "Classical Myth in Shakespeare's Plays," Elizabethan and Jacobean Studies Presented to F.P. Wilson, ed., H. Davis and H. Gardner (Oxford: Oxford University Press, 1959), 71.

[22] David Omerod, "A Midsummer Night's Dream: The Monster in the Labyrinth," Shakespeare Studies, XI (1978), 45.

[23] Frank Kermode, "The Mature Comedies," in Early Shakespeare, ed., J.R. Brown and B. Harris (New York: Schocken Books, 1966), 218.

[24] Ibid., 219.

[25] Ibid.

[26] P.G. Walsh, The Roman Novel, 190.

[27] McPeek, op. cit., 70-71, observed this parallel, but for the possibility that "palace" is really "pallet," a bed, see "Nashe and Romeo and Juliet," Notes and Queries, CCXXV (1980), 161-62.

[28] Usually dated 1594-95 with revision in 1597.

[29] Always allowing for the possibility that Romeo and Juliet precedes A Midsummer Night's Dream.

[30] See Brian Gibbons, ed., Romeo and Juliet (London: Methuen, 1980), 43.

[31] Stephen Booth, ed., Shakespeare's Sonnets (New Haven and London: Yale University Press, 1977), esp. Appendix 2, 551-54.

[32] The Riverside Shakespeare, 1745.

[33] Booth, Shakespeare's Sonnets, quoting from the Loeb translation. The death goddess is Libitina, although there is some doubt that Shakespeare would have known that fact.

[34] "Statues" has a capital "S" in the Quarto edition of 1609.

[35] Booth, Shakespeare's Sonnets, 227.

[36] W.G. Ingram and Theodore Redpath, ed., Shakespeare's Sonnets (London: Hodder and Stoughton, 1978), 122.

CHAPTER THREE

THE FALSTAFF PLAYS--AND DOGBERRY

Although it is not unlikely for a dramatist to wean himself from a source upon which he has been dependent in the interests of variety or from the principle of exhaustion, Shakespeare seems never to have relinquished his hold upon Apuleius in any period of his creative life. Certainly it is the case that Shakespeare varied the amount of his borrowings from The Golden Asse throughout his career, for different degrees of indebtedness to the novel are revealed in the Falstaff plays, 1 and 2 Henry IV and the Merry Wives of Windsor, and in the first of the Middle Comedies where Dogberry's humor is largely Apuleian, plays written between the heavily Apuleian-influenced early comedies and the still more consistently Apuleian-affected mature tragedies.

The ambivalence of 1 Henry IV on the levels of values and character is well recognized, if not ever to be perfectly understood. From the beastly transformation by the Welsh-women in the opening scene, through Hal's artificial and calculated loose behavior, to Falstaff's battle-field counterfeiting the play is full of double men who change as the occasion and their natures require. A very good deal of the words and phrases in the play come from a number of the pamphlets of Thomas Nashe,[1] but Apuleius himself in his novel of ultimate double-ness has provided incidents, and through Adlington's version, diction which has contributed to the lines of Hotspur, Hal, and most importantly, Falstaff.

When Northumberland rebukes his son over the latter's impatience at the treatment or non-treatment of his brother-in-law Mortimer, Hotspur responds with the appeal,

> Why, look you, I am whipt and scourged with rods,
> Nettled and stung with pismires, when I hear
> Of this vile politician, Bullingbrook.
> (I.iii.239-41)

There follows an exchange with his father which includes reference to "madcap" behavior (I.iii.244), a "castle" (I.iii.250), and to a "fawning greyhound" (I.iii.252). The diction in this scene has been affected by words and phrases in two consecutive chapters of The Golden Asse where first the death of the luxurious servant and then the experience of Lucius at the hands of the priestly flagellants are described. "Pismires" (I.iii.240) is unique in the canon and echoes the "Pismares" who are drawn to honey with which the servant has been annointed: "after they had felt the sweetnesse of the honey came upon his body, and by little and little . . . devoured all his flesh" (171). Hotspur's frustrations are largely self-inflicted, or at least self-intensified by his dwelling upon the loss of honor and the indignities suffered by the Percies, so that it is particularly appropriate that his being "whipt and scourged" should derive in its wording from the description of the behavior of the masochistic priest, "one more mad than the rest," who "tooke a whip and scourged his owne body" (174). It is of interest that on the single surviving sheet (C) of the first quarto edition (Qo) of 1598, which is "believed to be either Shakespeare's 'foul papers' or a transcript from them by another hand,"[2] the reading, which may represent Shakespeare's uncorrected recollection of the exact phrasing of Adlington, is "whip and scourg'd." That the politician Bolingbroke should be described as "vile" may be the result of those "mad" priests who practiced "vilde abominations" (175) when they have reached a "Castle" (174). The next stop after the castle is a house at which "a fat Bucke" given as a present is "eaten up by a gray hound" (176).

In addition, the mellifluous feast of the Pismares is recalled again during the king's lecture to Hal who has been guilty of "vile participation" (III.ii.87), like that of King Richard who mistakenly has

> Enfeoff'd himself to popularity,
> That being daily swallowed by men's eyes
> They surfeited with honey and began
> To loathe the taste of sweetnesse, whereof a little
> More than a little is by much too much.
>   (III.ii.69-73)

Hal's defense of himself is also Apuleian. He argues that his father is wrong to judge by the opinion of others. He assures the king who has likened Hotspur to 'Mars' (III.ii.112) and who thinks of Hal as "degenerate" (III.ii.128) that he is indeed the king's "son" (III.ii.134), that he will cover himself heroically with "blood" (III.ii.135), and that he will use Hotspur, this man of "renown" (III.ii.139) as his "factor" (III.ii.147), a factor who "shall render up every glory"

(III.ii.150). All this he promises to perform "in the name of God" (III.ii.153), never faltering until "the end of life (which) cancels all bands" (III.ii.157). The diction here comes from the episode in which Charite's fiancé Lepolemus disguises himself as a thief in order to join the band of thieves who have kidnapped her:

> As soone as he was entred in he said, God speed yee souldiers of Mars and my faithfull companions, I pray you make one of your band . . . yet thinke you not that I am an abject or a beggar, neither judge you my vertue and prowesse by ragged clothes . . . I am the renowned theefe Hemes . . . the sonne of Theron the noble theefe, nourished with humane bloud . . . finally I am inheritour and follower of all my fathers vertues, yet I lost in a short time all my company and all my riches, by one assault, which I made upon a Factor of the Prince. . . Howbeit I left not off for all this, nor did degenerate from the glory of my father . . . (140-41).

The king who "stole all courtesy from heaven" (III.ii. 50), not to mention the crown itself, makes a particularly good audience for the hitherto consciously deceptive Lepolemus as he inveigled the thieves into accepting him as a member in good standing. In the play, of course, Shakespeare has reversed the intention and provided Hal with a sincerity missing from the duplicitous Lepolemus. Hotspur does prove to be the prince's factor and Hal proves all too well that he is Henry's son.

Falstaff, too, shows the influence of Apuleius, both in terms of the company of soldiers he has pressed into service and in the infamous counterfeiting at the Battle of Shrewsbury. When he describes his shame at the appearance of his soldiers both the diction and the rhythm of the sentences reflect the description by the asinine Lucius of the workers in a poor bakery and of the servant animals. Falstaff, after beginning his description with terms partly derived from Barnabe Riche's Souldier's Wishe to Briton's Welfare,[3] continues,

> . . . gentlemen of companies -- slaves as ragged as Lazarus in the painted cloth, where the glutton's dogs lick'd his sores, and such as indeed were never soldiers,

> but disgarded unjust servingmen . . . ten
> times more dishonorable ragged than an old
> feazy'd ancient . . . you would think that
> I had a hundred and fifty totter'd prodigals
> lately come from swine-keeping, from eating
> draff and husks . . . Nay, and the villains
> march wide betwixt the legs, as if they had
> gyves on, for indeed I had most of them out
> of prison.   (IV.ii.25-42)

The Prince and Westmoreland share Falstaff's dismay at the appearance of these troops, with Westmoreland describing them as "exceeding poor and bare" (IV.ii.68-69), Falstaff pointing out that they had not "their bareness" (IV.ii.71) from him, and the Prince agreeing with Falstaff, "unless you call three fingers in the ribs bare" (IV.ii.73-74). Lucius, after his escape from the lascivious and masochistic priests who are put "in prison" (184) by the villagers, is driven to a 'bakehous' where he "saw a great company of horses" (184) and the human workers in the bakery:

> O good Lord what a sort of poore slaves
> were there; some had their shinne blacke
> and blew, some had their backes striped
> with lashes, some were covered with rugged
> sackes, some had their members onely hidden:
> some wore such ragged clouts, that you
> might perceive all their naked bodies, some
> were marked and burned in the heads with hot
> yrons, some had their haire halfe clipped,
> some had lockes on their legges, some very
> ugly and evill favoured, that they could
> scarce see, their eyes and face were so
> blacke and dimme with smoake, like those
> that fight in the sands, and know not where
> they strike by reason of dust: And some had
> their faces all mealy. But how should I
> speake of the horses my companions, how
> they being old and weake, thrust their
> heads into the manger: they had their neckes
> all wounded and worne away: they rated their
> nosethrilles with a continuall cough, their
> sides were bare with their harnesse and
> great travell, their ribs were broken with
> beating, their hooves were battered broad
> with incessant labour and their shinne
> rugged by reason of their lancknesse (185).

The "clouts" are a version of the "two napkins tack'd together" (IV.ii.43) and "yrons" and "lockes" suggest "gyves" (IV.ii.41), even as the "company of horses" echoes Falstaff's "company" (IV.ii.42), "ragged" echoes "ragged" (IV.ii.31), "legges," "legs" (IV.ii.40), and "bare," and "ribs" provide the stimulus for the Prince's jibe about ribs bare (IV.ii.74). In general, Lucius' description of his colleagues in the bakehouse, non-human and dehumanized, is a model for the still more extended description of the scarcely human soldiery who follow Falstaff as unwitting food for powder.

When Falstaff meets the Douglas, acts upon the principle that discretion is indeed the better part of valor, rises up, and then stabs the dead Hotspur, he is again Apuleian. In a further adventure in The Golden Asse, Lucius is the object of a struggle between his master a gardener and a soldier of limited courage. In the fight between them, the gardener so gets the advantage "that the souldier could not tell by what meanes to save himselfe, but by feining that he was dead" (201). Lucius adds that "the souldier afterwards rose up as one awaked from a drunken sleepe" (201), but would not complain of his defeat "lest he should be accused of cowardise or dastardnesse," (201). This example of deceit is relatively harmless, but it seems to have been fused in Shakespeare's mind with a far more corrupt version of deception earlier in the novel.

The story of Charite and her enterprising lover Lepolemus, (some of whose phrases have found their way into the lecture of King Henry and the response of Hal, as we have noted above) ends in the murder and suicide of the lovers when a treacherous rival enters the scene. Thrasillus is the traitor who, under the guise of friendship with Lepolemus, accompanies the latter on a hunt, described in an episode in the novel which Shakespeare had read sometime before he finished the composition of Venus and Adonis, as Starnes first noted. In his re-reading of the episode or in his recalling of it during the writing of 1 Henry IV, Shakespeare focused upon the method of treason. Having already hamstrung Lepolemus' horse when Lepolemus was on the ground, Thrasillus watched as Lepolemus was gored by the wild boar:

> Howbeit, Thrasillus was not sufficed to see him thus wounded, but when he desired his friendly help, he thrust Lepolemus through the right thigh with his speare,

the more because he thought the wound of
the speare would be taken for a wound of
the Boars teeth, then he killed the beast
likewise (161).

Following the burial of Lepolemus, "Thrasillus fained
much sorrow for the death of Lepolemus, but in his
heart he was well pleased . . . and to counterfeit the
matter he would come to Charites . . ." (162). However,
Charite is told by the ghost of Lepolemus that Thrasillus is a murderer. She resolves to revenge the murder
of her husband by killing Thrasillus whom she has drugged and then when this counterfeiter who wounded her
husband in the thigh

lay prostrate on the ground . . . Charites
. . . with manly courage and bold force
stood over the sleeping murderer, saying: Behold the faithfull companion of my husband,
behold this valiant hunter; behold me deere
spouse, this is the hand which shed my bloud,
this is the heart which has devised so many
subtill meanes to worke my destruction . . .
(164-65).

She then proceeds to prick out his eyes, saying that
the "death" (165) of this enemy will be sweeter than
life.

These materials have affected Falstaff's counterfeiting death and wounding of Hotspur, as well as Hal's
response to the spirit of the 'dead' Falstaff. We note
that Falstaff "falls down as if he were dead" (s.d.),
tells us that it was "time to counterfeit" (V.iv.113),
and then stabs the dead Hotspur "with a new wound in
(his) thigh" (V.iv.128), a phrase repeated in "this
wound in the thigh," (V.iv.151). We note further that
the counterfeiting, soon-to-be-thigh-stabbing Falstaff
is directly addressed as he lies "on the ground" (V.iv.
134) by the saddened Hal standing over him, Hal who
puns "Death hath not strook so fat a deer to-day,/
Though many dearer, in this bloody fray" (V.iv.107-8).
The image used by McPeek to describe Shakespeare's use
of the Psyche myth in A Midsummer Night's Dream is apt
here in a more modest scope: the story of Thrasillus'
treachery and punishment is broken into fragments and
reformed into a design with a very much lighter coloring. Shakespeare noted especially the deceptive wounding in the thigh, the counterfeiting of behavior, the
direct address over the prostrate body of the counterfeiting thigh-stabber, and the punning potential of

"deere," enhanced by the analogous "heart." Falstaff does not murder Hotspur, his counterfeiting is self-defensive, his threatened embowelling is never carried out, and as a fat deer he will rise again to wear horns in The Merry Wives of Windsor. He is not a Thrasillus, indeed as a miles gloriosus he is the opposite of Thrasillus whose name as we have noted means "over-bold". Yet when Falstaff has his genealogy described it should include in the family tree Thrasillus as well as Thraso.[4]

Before Falstaff acquired his antlers, he continued to be affected by Apuleian material as a close look at 2 Henry IV reveals. The themes of doubleness and of metamorphosis continue with Hal descending into "a lower transformation" (II.ii.174-5) as a drawer before his consummate and lasting change from boon companion to responsible monarch, and Falstaff trying to transform memory into desire and the rawest recruits into the king's soldiers. These recruits, perhaps because they are examined individually, are not described in the terms derived from Apuleius which make memorable their predecessors who marched to Shrewsbury. Indeed, the Apuleian material is confined to two scenes of the Second act.

Mistress Quickly's remark that there is no honesty "unless a woman should be made an ass and a beast" (II.i.37) and Falstaff's reference to Mistress Quickly as "the quean" (II.i.47) ten lines later together suggest that Shakespeare was recalling the episode in Chapter Forty where Lucius as ass watches the baker's wife in her adultery when she is described as a "mischievous queane" (187,191) and a "wicked queane" (192) whose love is interrupted before "he had scarce eaten the first morsell" (191). Compare Falstaff's subsequent reference to "the sweetest morsell" (II.iv.367) he must leave unpicked. However, these echoes seem casual. More consciously derived is the diction in the brief exchange amongst Bardolph, the Boy, Poins, and the Prince in which Poins calls the Boy already feared 'transform'd' (II.ii.72) by Falstaff, a "virtuous ass" (II.ii.75), the Prince observes that "the boy" has profited (II.ii.84) and asks Bardolph "how doth thy master" (II.ii.98), and the page boy himself makes a confused reference to the story of Meleager (which Shakespeare had used in 2 Henry VI) in "Althaea's dream," (II.ii.87) and "Althaea dreamt she was deliver'd of a fire-brand" (II.ii.89-90). This exchange echoes speech and description in Chapter Thirty-One where

Lucius is victimized by the vengeful mother of a boy
who has been killed by a bear. The mother blames Lucius
for not protecting her son. The reverberant words are
"the boy" (154), "thy good Master" (155), "a firebrand"
(155), and "so I enforced the queane to leave off,
otherwise I had died as Meleager did by the sticke,
which his mad mother Althea cast in the fire" (155).
Bardolph's nose has become the firebrand of Althaea,
-- Bardolph, in the words of "the quean" Mistress
Quickly (who spoke of a woman "made an ass"), who has
an "arrant malmsey-nose" (II.i.39).

    Just before Hal undergoes his voluntary "transformation" into a drawer, Falstaff, Pistol, Bardolph, Mistress Quickly and Doll Tearsheet are involved in a tumultuous exchange ending in drawn swords and the flight of Pistol and Bardolph. Some of the terms used in this exchange derive from the first episode of The Golden Asse in which Lucius listens to the story of how Aristomenus shared a room in an inn with Socrates, a commercial traveler who is the victim of his own lechery and the power of the witch Meroe ("being so named because she was a Taverner, and loved wel good wines," (28) -- Mistress Quickly is Taverner of the Boar's Head). The episode involves Aristomenus watching as the witches Meroe and Panthia (compare the benign ladies Mistress Quickly and Doll Tearsheet) combine to punish the unfaithful Socrates, "the companion of Aristomenus," by cutting his throat in his sleep, withdraw his heart, stop up the wound, and before leaving punish also the witness Aristomenus by urinating upon him. Of particular interest are the words "naked sword" (27), "sister" (28), "Calipso" (28), "thrust" (28), "dolefull" (28), "ghost" (28), "wide wound" (28), "Gallowes" (29,30), "asleepe" (29), "murthered" (29), "Dog Cerberus" (30), "imbrued" (31),[5] and "belly" (31). These terms recur in 2 Henry IV, II,iv as "Cerberus" (II.iv.168), "dogs" (II.iv.174), "Calipolis" (II.iv.179),[6] "thrust" (II.iv.188,190,211), "Galloway" (II.iv.189),[7] "imbrue" (II.iv.196), "asleep" (II.iv.197), "doleful" (II.iv.197), "ghastly" (II.iv.198), "gaping wounds" (II.iv.198), "Sisters" (II.iv.199), "murder" (II.iv.206), "naked weapons" (II.iv.207), and "belly". In addition, the associative echo of 'pisse' in "Pistol" may be of significance in understanding why it is Pistol who asks the question "shall we imbrue," for in Adlington's version Aristomenus speaks of the "stinke of the pisse wherewith those Hagges had embrued me" and Socrates tells Aristomenus that "thou art imbrued with stinking pisse." "Imbrue" occurs in the canon only here and in the heavily Apuleian A Midsummer Night's Dream, just as 'blubber'd' occurs only here in 2 Henry IV at the end of this scene and quite later in The Two Noble Kinsmen. Doll is described at II.iv.390 as "blubber'd" over the departure of Falstaff. Socrates' wife grieves at the loss of her husband, "with face and visage blubbered with teares" (22).

Shakespeare held in volatile solution the elements of sexuality, drunkenness, for Aristomenus admits to having been "overcome with wine" (31), violence, a place, a vocation, an Inn, a Taverner, two women of some maturity, murder and micturition, making light the tone as he moved those elements from the inn in Thessaly to the Boar's Head of London. Some further indication that the Thessalian inn fitted with Shakespeare's view of the Boar's Head exists earlier in Mistress Quickly's response to Falstaff's extempore performance in the character of King Henry in 1 Henry IV. Mistress Quickly is so delighted by the playlet, "O Jesu, this is excellent sport, i'faith" (II.iv.390), that tears of laughter run down her face. Falstaff takes advantage of these tears of laughter with a regal command, "Weep not, sweet queen, for trickling tears are vain" (II.iv.391). "Trickling" is unique in the canon, and it appears to be the result here of Shakespeare's recalling Aristomenus' own tears of laughter in the Thessalian inn as he inadvertently acts the role of a snail: "for as tears oftentimes trickle down the cheeks of him that seeth or heareth some joyfull newes, so I being in this fearfull perplexity, could not forbeare laughing, to see how of Aristomenus I was made like unto a snaile in his shell" (27).[8]

The death of Falstaff in Henry V is paralleled by a loss of Apuleian materials in that play. There is the unique "inheritrix" of I.ii.51 which might have been prompted by the description of the baker's daughter as "inheritrix to her father" (195) in Chapter Forty-One of the novel, for the legalisms in the appropriate passage in Holinshed which Shakespeare borrowed from quite directly do not use the word.[9] And there is Pistol, who in 2 Henry IV had borrowed "imbrue" from the story of Aristomenus and Socrates, and may have borrowed again in his threat to "cut" the "throat" (IV.iv.32) of his French captive to "couper" his "gorge" (IV.iv.36) from the same story of Socrates who had his "throat cut" (28) and of Aristomenus who hoped to explain away his experience as the result of over-eating and excessive drinking, of being like those "as fill their gorges" (31). Such a conflation and compression of proximate terms in a source is characteristic of Shakespeare's general tactical practice, but even this possible borrowing from The Golden Asse is scarcely sufficient to raise Henry V to the level of 1 and 2 Henry IV as a text of significant Apuleian material.

Far closer to the novel in broad comic spirit is The Merry Wives of Windsor, a play with many references to transformation and to asses. It is particularly fitting that the play owe something to the novel for it celebrates the Knights of the Order of the Garter,[10] and we know that Adlington dedicated his translation, The Golden Asse, in 1566 to "Thomas Earle of Sussex, Viscount Fitzwalter, Lord of Egremont, and of Burnell, Knight of the most noble Order of the Garter" (3).

Various characters in the comedy liken themselves to an ass or are likened by others to the same animal. Slender for all his imbibing is confident enough of his memory to say, "yet I am not altogether an ass" (I.i. 172). Ford is sure that "Page is an ass, a secure ass; he will trust his wife, he will not be jealous" (II.ii. 300-301). Bardolf refers to the Germans as "three Doctor Faustuses" (IV.v.69-70) in a pronunciation which is revealed by the Folio reading, "Faustasses." And Falstaff himself in the midst of a dawning self-awareness says that "I do begin to perceive that I am made an ass" (V.v.119). Falstaff is also worried that Evans will "transform" him "into a piece of cheese" (V.v.82) and suggests that "'Tis time I were chok'd with a piece of toasted cheese" (V.v.138-39), good jokes on the proverbial enthusiasm of the Welsh for cheese, but also reflective of the bewitched Socrates whose tormenting witch Meroe "transformed" her lover, and of Aristomenus who hears the story of Socrates which begins with adventures through Thessaly trying to sell "new cheeses" (22), eating meat "fried with the flower of cheese and barly" which sticks in his throat "that I was well nigh choked" (21). Socrates dies after eating "a whole Cheese" (32). Aristomenus is "imbrued with stinking pisse" (31), a condition which may have prompted Shakespeare's giving to Falstaff at the opening of this scene the rare "piss" (V.v.14).[11] Without considering Falstaff as a mock Socrates in his earlier career, meeting a parodic Socratic death in Henry V,[12] we may note that the juxtaposition of transformation, cheese, choked, and pisse in an episode already used in 1 and 2 Henry IV suggests that Shakespeare has used these terms again in another episode of transformation.[13] Indeed, Falstaff's earlier transformation into "the old woman," (IV.ii.85,181), the witch of Brainford, with the jealous Ford's unexpected return home and his terms of abuse for the old woman, "witch," and "quean" (IV.ii.172) recalls the series of hidden and discovered adulteries in the episode of the baker's wife, who hires a "witch" (194), confides in a bawd, "the old woman," (187) and is herself called a "queane" (187,192). Shakespeare has practiced his tactic of reversal, for whereas the wives in Apuleius are guilty, Mistress Ford, in keeping with the tone of this sportive comedy, is innocent.[14]

Of course the prime transformation in The Merry Wives of Windsor is of Falstaff into a stag. Although Falstaff seems to recognize the ambiguity of his metamorphosis, that he is as much "ass" (V.v.119) as stag, the Actaeon-like transformation as much as the metamorphic asinine change is at least partly Apuleian. Pistol addresses Ford as "Sir Actaeon" (II.i.118) and Ford thinks of Page as a "willful Actaeon" (III.ii.43), and we know that the myth of Actaeon itself was one of Shakespeare's favorites.[15] It is also a myth of importance in The Golden Asse.

Shortly following the page of the dedication to "Thomas Earle of Sussex . . . Knight of the most noble Order of the Garter" (3), Adlington justifies the moral worth of his translation by pointing out that myths and fables have ethical significance hidden within them. He cites several examples of such fables, the first of which is that of Actaeon:

> For by the Fable of Actaeon, where it is feigned that when he saw Diana washing her selfe in a Well, hee was immediately turned into a Hart, and so was slain of his owne Dogs; may bee meant, That when a man casteth his eyes on the vaine and soone fading beauty of the world, consenting thereto in his minde, hee seemeth to bee turned into a brute beast, and so to be slaine through the inordinate desire of his owne affects (5).

In the novel itself when Lucius visits his aunt Byrrhena's house he sees marble statues in the garden, the most prominent of which is of "the goddesse Diana." A lengthy description of her dogs follows and then

> Amongst the branches of the stone appeared
> the image of Actaeon: and how that Diana
> (which was carved within the same stone,
> standing in the same water) because he
> did see her naked, did turne him into an
> Hart, and so he was torne and slaine of
> his owne hounds (43).

Byrrhena warns Lucius of the dangers of Pamphile and her lust, but he immediately returns to Fotis as she is stirring the pottage and subsequently allows his curiosity to be added to his sexuality, with the result that he is punished with asinine transformation. Falstaff is something of an antlered Bottom who is punished for his "sinful fantasy" (V.v.93), his "lust and luxury" (V.v.194).

The laughter at the expense of Falstaff which fills so large a part of the final scene could have been enhanced by elements of the Risus festival at which Lucius is made the butt of communal joking, but it is not. Yet, The Merry Wives of Windsor in its idea of a punitive transformation (in which he who would cuckold is made to wear the horns), its particular focus upon the myth of Actaeon, its celebration of the Order of the Garter, and its reference to witches and queans is as much influenced by elements in The Golden Asse as those plays which featured Falstaff in a less farcical mode, 1 and 2 Henry IV.

The asininity of Dogberry in Much Ado About Nothing is Apuleian in origin, but not completely so. In fact the constable's humor in the play derives from the comic Watch in King Leir, the apologia of Gabriel Harvey in Pierce's Supererogation, and the trial scene in the Risus episode of The Golden Asse. In King Leir, as Jacqueline Pearson has shown,[16] there is not only an abuse of the English language by the Second Watchman in pre-Dogberrian fashion with "follow my vice"[17] when he means 'advice,' but also a reference to a man's being accused of asininity: "I hope you do not call me asse by craft, neighbor," (2452) says the First Watchman to the Second. This brief exchange may have stimulated Shakespeare to the point of expanding the joke on 'ass'-calling. Yet he had also before him the case of "little Apuleius," Nashe having called Harvey an "ass" and Harvey's heavy-handed and inconsistent defense of the dignity of asses in general and therefore of himself in particular.[18] Harvey is especially anxious to have it recorded that Nashe has named him an ass: "Be it knowne

unto all men by these presentes, that Thomas Nashe, from
the topp of his witt looking downe upon simple creatures, calleth Gabriell Harvey a Dunse, a foole, an
ideot, a dolt, a goose-capp, an _asse_, and soe fourth"
(31)[19]. Harvey goes on to say "If I be an _Asse_, I have
company enough . . . He . . . shall have much adooe
. . . (36) . . . Some complexions have much adoe to alter their nature . . . (37) . . . I were indeede a notorious insensate . . . I will prove miselfe no _Asse_
. . . (39) . . . they are rare, and dainty wittes, that
can roundly call a man _Asse_ at every third word . . .
(157) . . . but what an _asse_ am I . . ." (167), and
much, much more. Further, in his counter-attack upon
Nashe, Harvey plays with variations upon the word
"Dogges-meate," (30,31,32,35), "Dogs'head" (30), and
"Dogged" (31) with the result that the constable's name
"Dogberry" itself as well as his concern to be written
down an ass derive from the defense of the victim of
little Apuleius.

Such an origin for "Dogberry" is in keeping with
the just opinion that in the midst of this very Italian-
ate play, the humorous constable is "undeniably English."[20] Aubrey went so far as to state that "the Hu-
mour of the Constable . . . he happened to take at Gren-
don in Bucks . . . which is the roade from London to
Stratford."[21] Perhaps Shakespeare did find some inspi-
ration from such a personal encounter, perhaps the figure of an asinine Harvey walking in the garden of
Christ's College was a helpful addition, but in either
or both events _The Golden Asse_ itself provided considerable material for the comedy.

Apart from his delightful verbal errors, Dogberry
is most memorable for (1) the care he shows for his role
as leader of the watch and (2) his related concern that
the testimony in which he has been called an ass be duly
recorded. At the end of Book II of _The Golden Asse_
Lucius, soon to be literally an ass, kills or thinks he
kills three men of great stature while they were attempting to break into the house of his host. In Book
III Lucius is brought before the bar of justice as a
homicide by the captain of the watch:

> And thinke you not that I am moved here-
> unto by envy or hatred, but by reason of
> my office, in that I am captain of the
> night Watch, and because no man alive
> should accuse mee to bee remisse in the

> same, I wil declare all the whole matter,
> orderly as it was done this last night (65).

There are striking parallels between the Dogberry episodes and that of Lucius on trial in the Apuleian novel. First, it is following this particular experience that Lucius involves himself in the machinations which turn him into an ass. Dogberry is called an ass by Conrad (IV.ii.73) and six times in the play identifies himself as an ass:

> O that he were here to write me down an ass!
> But, masters,
> remember that I am an ass; though it be not
>   written down, yet
> forget not that I am an ass.
>   (IV.ii.75-8)

> O that I had been writ down an ass!
>   (IV.ii.86-7)

> . . . and, masters, do not forget to specify,
>   when time and place
> shall serve, that I am an ass
>   (V.i.255-56)

> . . . this plaintiff here, the offender,
>   did call me ass
>   (V.i.305-06)

Second, the captain of the watch in *The Golden Asse* is "an old man" and is specifically cited as such by Adlington in his caption for Chapter 13, "How Apuleius was accused by an old man (my italics), and how he answered for himselfe." In *Much Ado*, Verges, Dogberry's assistant constable, is called by Dogberry "an old man" (III.v.10) and himself proudly states: "Yes, I thank God I am as honest as any man living, that is an old man, and no honester than I" (III.v.13-15). 'Verges' is a name unique in the canon and is one clearly suggestive of the role of the rods-carrying assistant to a Roman magistrate. Adlington uses the word in the early episode when Lucius meets his friend Pithias, "the Clerke of the market" (36). The final syllable of 'Pithias' may have put him in Shakespeare's mind when he gave the name "Verges" to a lesser Magistrate associated with "ass." Certain it is that Pithias is with "Servitors" who carry "these rods or verges" (36).

Third, the defendants in both cases are associated with drunkenness. Borachio has a name which indicates his nature, while Lucius confesses to " . . . (beeing well tipled with wine, which I will not deny) . . ." (65).

Fourth, there is the theme of imagined death. The thieves were not men killed by Lucius, but bladders; Hero is not dead, nor her "cousin," but truly alive with her reputation restored.

Fifth, there is the issue of suspected thievery. Dogberry and the watch have the following exchange:

> Dog. If you meet a <u>thief</u>, you may suspect him, by virtue of your office, to be no true man; and for such kind of men, the less you meddle or make with them, why, the more is for your honesty.
>
> (2) Watch If we know him to be a <u>thief</u>, shall we not lay hands on him?
>
> Dog. Truly by your office you may, but I think they that touch pitch will be defil'd. The most peaceable way for you, if you do take a <u>thief</u>, is to let him show himself what <u>he is</u>, and steal out of your company (III.iii.50-60).

Lucius states that when he saw the three men (who are no true men) breaking into his host's house " . . . they gave me occasion, and not without cause, to thinke that they were strong <u>theeves</u>" (60).

Sixth, there is a direct examination in both texts, Lucius by the captain of the watch, and Borachio by Dogberry in the company of the watch.

Seventh, in both texts there is a tragi-comic calumniation, of Hero in <u>Much Ado</u>, and of Lucius in <u>The Golden Asse</u>.

Eighth, there is the interjection, "<u>tush</u>," not rare, but as an added element in the series of parallels of some significance, which appears in <u>Much Ado</u> and in this episode of <u>The Golden Asse</u>. Lucius quotes the leader of the thieves as having said, " . . . <u>Tush</u> you are but boyes, take men's hearts unto you . . ." (66). Borachio in <u>Much Ado</u> says, "<u>Tush</u>! I may as well say the fool's the fool" (III.iii.123). Leonato and Claudio also use this interjection at V.i.58 and V.iv.44.

Ninth, the confused numbering of accusations and defenses at V.i.215-23 owes something to Lucius' numbering of his defenses:

> Dog. Marry, sir, they have committed false report; moreover they have spoken untruths; secondarily, they are slanders; sixt and lastly, they have belied a lady; thirdly, they have verified unjust things; and to conclude, they are lying knaves.
>
> D. Pedro First, I ask thee what they have done; thirdly, I ask what's their offense; sixt and lastly, why they are committed; and to conclude, what you lay to their charge.
>
> And . . . since first I was Mooved to set upon the theeves by just occasion. Secondly, because there is none that can affirme, that there hath been at any time either grudge or hatred between us. Thirdly, we were men meere strangers, and of no acquaintance. Last of all, no man can proove that I committed that fact for lucre or gaine (66-67).

Tenth, the atmosphere, themes, and tactics of the Apuleian episode on a general level are most like those of Much Ado. Geoffrey Bullough accurately sums up the play as "a tale of credulity in which Shakespeare makes good use of his favorite device of deception; here it is deception by substitution and disguise, by the faulty interpretation of things seen and heard, by false report."[22] Such a description fits precisely the trial scene in The Golden Asse.

Dogberry may well owe his origin to the Bucks constable Aubrey mentioned, to the watch in King Leir, and to Gabriel Harvey, but we have long since learned that Shakespeare made use of a coalescent imagination which fused disparate source materials. In Much Ado About Nothing Shakespeare has allowed this constable, so concerned to be called an ass, a descent not only English, but Milesian.

In these plays Falstaff has drawn the greatest amount of material, thematic and descriptive, from The Golden Asse. As counterfeiting stabber, player king, and captain of a tatterdemalion company, he has absorbed words and phrases belonging to Lucius, Aristomenus, and Thrasillus. As an asinine stag he is a corpulent version of that Actaeon whose image was shown as an unheeded warning to the pre-asinine Lucius.

But even as Shakespeare was willing to give the same character words and acts from several characters of discrete episodes in the novel, so he extended the same kinds of material to other characters, major and minor, in these dramas. Hal and Hotspur, especially in their dialogues with their fathers, and Pistol, Bardolph, and Mistress Quickly, each of whom is transformed himself or watches others in various acts of transformation, derive words and phrases, images and even acts, from The Golden Asse. Hotspur is not a lascivious servant, but he is tortured by thoughts as fierce as the pismires in the novel. Hal is not truly a thief, although crowns and thieving belong to the world of his father, but he is like Haemus in his calculated disguise and he does make Hotspur his "factor." Mistress Quickly and Doll Tearsheet are hardly on the level of the witches Panthia and Meroe, but the language in the Boar's Head is that of the Thessalian tavern.

The multiplicity of episodes in the novel always had the potential for varied exploitation by Shakespeare, but in these history plays and in Much Ado where Dogberry is so perfectly asinine, a very model for his younger colleague Elbow in Measure for Measure, Shakespeare has outdone himself in both the variety of borrowings and the number of episodes placed under levy.

CHAPTER THREE

[1] See, for example, The New Variorum Supplement to Henry IV, Part 1, ed. G. Blakemore Evans, The Shakespeare Quarterly, VII (New York, 1956), and my "Nashe and 1 Henry IV," Notes and Queries, ccxxiii (1978), 129-131.

[2] The Riverside Shakespeare, 881.

[3] A.R. Humphreys, ed., The First Part of King Henry IV (1960: rpt. London, Methuen, 1974), 128.

[4] "Nashe and 1 Henry IV," Notes and Queries, ccxxiii (1978), 130.

[5] The form "embrued" occurs on the previous page (30).

[6] It is acknowledged that "Calipolis" itself derives from Peel's Battle of Alcazar, a popular piece for parody, but the suggestive link is provided by the first syllable.

[7] Again, as with "Calipolis" the suggestive first syllable in Apuleius is the creative link.

[8] Note the Hostess' references to "searching wine" (II.iv.27) and to "blood" (II.iv.28) and Aristomenus' description of Meroe, the taverner witch, "searching about" and letting "blood" on the following page in the novel (28).

[9] See Richard Hosley, Shakespeare's Holinshed (New York: Capricorn, 1968), 120-21.

[10] The Folio, but not the quarto edition includes the Garter references.

[11] As a verb used only once elsewhere in the late and vexed The Two Noble Kinsmen, III.v.57.

[12] Sack kept Falstaff alive, while hemlock killed Socrates, but as (mis-)-leaders of youth they have something in common.

[13] Note Meroe's comment to Panthia about Socrates, "my deare and sweet heart" (28), and Mrs. Ford's address to Falstaff, "my dear . . . my male deer" (V.v. 16-17).

[14] An added link between play and episode in which Aristomenus sees Panthia and Meroe cut the throat of Socrates is provided by the Host's reference to Falstaff's "truckle-bed" (IV.v.7), the very kind of bed under which Aristomenus tried to hide as the tears began to "trickle down" (27), "my bed whereon I lay being a truckle-bed" (27).

[15] For allegorical meanings of Actaeon in the Renaissance, see Walter R. Davis, "Actaeon in Arcadia," Studies in English Literature, 2 (1962), 100-104.

[16] Jacqueline Pearson, "Much Ado About Nothing and King Leir," Notes and Queries, ccxxvi (1981), 128-29.

[17] Line numbering from King Leir in the Malone Society reprint, ed., W.W. Greg (London, 1907).

[18] I owe the suggestion of a link between Harvey and Dogberry to Professor G.B. Evans.

[19] Gabriel Harvey, Pierce's Supererogation (1593, London: Scholar Press, facs., 1970).

[20] F.P. Wilson, Shakespearian and Other Studies (Oxford: Oxford University Press, 1969), 87.

[21] Aubrey's Brief Lives, ed., Oliver Lawson Dick (London: Penguin Books, 1949), 334.

[22] Geoffrey Bullough, ed., Narrative and Dramatic Sources of Shakespeare (London: Routledge & Kegan Paul, 1957-75), II, 74.

CHAPTER FOUR

THE GREAT TRAGEDIES (1)

As Shakespeare began the sequence of tragedies which mark the height of his achievement, his use of The Golden Asse became still more marked and ultimately more significant than in almost all but a few of his earlier works. His familiarity with all aspects of the novel and his experience in using most of them allowed him to return to those which had proven most malleable and in ways which made the Apuleian material still more completely woven into the texture of the plays.

Julius Caesar written at about the same time as Henry V, which was most modestly influenced in terms of diction by The Golden Asse and As You Like It which seems to have been influenced by the novel not at all, has an entire scene essentially drawn from the adventures of Lucius. The short proscription scene, IV.i., which serves not only to qualify our admiration for Antony but also to educate us still further in the brutality of power politics, derives from that section of Plutarch's Life of Marcus Antonius labelled in the margin of North's translation "the proscription of the Trimuviri."[1] However, Plutarch does not provide any discussion of the imminent exclusion of Lepidus or any imagery of Lepidus as donkey and horse. I suggest that Shakespeare derived much of the diction for this scene, as well as the theme of odd-man-out from the episode of the adventures of Lucius in which he is the weakest in a bestial trio. It is important to note that in Plutarch's account the outstanding victim of the proscription who escapes death is Lucius Caesar, Antony's uncle. In a play otherwise quite faithful to its Plutarchan sources, Shakespeare seems to have gone out of his way to suppress reference to Lucius Caesar, substituting the unhistorical nephew, Publius, at line 4. Adding a second Lucius would have caused him no more confusion than that provided by the two Bruti and two Cinnas; perhaps a Lucius here in IV.i. would have revealed too clearly the source of the asinine reference.

Elements of diction and circumstance in this scene present in the prose of Adlington include: "prick'd" (1.16), "consent" (11.2,3), "Caesar's" (1.7), "determine" (1.8), "cut off some charge in legacies" (1.9), "Is it fit/The threefold world divided, he should stand" (11.13-14), "bear them as an ass bears gold,"

(1.21), "driven" (1.23), "our treasure where we will" (1.24), "take we down his load" (1.25), "Like to the empty ass, to shake his ears/And graze in commons" (11. 26-7), "valiant soldier" (1.28), "So is my horse" (1. 29), "I do appoint him a store of provender" (1.30), "fellow" (1.36), "one that feeds" (1.36), "our means stretched,/And let us presently" (11.44-45), and "perils" (1.47). Compare the words and phrases from the narrative of the newly metamorphosed Lucius in his dealings both with the hostile ass and horse (once his own when he had his human form) and with the thieves who capture him as a beast of burden for their stolen treasure: " . . . hee would not rise neither with beating nor pricking . . . (86) -- the word 'prick'd' is clearly used by Shakespeare in the sense of "picked out," "noted on a list," but in North's version of this proscription, and those of the same scene in the lives of Cicero and Marcus Brutus, the word "pricked" does not occur -- "for my horse and the asse as it were consented to work my harm . . ." (77), " . . . I determined with myself to seek some civil remedy . . . I thought to call upon the renowned name of the Emperor, and to say, O Cesar, and cried out aloud, O, but Cesar I could in no wise pronounce" (79), " . . . I gave charge of my horse . . ." (78), " . . . and then they drew out their swords and cut off his legs . . ." (86), "what should we stand here so long about a dead, or rather a stony asse? let us bee gone: and so they tooke his brethren, and divided some to mee, and some to my horse" (86) -- this sentence immediately follows that which contains the word "pricking," is immediately followed by the sentence with the words "cut off his legs," and is in the form of a rhetorical question, just as are Antony's lines 12-14 with the similar diction, -- "all the treasure of Milo . . . that they could beare away . . . and took us two poore asses and my horse and laded us with greater trusses than we were able to beare" (78), " . . . and they tooke the trusse from my backe, . . . and gave them part of the Treasure . . . and after that we were unladen of our burthens they let us loose into a meadow to pasture, but myne own horse and Miloes Asse would not suffer me to feed there with them, . . ." (83), " . . . shaking myne head . . ." (77), " . . . one of them more valiant than the rest . . . valiant captains . . ." (87), " . . . and driven away . . ." (78), " . . . first store of bread . . ." (87), " . . . we came to our appointed place . . ." (86), " . . . fearing lest I should eat up their provender . . ." (77), " . . . and willed one of their fellows . . ." (79), " . . . why I determined to doe . . . upon my fellowes . . ." (85) " . . . stretching out my neck . . . the boy to whom I gave charge of my horse came presently in . . ." (78), " . . . our perillous labors . . ." (87), and " . . . our present peril . . ." (88). In addition certain of the verbs used by Antony as he describes what will be done to the ass/horse Lepidus, "turn," "wind" and "run" in "It is a creature that I teach to fight,/To wind, to stop, to run directly on" (31-32), follow the sequence of participles used to describe the landscape through which Lucius passes, "turning bottoms . . . winding . . . vallies . . . running water . . ." (86).

The sequence of animal imagery from the ass and then horse references to Lepidus to the bear at the stake comparison of Octavius ("for we are at the stake,/ And bay'd about with many enemies," (IV.i.48-9) follows that of the order of animal transformations in this section of The Golden Asse: Lucius is transformed into an ass (77), thinks himself " . . . no more an Asse, but a swift coursing horse . . ." (84), and listens to the last of the thieves' stories, that of the brave Thrasileon who died in the role of a beseiged bear (94). What is of particular and supporting interest is the fact that Shakespeare was returning to a familiar episode in the novel, one of proven malleability, for he had used the beginning of Lucius' career in these pages (esp. 83-4) for much of his version of the death of Jack Cade in 2 Henry VI (IV.x.)[2] So reworkable was this episode that later Shakespeare would return in Macbeth (V.vii) for the death of his protagonist to the death of the last of the thievish captains, Thrasileon, as is noted below.

It is a truism that "plays are made of scenes before they are made of words."[3] What is of especial interest here is that in Julius Caesar (IV.i) Shakespeare has envisioned an entire scene in dramatic terms on the basis of a narrative episode in The Golden Asse, an episode itself of considerable dramatic quality -- and he has filled the scene with the words of the prose episode. Further, the theme of victimization at the hands (hooves!) of numerical superiors was of such importance to a dramatist who throughout his career dealt with versions of injustice that he did not forget that even the victimizers themselves can be punished in the form in which they sinned. For in Antony and Cleopatra, a work heavily influenced by Apuleius, Cleopatra as she prepares to frustrate Octavius' plan, refers to him as an "ass/Unpolicied" (V.ii.307-8).

That Shakespeare should have recalled in his kaleidoscopic memory The Golden Asse when he was composing Hamlet is not surprising when one considers the number of episodes in the novel which parallel events in the tragedy: the murder of a husband by poison in the interest of adultery (Book II), a widow warned by the ghost of her husband to abstain from sexual intercourse with his murderous would-be successor and that widow's calculated concern with the unseemliness of too hasty a remarriage (Book VIII), and parricide, adultery, and sexual tension between a stepson and stepmother in a bedchamber interview together with the attempted murder of the stepson by a poisoned drink mistakenly quaffed by another (Book X). The certainty that Shakespeare had Apuleius in mind during the writing of Hamlet is evidenced by the presence of words and phrases in this tragedy, unique in the canon, but which occur in Adlington, often in contexts analogous to those of the play. Among these terms are "fishmonger" (II.ii.174,189), "fardels" (III.i.75), "baker's daughter" (IV.v.43) and "flaxen" (IV.v.196).

The usual gloss on "fishmonger" is "bawd" or "pimp," but to quote the most recent edition of the works: "no evidence has been produced for such a usage in Shakespeare's day."[4] I suggest that the term is used by Shakespeare not in any sense of sexual corruption,[5] although by extension that can be read into the term, but rather in the sense of absolute dishonesty, dishonesty which Shakespeare would have recalled from the example of the corrupt fishmonger of Book I of The Golden Asse, the seventh chapter: "How Apuleius, going to buy fish, met with his companion Pythias," the Pythias whose servants carry the verges of his office as we have noted above in our discussion of Much Ado About Nothing:

> But Pithias when he espied my basket wherein my fish was, tooke it and shaked it, and demanded of me what I payd for all my Sprots. In faith (quoth I) I could scarse enforce the fishmonger to sell them for twenty pence. Which when he heard, he brought me back again into the market, and enquired of me of whom I bought them, I shewed him the old man which sate in a corner, whome by and by, by reason of his office hee did greatly blame, and sayd, Is it thus that you serve and handle strangers, and specially our friends? Wherefore sell you this fish so deare, which is not worth a halfepenny?

> Now perceive I well, that you are on
> occasion to make this place, which is the
> principall city of all Thessaly, to be
> forsaken of all men, and to reduce it into
> an unhabitable Desart, by reason of your
> excessive prices of victuals, but assure
> your selfe that you shall not escape with-
> out punishment, and you shall know what
> myne office is, and how I ought to punish
> such as offend (36).

Like the fishmonger Polonius is an old man and like him he is dishonest. And like the fishmonger Polonius is punished for his deception. It is of supporting interest to note that just after Polonius has left the stage, Hamlet addresses Rosencrantz and Guildenstern with "dear friends, my thanks are too <u>dear</u> <u>a</u> <u>half-penny</u>" (II.ii.273-74), partially echoing Pythias' indictment of the old fish seller. And it will be recalled that Hamlet implicitly identifies himself with Pythias when he later refers to his trusted friend Horatio as "Damon" (III.ii.281).

"<u>Fardels</u>" occurs in the midst of Hamlet's most celebrated soliloquy and nowhere else in Shakespeare's works in exactly the same form. It does occur as "far-thel" in The Winter's Tale, IV.iv.754,756, when Autolycus speaks to the Shepherd at the beginning of a particularly Apuleian passage. Hamlet speaks of

> The insolence of office, and the spurns
> That patient merit of the unworthy takes
> When he himself might his quietus make
> With a bare bodkin; who would <u>fardels</u> beare,
>   (III.i.72-5).

The dramatist seems to have recalled the tribulations of Lucius the ass in Book VII of the novel and has allowed the prince to identify himself in all his frustration as an "<u>ass</u>" (II.ii.582) and later to pun on conjunctions and donkeys in "And many such-like <u>as's</u> of great charge" (V.ii.43). Lucius as ass was mistaken in the hope that he would be freed of his burdens:

> then he that had in charge to keepe the
> horse, was called for, and I was delivered
> unto him with great care, insomuch that I
> was right pleasant and joyous, because I
> hoped that I should carry no more <u>fardels</u>
> nor burthens (146).

The likelihood that Shakespeare had the prince recalling the unfair burdens of Lucius is increased when one notices that "the insolence of office," another abuse cited three lines earlier by the Hamlet who extrapolates from his own difficulties to speak of those of common men, is parallelled in Book II of The Golden Asse:

> To whom he answered, Madam you in the office of your bounty shall prevaile heerin, but the insolencie of some is not to be supported (53-4).

Hamlet concludes his most famous soliloquy when he sees Ophelia:

> Soft you now,
> The fair Ophelia. Nymph, in thy orisons
> Be all my sins rememb'red
> (III.i.87-9)

In The Golden Asse Venus is offered an "orison" by Psyche (121) who is thought to be one of the "Nymphs" (116). Indeed, Ophelia's general passivity and vulnerability, her social inequality in comparison with Hamlet, her possible future pregnancy as feared by her father, and her suicide by drowning are modelled upon the passive Psyche's mortality in the face of Cupid's immortality, her actual pregnancy, and her attempted drowning.

In her later distraction Ophelia speaks some quite puzzling lines. One of her most puzzling occurs in her exchange with the king:

> King. How do you pretty lady?
>
> Ophelia. Well, God dild you! They say the owl was a baker's daughter. Lord, we know that we are, but know not what we may be. God be at your table!
>
> King. Conceit upon her father
> (IV.v.41-5)

The usual gloss on the baker's daughter turned owl is to the Gloucestershire legend of Christ's having punished an ungenerous girl who objected to the amount of bread given Him. Ophelia in her confusion may say whatever comes into her head, yet I suggest that there is a method in madness even for Ophelia. Shakespeare stressed that Claudius believes here and thirty lines later that the madness stems from her grief over her father's death. It is far from clear that Claudius is completely correct in his assessment, although there is no doubt that the death of Polonius is at the least a major factor in her upset. It is still more unclear why she should be put in mind of this legend unless it were that her creator had remembered another distraught baker's daughter, one whose father had been murdered. In Book IX of The Golden Asse the adulterous baker's wife, the mischievous "queane," frustrated by the constraints and hostility of her husband, hires an enchantress to bring about either a reconciliation or the death of her husband. The enchantress, unable to change her husband's heart and fearful of losing her salary, kills him. His servants discover the body of the baker hanging from a rafter, take it down, lament, and bury it -- all before the daughter learns of the death of her father:

> This woman tooke the Baker by the hand, and faining that she had some secret matter to tell him, went into a chamber, where they remained a good space, till all the corne was ground, when as the servants were compelled to call their master to give them more corne, but when they had called very often, and no person gave answer, they began to mistrust, insomuch that they brake open the doore: when they were come in, they could not find the woman, but onely their master hanging dead upon a rafter of the chamber, whereupon they cryed and lamented greatly, and according to the custome, when they had washed themselves, they tooke the body and buried it. The next day morrow, the daughter of the Baker, which was married but a little before to one of the next Village, came crying and beating her breast, not because she heard of the death of her father by any man, but because his lamentable spirit, with a halter about his necke appeared to her in the night, declaring the whole circumstance of his death, and how by enchantment he was descended into hell, which caused her to thinke that her father was dead (195).

Here we have a true baker's daughter in circumstances analogous to those of Ophelia with a murdered father buried hugger-mugger. But why "<u>owl</u>"? It was an enchantress who killed the baker and it was an enchantress, Pamphile, who in Book III transformed herself into a bird, specifically, "she became an Owle" (75). Lucius also wants to become an owl, but meets with resistance from the chambermaid Fotis who can obtain the necessary ointment. She is fearful that he will fly away and desert her:

> Then said Fotis, Wil you go about to deceive me now, and inforce me to work my own sorrow? Are you in the mind that you wil not tarry in Thessaly? if you be a bird, where shal I seek you, and when shal I see you? Then answered I, God forbid that I should commit such a crime, for though I could fly in the aire as an Eagle, or though I were the messenger of Jupiter, yet would I have recourse to nest with thee: and I swear by the knot of thy amiable hair, that since the time I first loved thee, I never fancied any other person: moreover, this commeth to my minde, that if by vertue of the oyntment I shall become an Owle, I will take heed that I come nigh no mans house: for I am not to learn, how these matrons would handle their lovers, if they knew that they were transformed into Owles (75-6).

I suggest that the idea of desertion -- the central theme of Ophelia's Saint Valentine's day song which follows immediately upon her 'baker's daughter' reference -- coupled with enchantresses' turning bakers into dead men and lovers into owls, led to the allusion to the legend of the owl who was a baker's daughter.

The word "flaxen" in Ophelia's last song (IV.v.196) is unique in the canon. I suggest that when Ophelia uses the term to describe, ostensibly, the appearance of her late father Polonius she is in fact continuing that revealing ambiguity begun with her first entrance in this scene. The most recent editor of Hamlet comments on IV.v.23-40: "in these snatches of ballads Ophelia seems to be confusing recollections of her lost lover with her dead father. They hint that the cause of her madness is not only her father's death but her estrangement from Hamlet and his banishment."[6]

Ophelia's very real confusion has a source in the confusion created by the "white lie" told by Psyche in the fairy tale of Cupid and Psyche which occupies the centre (Books IV-VI) of The Golden Asse. Psyche, under orders from Cupid, her mysterious and as yet unseen husband, not to reveal his true nature, deceives her envious sisters first by saying that her husband is a handsome young man "with a <u>flaxen</u> beard" (106) and later, forgetting her earlier <u>version</u>, by telling them that he is a "man of middle age, having his beard interspersed with gray haires" (110). In her distraction Ophelia repeats the pronoun "he" in the line following "All flaxen was his poll." "<u>He</u> is gone, <u>he</u> is gone" may well be the iterative of the ballad which she is echoing, but the repetition certainly admits of ambiguity in the mind of the audience where one "he" is Polonius, the other "he" Prince Hamlet, each guilty of a kind of desertion of her, the one whose "beard was white as snow," the other whose poll was "all <u>flaxen</u>."[7]

Adding to the probability that Ophelia's "<u>flaxen</u>" derives from the "<u>flaxen</u>" of Psyche is the clear parallel between the two <u>girls</u>, a parallel in Act I, scene iii with Polonius' lecture to Ophelia on the danger of a pre-marital pregnancy resulting from too intimate a relationship with her socially superior lover. Polonius is expressing the same fears as did Venus in <u>The Golden Asse</u> when she worried over the potential embarrassment to herself which would be caused by any offspring from the morganatic union of the immortal Cupid and the mortal and pregnant Psyche. Polonius' crude punning on "<u>tender</u>" (I.iii.107-09) may have been stimulated by Venus' social anxiety over the effects of Cupid's passion, "Forbeeing of <u>tender</u> and unripe yeares, thou hast with too licentious <u>appetite</u> embraced my most mortall Foe, to whome I shall bee made a mother, and shee a Daughter" (117). The parallel is concluded in IV.vii where Ophelia's suicidal drowning is modelled upon the near-suicidal drowning of Psyche following her having been deserted by Cupid.

Hamlet may have feared that Ophelia in her appetites and fidelity was or would turn out to be the same kind of girl who had married his father. But it is Ophelia, too, who reads her love in the light of her surviving parent. With pathetic result the images of father Polonius and lover Hamlet merge at the point of male desertion. In her psychologically understandable confusion Ophelia uses the ambiguous pronoun "he" and the equally ambiguous pronomial adjective "his" ("His beard . . . his poll," IV.v.195,196), moving from the memory of her father's "white" beard to her lover's "<u>flaxen</u>" poll, the tactile as well as visual adjective which belonged to only the younger one of her source sister Psyche's unreal husbands.

There are three other matters of Apuleian derivation surrounding the career of Ophelia: the solution to the textual crux of "bonds"/"bawds," Ophelia's response to Laertes' warning, and Gertrude's description of Ophelia's death.

Editors still differ over the "pious <u>bonds</u>" or "pious <u>bawds</u>" cited by Polonius in order to characterize the <u>vows</u> given by Hamlet to Ophelia (I.iii.130). Theobald's inspired emendation, "<u>bawds</u>," seems still more justified when one adds a consideration of Shakespeare's source for this scene to the usual textual argument that the "u" in "bauds" (an Elizabethan variant of "bawds") was turned or mistaken for an "n". We have noted that Polonius' coarse warning to Ophelia with its play on "<u>tender</u>" is prompted less by concern for Ophelia than by his embarrassment over the prospect of becoming the grandfather of an illegitimate child. Polonius' behavior is modelled upon that of the socially conscious Venus who is anxious lest she become the grandmother of an illegitimate child: "Behold she thinketh (that by reason of her great belly, which she hath gotten by playing the whore) to move me to pitty, and to make me a grandmother to her childe" (122).

Venus addresses Cupid as a "<u>trifling</u> boy" (117), stresses his youth, and hears her sister goddesses call him "<u>young</u>" (118). We recall that Laertes cites the <u>trifling</u> of Hamlet's favor (I.iii.5) and that Polonius urges Ophelia to believe of Hamlet "that he is '<u>young</u>'" (I.iii.124). In the paragraph before that in which she cites Cupid's "tender" years Venus asks the rhetorical question, "Is this an honest thing, is this <u>honourable</u> to thy parents." Ophelia attempts to resist the implication of the scenario painted by her father with her poignant "My lord, he hath importun'd me with love/In <u>honorable</u> fashion" (I.iii.110-11).

In the immediately preceding paragraph in which Venus first learns that Psyche is Cupid's love, the very girl to whom the goddess had sent her son as an agent of retribution, the irate deity's last words before "Is this an honest thing, is this <u>honorable</u> to thy parents" are "What did he think that I <u>was a bawd</u>, by whose shew he fell acquainted with the maid" (116). It may be that Polonius uses the word "<u>bawds</u>" so easily because he is projecting onto Hamlet his own amorous history ("I do know,/When the blood burns, how prodigal the soul/Lends the tongue vows" I.iii.115-7) or that he expresses himself in this way because his own subsequent loosing of Ophelia to Hamlet has more than a touch of the pander about it, but the probability is that Polonius' creator who thought in terms of the Venus-Cupid-Psyche tensions when he wrote of Polonius-Hamlet-Ophelia and gave so many terms from Apuleius/Adlington to the old counsellor, to his son Laertes, and to his daughter when they discussed the Prince, including "honourable," "trifling," "tender," "young," "dalliance," etc., introduced also the idea of a sexual go-between in the word "bawd," a term made plural by Polonius.

Indeed, although Pope tried to make an ass of Theobald in The Dunciad, we may note that Theobald deserves the last, perhaps braying laugh as The Golden Asse lends probability to his celebrated emendation of "bawds" for "bonds."[8]

Shakespeare's practice of looking at both the Adlington version and the original Apuleian Latin contributed to the one spark of independence which we see Ophelia display. The influential passage is that in which Psyche prepares to drown herself rather than face yet another impossible task set for her by Venus:

> Psyches arose willingly not to do her commandment, but to throw her selfe headlong into the water to end her sorrows. Then a green reed inspired by divine inspiration, with a gratious tune and melody gan say, O Psyches I pray thee not to trouble or pollute my water by the death of thee . . . (123-4)

This episode of the near suicidal drowning of a gentle girl with the strong word "pollute" echoed in Shakespeare's mind when he wrote of the aftermath of Ophelia's suicidal drowning. Note Laertes' graveside "Lay her i' th' earth,/And from her fair and unpolluted flesh/May violets spring" (V.i.238-40). When Ophelia had listened sufficiently to her brother's argument that she should avoid the sexual danger represented by the socially superior Hamlet, she reminded Laertes of his own need to avoid hypocrisy:

> I shall the effect of this good lesson keep
> As watchman to my heart. But, good my brother,
> Do not, as some ungracious pastors do,
> Show me the steep and thorny way to heaven,
> Whiles, like a puff'd and reckless libertine,

> Himself the primrose path of dalliance treads,
> And reaks not his own rede.
> (I.iii.45-51)

These lines contain terms which are also present in the Apuleian episode in which Venus, after seeking the help of her brother in finding Psyche, punishes the girl with the second in a series of seemingly impossible tasks. First, "my brother" recalls Venus' address to Mercury, O my brother (121). Second, "dalliance" echoes "in the meane season, Cupid was closed fast in the surest chamber of the house, partly because he should not hurt himself with wanton dalliance" (123). Some added suggestion that Shakespeare thought in terms of the Venus-Cupid-Psyche story when he wrote Ophelia's lines exists in the word "treads" (I.iii.150) for earlier in his career Shakespeare had used the word in the anti-Petrarchan sonnet 130, "I grant I never saw a goddess go,/My mistress when she walks treads on the ground." Third, the "thorny way" suggests the thickets . . . bushes . . . briers . . . (124) which Psyche must enter to satisfy the command of Venus, while the leisured Venus herself gives the command the morning after she has returned from a marriage banquet in a libertine manner, "wel tippled with wine, smelling of roses" (123). Fourth, "pastors" puts us in mind of " . . . the great sheepe . . . kept by no manner of person . . ." (123) which Psyche was to chase. The Latin of Apuleius is: "Oves ibi . . . incustodito[9] pastu" (Met. 6.ii.16,17).[10] It is important to recall that "pastors" is rare in the canon.[11] Fifth, although " . . . reaks not his own rede . . ." does mean "heeds not his own advice," the line is punningly close to the situation of Psyche who does heed the advice of her reed not to expose herself to danger. Finally, we should note Ophelia's response to her brother's request to avoid the danger of Hamlet: "'Tis in my memory lock'd/And you yourself shall keep the key of it" (I.iii.85-6). Psyche is as obedient to the reed as Ophelia is to Laertes:

> Then spake the gentle and benigne reed, shewing a mean to Psyches to save her life, which she bore well in memory, and with all diligence, went and gathered up such lockes as she found . . . (124).

The life of Ophelia ends in Gertrude's description of the girl's watery death. Because Psyche only threatens suicide by drowning, there is not in this episode of the novel a description of death by water. However, earlier in the tale of Cupid and Psyche there is a description of a kind of floating by Psyche which seems to have affected the diction and overall image in Gertrude's story of Ophelia's demise.

We remember that when Venus had for the moment succeeded in preventing any suitors coming to Psyche the effect upon Psyche was that "she lamented her solitary life, and being disquieted both in mind and body, although she pleased all the world, yet hated shee in her selfe her owne beauty" (100). Her father then visits the Oracle of Apollo and is commanded "Let Psyches corps be clad in mourning weed" for her marriage with a "Serpent dire" whose powers are superior to those of the gods such that "The rivers blacke, and deadly flouds of paine,/And darkness she, as thrall to him remaine" (101). There is no doubt that "corps" means "body" and not "dead body" and "weed" means "garment" and not "vegetative growth," although the theme of the passage allows for both meanings in each word, as is very clear in the former case from "they went to bring this sorrowful spowse, not to her marriage but to her final end and buriall" (101). In the event, of course, Psyche is brought from the mountain top to the palace of Cupid:

> Thus poore Psyches being left alone, weeping and trembling on the toppe of the rocke, was blowne by the gentle aire and of shrilling Zephyrus, and caried from the hill with a meek winde, which retained her garments up, and by little and little brought her downe into a deepe valley, where she was laid in a bed of most sweet and fragrant flowers (102).

The motion of floating (in air in The Golden Asse, in water in Hamlet), and then gradual descent ("and mermaid-like awhile they bore her up," IV.vii.176), the flowers surrounding the girl (particularized by Shakespeare), the principle of envy (Venus' envy which led to the isolation of Psyche, the "envious sliver" IV.vii.173 which breaks), Psyche as weedy trophy and Ophelia as covered with "weedy trophies" (IV.vii.174), and the "weeping" Psyche with Ophelia fallen into the sympathetically "weeping brook" (IV.vii.175) combine to suggest that while it is possible that the author of the Ur-Hamlet, not finding the death by drowning of the Ophelia figure in either Saxo Grammaticus or Belleforest,[12] created the episode, it is far more likely that Shakespeare taking whatever hint he cared to from the <u>Ur-Hamlet</u> modelled the watery descent of Ophelia upon the airy flight of Psyche.

Gertrude herself has a distinctly Apuleian quality. Belleforest had added a considerable misogynistic aspect to the story of Hamlet as he had received it from the version of Saxo Grammaticus.[13] Shakespeare accepted the misogyny and added to it from descriptions in little Apuleius' <u>Christ's Teares over Jerusalem</u>[14] and in Apuleius' novel, particularly from the episode of the adulterous stepmother of Book X.

In the same sequence of stories dealing with sexuality and its attendant dangers (which featured among others the baker's daughter), Apuleius tells the tale of a stepmother who loved her "sonne in law" (206) to the point of sexual desire, finds herself rebuffed by him, resolves to kill him in revenge by poisoning his cup of wine, has her own son mistakenly drink the poisoned wine, blames the stepson for the death of her own child, and is discovered by the agency of the ancient physician who had, it turns out, saved her sons by substituting a sleeping potion for poison. The last part of the episode Shakespeare had recalled as he was developing the character of Friar Lawrence in <u>Romeo and Juliet</u>, as we have noted above, and below we will see his use of the episode in both <u>Othello</u> and <u>Cymbeline</u>. Here in <u>Hamlet</u> we may note the diffraction of this narrative into the elements of the sexual tension between a son and a mother (one married to the son's stepfather), a bedchamber interview, and the subsequent mistaken drinking of poisoned wine by an unintended victim. We begin by noting the obvious fact of Hamlet's bitter anguish over his mother's remarriage, a remarriage described as incestuous (III.iii.90 and elsewhere), and in terms sufficiently graphic so as to reveal an extraordinary fixation upon Gertrude's sexual behavior by her son. Second, we see that when Guildenstern tells Hamlet that "The Queen . . . in most great <u>affliction</u> of spirit," (III.ii.311-12) has sent him with the request that Hamlet speak with her in her closet, a request described as "your <u>mother's commandment</u>" (III.ii. 316-17), he is using words derived from description of the meeting between stepson and stepmother in <u>The Golden Asse</u>. She sends for him only after "she had been long time tormented in her <u>affliction</u>," and he complies for he is "nothing disobedient to the <u>commandment</u> of his <u>mother</u>" (206). The Prince responds with "We shall obey, were she ten times our <u>mother</u> (III.ii.333-34).

Next, we note that when Hamlet enters the Queen's closet for the interview, his mother tells him, "Hamlet, thou hast thy father much offended." In The Golden Asse the stepmother's first words are "Thou, thou art the originall of all my dolour" (207) and she goes on to say "neither let my conscience reclaime to offend thy father" (207). Further, some of the diction in the exchange between mother and son in this final scene of the Third Act, relatively insignificant in itself, appears in sequence as a significant reflection of terms in the Apuleian episode. Among these are "pale" (206), the countenance of the stepmother transferred in the play to the ghost in how "pale he glares" (III.iv.125), "schoole" (208), the origin of the other son who comes to drink unwittingly the poisoned wine and "schoolemaster" (206), the agent of the stepmother's revenge against the stepson, together affected the agents of Claudius, "my two school-fellows" (III.iv.202), "custom" (209), the habit of judicial Athens, turned to the "monster custom" (III.iv.161) which yet has benefits for Gertrude, the "counsellors" (209) who judge the case become the slain Polonius, "this counsellor" (III.iv. 213), "all this matter" (209) understood by Lucius, mirrored in "all this matter" (III.iv.186) to be kept from Claudius, "an Ape" (210) in the group of animals parricides were sewn up with stimulated the mysterious "ape" (III.iv.194) who crept "in the basket" (III.iv. 195)[15] rather than into the place of the Apuleian simian who was sewn "in a skin" (210), and the "sealed" purse (211) turned "seal'd" letters at III.iv.202.

Finally, the plot to kill the stepson by "poyson . . . mingled with wine to the intent he (the schoolmaster) would give it to the young man to drinke" (208), which fails when the other son does the drinking of the wine mixed with "venim" (208), is reflected in the back-up plan of Claudius with the poisoned wine for Hamlet's "drink" (IV.vii.159) in the event that the Prince escapes Laertes' "venom'd stuck" (IV.vii.161). This plan fails too when Gertrude ignorantly drinks the poisoned wine. In Apuleius the agent of the stepmother falsely states that the stepson "went himselfe and bought poyson, and after tempered it with wine" (209-10). In the play Laertes, the agent of Claudius, correctly states that the King has deserved his fate for "It is a poison temper'd by himself" (V.ii.328). In the novel the Physician who substitutes a sleeping potion for the poison does so partly because his vocation is to cure by "medicines" (212) and he had been afraid that the would-be-murderer would achieve his evil purpose "with a sword" (212) or some other instrument. In the play Laertes, who tells Hamlet that "No med'cine in the world" (V.ii.314) can help him, used a poison-tipped rapier, a version of a sword. When Hamlet does kill Claudius, he returns first to the themes central to the Apuleian episode, "thou incestuous, murd'rous, damned Dane" (V.ii.325) and refers to the "union" Claudius said he would place in the drinking cup. There is no "union" in Adlington's version, but in the Apuleian Latin the response to the discovery of the poisoned cup by the stepmother is one of especial malice involving a plan for the destruction of her entire family. Apuleius describes the singular malice as "exemplar unicum" (10.5.13) a phrase sufficiently suggestive to have prompted the adulterous and incestuous Claudius to speak of the "union" which paradoxically destroys his entire family.

Shakespeare's pervasive use of The Golden Asse in Hamlet is quite clear. It has been argued that even "Lucianus," the nephew to the King in the play within the play, is a Latinate version of Lucian whose work Shakespeare knew when he composed Timon of Athens, a great favorite of the ironic Christian humanists Erasmus and More, and one to whom the Renaissance mistakenly credited the source of Apuleius' novel, Lucius or the Ass.[16] Without building on this possibility and its ramifications, we may say that the great length of Hamlet has made possible a great deal of Apuleian material, more than in almost any other play. Indeed, we may note in conclusion that repeated study of the two works is likely to uncover still other instances of Apuleian influence upon the play as in the great soliloquy of III.i. where "fardels" and "the insolence of office" and the subsequent "nymph" and "orisons" already revealed as Apuleian, are joined by the unique "contumely." We recall that in the story of the fishmonger Pythias in the original Latin is pleased by the "contumelia" (1.25.17) he has shown to the old man, and that in the tale of the adulterous baker's wife the asinine Lucius "spurned off the flesh" (193) of the fingers of the wife's hidden lover who was then "whipped" (194) while she was "offended at this great contumely" (194). The Prince has recalled and elevated the context of these words in his "whips and scorns of time" (III.i. 69), the proud man's contumely" (III.i.70), and "the spurns/That patient merit of the unworthy takes" (III. i.72-73).

Othello, the tragedy written next after Hamlet, perhaps more than any other of the tragedies parallels the theme of The Golden Asse with its transformation of a man into an ass as punishment for his excessive curiosity about sexual appetite. In addition, there is the fact of Shakespeare's use in Othello of another work of Apuleius, his Apologia, for Othello's defense of himself against the charge of having practiced witchcraft in order to win Desdemona. The Apologia is Apuleius' rather confident defense of himself against the charge that he had gained the love of his wife by the use of charms, drugs, and magic. Material common to both Othello and the Apologia include: 1) the charge of witchcraft introduced for the purpose of annulling a marriage; 2) the central concern with reputation; 3) a magical handkerchief; 4) a marriage of persons disproportionate in age and country; and 5) a marriage which begins in a kind of elopement.[17]

The totality of Apuleian influence is first reflected in the pattern of "ass" puns and references which are most clearly manifested in Iago's two statements that Othello can "as tenderly be led by th' nose/ As asses are" (I.iii.401-02) and that he will reward Iago "for making him egregiously an ass" (II.i.309), but revealed also to the attentive listener/reader in the terms "ass," "assails," "assault," "assay," "assays," "assign," "assist," "assur'd," "assure," and even Iago's noun vocative pun on the conjunction "as" in "as (to be bold with you)" at III.iii.228.[18]

Within the drama there are terms both unique or occurring for the first time in the canon and also present in The Golden Asse. Among these are "mandragora," "poppy," "castigation," "circumstanced," and "incontinently." Further, the two statements by Iago about Othello's asininity are themselves strikingly close to phrases in the Latin original of The Golden Asse.

First, in some of his most memorable lines Shakespeare has Iago, Othello's "ancient," analyze the effect of his having implanted jealousy in the mind of the Moor:

> The Moor already changes with my poison:
> Dangerous conceits are in their natures
>   poisons,
> . . . .
> Not poppy, nor mandragora
> Nor all the drowsy syrups of the world

>   Shall ever medicine thee to that sweet sleep
>   Which thou ow'dst yesterday.
>
>   (III.iii.325-26
>   330-33)

L.P. Wilkinson has offered the sensitive comment that "poppy" and "drowsy" were inspired by Georgics I.78: "Lethaeo perfusa papavere somno."[19] I suggest that the lines owe still more to The Golden Asse, Book X, where there is the episode already familiar by virtue of its use in Romeo and Juliet and Hamlet of the apparent murder by poison in which a physician is called upon to defend himself, "but there arose a sage and ancient (my italics) Physician" (210). He refutes his accusers by pointing out that he had suspected a crime and therefore had substituted a sleeping potion for poison. Some of the diction in the physician's apologia is strikingly parallel to the words of Iago:

> for I will give you an evident proofe and argument of this present crime. You shall understand, that when this caytiffe demanded of me a present and strong poyson, considering that it was not my part to give occasion of any others death, but rather to cure and save sicke persons by meane of medicines: and on the other side, fearing lest if I should deny his request, I might minister a further cause of his mischiefe, either that he would buy poyson of some other, or else returne, with a sword or some dangerous weapon, I gave him no poyson, but a doling drinke of Mandragora, which is of such force that it will cause any man to sleepe, as though he were dead . . . he is yet alive and doth but sleepe, and after his sleepe, he shall returne to life againe, but if he be dead indeed, then may you further enquire of the causes of his death. The opinion of this ancient Physitian was found good . . . the father of the child . . . soporiferous sleepe (211-12).

Perhaps the "evident proofe" which the good physician offers inspired Othello's request for "ocular proof" (III.iii.360). What is clear is that, although Shakespeare may well have recalled Virgil for his "poppy" (but recall that "poppy" is one of the seeds culled by Psyche, 122), nevertheless for his "mandragora," "poison," "medicine," "sleep," and "drowsy" ("soporiferous") he went to Apuleius in translation where he could take from an "ancient" just physician words which Othello's unjust "ancient" would rephrase in immortal fashion.

Second, "incontinently" of "I will incontinently drown myself" (I.iii.305) is unusual in that Shakespeare everywhere else in the canon uses the adjective "incontinent" adverbially as "he says he will return incontinent" (IV.iii.12). The form of the adverb used to describe the directness with which Roderigo seeks to drown himself may have been suggested by the pervasive use of the adverb "incontinently" by Adlington throughout The Golden Asse.

Third, we know that Shakespeare looked at both Adlington's version and the Latin original. The word "castigation" in English is as old as Chaucer, but Shakespeare never had used it before "A sequester from liberty: fasting and prayer,/Much castigation, exercise devout" (III.iv.40-41). I suggest that Shakespeare was prompted to increase his active vocabulary with this term because he recalled the number of times that "castigare" and its forms appear in the Metamorphoses. The probability of such a derivation is increased when we note that the unique "sequester" of the previous line, the presence of which results in two unusual terms in absolute propinquity, in a context of mendacity, has a parallel in "sequestro" (admittedly not a verb form) at Met.6.31.18 following a "castiget" at Met.5.30.16 and a "castigans" at Met.7.15.14, "nunc etiam mendaci fictae debilitatis et virginalis fugae sequestra ministroque."

Fourth, "circumstanc'd" in Bianca's "'Tis very good: I must be circumstanc'd," (III.iv.201) is not used as a verb elsewhere in Shakespeare, but the versions of the Latin verb "circumsto" are used by Apuleius in the Metamorphoses at 1.12.9 where the witches stand around the sleeping Socrates and at 9.11.22 where Lucius is forced to a mill surrounded by men with sticks.

Fifth, Iago's two phrases describing Othello's asininity at I.iii.401-2 and II.i.309 may owe something to Apuleius' Latin. An ass is a metaphor for a fool. In the context of trickery during the Cupid and Psyche episode (Met.6.19.12) there occurs the phrase "hunc offrenatum unius offulae praeda" in reference to Cerberus who is associated in the episode with a lame ass. I suggest that the image of Othello as an ass led by the nose involves a humiliating bridling, an image inspired by the concrete meaning of "offrenatum." The second phrase where Iago gloats over the prospect of having the Moor reward him "for making him egregiously an ass," recalls the similar collocation of words, if not grammar, in the Latin text of the Metamorphoses where Haemus is the savior of the girl Charite and Lucius the ass, "et asini sospitator egregius" (Met.7.10.2).

Sixth, Iago's reference to the future grandchildren of Brabantio as "gennets" uses a term unique in the canon. The ancient speaks of the Senator's "daughter cover'd with a Barbary horse" (I.iii.111-12) and of "the beast with two backs" (I.iii.116), while Roderigo cites Desdemona's being in "the gross clasps of a lascivious Moor" (I.iii.126). Lucius in describing his adventures with the lascivious Matron and her immediate successor speaks of his new master's bringing "Beasts" (216), of "Thessalian Horses or Jenets . . . trimmed with . . . barbs of gold . . . and purple coverings" (217), and of a "Coverlet" (218), of bearing his Master upon his "backe" (217), of the grotesque embrace between himself and the Matron (218), of the matron's successor who had murdered her "daughter" (219), and, at the end of the story of the second woman, of a man dressed in the "vestments of Barbary" (224). The idea of a lascivious embrace between a brute male and a tender female is common to both passages, with the male beast particularized as an equine lover. The parallelism implies a sexuality on the part of Desdemona bordering on the unnatural, exactly the suggestion which Iago is making and which Brabantio had already feared ("This accident is not unlike my dream," I.i.142). This image of bestial/human intercourse in the novel had been treated in a far more benign fashion in the delicate relationship between the assified Bottom and Titania in A Midsummer Night's Dream. Here the image has drawn in its train some of the surrounding diction, including the unique "Jennets"/"gennets." It will take Othello's noble defense two scenes later, a defense drawn largely from Apuleius' Apologia and supported by Desdemona's testimony, before we forget this image of mutual lasciviousness. And then in the temptation scene of III.iii Iago will resuscitate the idea within the image for the benefit not of Brabantio but of Othello himself.

Finally, not only does Iago's Spartan taciturnity in the face of torture at the end of the play derive from the behavior of the guilty servant exposed by the ancient physician who prescribed the mandragora instead of poison, but the flaming minister speech which opens

the final scene is also Apuleian. It will be remembered
that Ludovico describes Iago's murderous "work" as an
"object (which) <u>poisons</u> sight" (V.ii.364), and that both
he and Gratiano <u>speak of</u> "cruelty/That can <u>torment</u>"
Iago (V.ii.334) and the "<u>Torments</u> (that) will ope"
Iago's lips (V.ii.306) after the villain has promised
that he will never speak of the reason why he had en-
snared Othello's soul and body, a promise we believe
that he will fulfill. The evil servant had "abused"
the judges "by invented lyes and tales" (210) and when
discovered, "neither the feare of the wheele or any
other <u>torment</u> according to the use of the Grecians,
which were ready prepared, no, nor yet the fire could
enforce him to confesse the matter, so obstinate and
grounded was he in his mischievous mind" (211). The
economy of Shakespeare's art is thus shown quite clearly, as Iago, the ancient, who was given the diction of
the ancient Physician in his mandragora passage in III.
iii is finally presented in terms of the villainous and
lying servant who was exposed by that same ancient
Physician.

The address to the light in <u>Othello</u> at V.ii.1-22
has a parallel in Psyche's would-be slaying of Cupid
and her address to the lamp in Book V, Chap. 22 of <u>The
Golden Asse</u>. This is the episode from which Shakespeare borrowed for Tyrrel's description of the murder
of the innocent princes in <u>Richard III</u>, IV.iii.1-22, in
a passage of identical length. Shakespeare seems to
have borrowed from <u>The Golden Asse</u> in the history play,
then borrowed from <u>himself</u> and <u>The Golden Asse</u> yet
again in the tragedy.

Both Othello and Psyche are in bed chambers. Both
are bent on execution. Both hesitate. Each repeatedly
kisses the intended victim. Each addresses the bedside
light (a "flaming <u>minister</u>" in <u>Othello</u> V.ii.8, and "the
vile <u>ministry</u> of <u>love</u>" in Adlington's translation, 113).
Each notices the whiteness of the victim's skin ("that
<u>whiter</u> skin of hers <u>than</u> snow," V.ii.4, and "his neck
more <u>white</u> <u>than</u> milk," 113). Both raise the issue of
repentence with the same verb form ("Should I <u>repent</u>
me," V.ii.10, and "it did not <u>repent</u> Venus to beare
such a childe," 113). Both are active in contexts of
broken faith, Othello in his tragically erroneous view
of Desdemona and Psyche in breaking her pact with Cupid
("The god beeing burned in this sort and seeing that
promise and faith was broken," 113). Both would-be victims wake in the midst of the addresses to the light.
Both engines of death refuse to function: the sight of

Desdemona can "almost persuade/Justice to break her sword," V.ii.16-17, and at the sight of Cupid "the razor turned his edge" (113). In addition, just as the <u>roses</u> on the lips of the Yorkist princes were affected by the "<u>rosei</u>" of the original, so the celebrated "<u>relume</u>" of V.ii.13 seems to have been influenced by the Apuleian "<u>lumen</u>" behind Adlington's "light," (113). Finally, even the drop of burning oil which falls upon Cupid and wakes him ("There fell out a droppe of burning oyle from the lampe upon the right shoulder of the god," 113) is paralleled in Othello's falling tear which wakes Desdemona ("This sorrow's heavenly,/It strikes where it doth love. She wakes," V.ii.21-2).[20]

The parallels of situation, diction, and of theme are clearly the result of calculation. The use of <u>The Golden Asse</u> in the tragedy is scarcely surprising when one considers that the story of a man's transformation into an ass might well have been uppermost in Shakespeare's mind when he created a man who is "led by the nose as asses are" and made "egregiously an ass." But the use of this particular episode of proven malleability is especially appropriate to <u>Othello</u> for the traditional moral allegorical reading of the tale, an approach elsewhere in the canon usually scanted by Shakespeare, to the effect that true love is blind[21] (a theme we have noted above in <u>Love's Labor's Lost</u> and <u>A Midsummer Night's Dream</u>) seems to have been appreciated fully by the dramatist in this tragedy of a jealous man so dependent for happiness upon "ocular proof." Like Psyche, Othello now has lost his love and does not receive his source model's second chance. Finally, the roses which Lucius eats to regain his human form have a pale reflection in Desdemona as the rose Othello kisses before and after he kills her, regaining in the final kiss of mortal union a measure of the original dignity from which he had been transformed by his jealousy.

In these first of the great tragedies Shakespeare had learned to construct an entire scene of human dealings upon a model of animal actions in <u>The Golden Asse</u> with the proscription scene IV.i. in <u>Julius Caesar</u>. For the political demise of Lepidus, odd-man-out in a political troika, is described in imagery drawn from Lucius' first experience as an ass, one turned against by his asinine and equine brethren. He had in <u>Hamlet</u> created a parallel constellation of lover, loved, and fearful parent in Hamlet, Ophelia, and Polonius modelled upon the same configuration in the novel of Cupid, Psyche, and minatory Venus. This parallel adds considerable weight to the argument that the relationship between Ophelia and Hamlet has been one of considerable intimacy and that Polonius' anxiety, however grossly and selfishly expressed, was quite well-founded. In addition, Shakespeare found in the novel diction and circumstance for the dialogue between son and mother in the play, as well as for that in the plot against the protagonist with its bizarre outcome. In Othello [22] Shakespeare demonstrated a recidivist's enthusiasm for certain episodes in the novel, especially those of the lecherous matron (previously used in A Midsummer Night's Dream), the adulterous step-mother and saving Physician (used immediately before in Hamlet),[23] and the would-be murder of Cupid by Psyche (first used in Richard III), and treated each in a new way by shifting tone in the first and third instances and reflecting different features of the second episode in an elegant economy of energy. Finally, he allowed himself a near-allegorical presentation of the Cupid and Psyche story in the opening of the final scene, an approach he never seems to have allowed himself before, except in A Midsummer Night's Dream, and perhaps Love's Labor's Lost, and there with the same theme that love is blind.

Except in the case of Julius Caesar, Shakespeare again has shown that wherever else in the course of a play he wished to transform Apuleian material, it was in the final scene, usually a setting with multiple deaths, that he borrowed with special enthusiasm from analogous scenes in The Golden Asse.

CHAPTER FOUR

[1] See Geoffrey Bullough, ed., Narrative and Dramatic Sources of Shakespeare (London: Routledge & Kegan Paul, 1957-75) V, 268.

[2] All the diction occurs within pages 77-88, a unit of text quite compact, as pages 80 and 81 are blank and page 82 has only an indication of book numbers.

[3] Emrys Jones, Scenic Form in Shakespeare (Oxford: Clarendon Press, 1971), 3.

[4] The Riverside Shakespeare, 1, 154.

[5] See Harold Jenkins, "Hamlet and the Fishmonger," Jahrbuch der deutschen Shakespeare -- Gesellschaft West, CXI (1975), 109-20.

[6] T.J.B Spencer, ed., Hamlet (Harmondsworth: Penguin Books, 1980), 312.

[7] Spencer glosses "flaxen was his poll" as "his head was pale like flax."

[8] See especially the link between Theobald and asininity on the title page of the first edition of The Dunciad Variorum of 1729.

[9] Where Apuleius seems to be playing upon the central theme of who guards the guards themselves.

[10] Line numberings are to the Loeb edition of S. Gaselee (London: Heinemann, 1915).

[11] "Pastors" is unique in the canon, unless one accepts the reading of Q1 of Richard II at III.iii.100.

[12] See Kenneth Muir, The Sources of Shakespeare's Plays (London: Methuen, 1977), 160.

[13] See Anne Righter Barton in the Preface to New Penguin Hamlet, 9.

[14] See especially the attack upon women's painting and the prostitutes "in theyr nunnery" in Christ's Teares over Jerusalem, ed., R.B. McKerrow (Oxford: Basil Blackwood, 1904-10, rpt. 1958) III.152. For the criticism of the queen's closet as a bedroom, see Michael

Cameron Andrews, "His Mother's Closet: A Note on Hamlet," Modern Philology, 80 (1982), 164-66.

[15] No one seems to know this story today.

[16] See Wm. Montgomerie, "Lucianus, nephew to the King," Notes and Queries, cxcvi, 149-51.

[17] For the development of this argument see Appendix B.

[18] See I.i.47; II.iii.204; V.ii.258; I.iii.18; II.i.120; II.iii.207; I.iii.285; I.iii.246; I.ii.11; III.iii.1; III.iii.11; IV.i.30; III.iii.20; IV.ii.199.

[19] L.P. Wilkinson, The Georgics of Virgil (Cambridge: Cambridge University Press, 1969), 295.

[20] The mixture of passion and respect may have the added ingredient in the description of the union of Lucius and the Corinthian matron with the words, "light," "lampe," "skinne," "balme," and "kissed" (218).

[21] See Edgar Wind, Pagan Mysteries in the Renaissance (London: Peregrine Books, 1967), 53-80.

[22] The exactness of the parallels in the final scene between the sexually experienced lovers Cupid and Psyche and Desdemona and Othello makes one hesitate to accept the recent persuasive argument that the marriage between Desdemona and Othello was never consummated.

[23] More recent than T.J.B. Spencer's edition of Hamlet is Harold Jenkins' magisterial New Arden volume, one full of riches, but while strong on "little Apuleius" as a source denies any role to Apuleius.

CHAPTER FIVE

THE PROBLEM PLAYS

Shakespeare's Problem Plays, whatever their final number and titles, have always included at least All's Well That Ends Well, Measure for Measure and Troilus and Cressida. Some critics have included Hamlet and some Timon of Athens. We have already discussed Hamlet as part of the tragedies and now accept the inclusion of Timon of Athens among these Problem Plays, for it, like the generally accepted trio of All's Well That Ends Well, Measure for Measure and Troilus and Cressida, has "a language . . . often extremely hard to construe . . . for all readers this is the first and most vital 'problem.'"[1] Sometimes this tortuous language is marked by Apuleian elements.

Troilus and Cressida was written at about the same time as Hamlet and its tone and imagery is often similar to the tragedy. Hamlet as we know is heavily Apuleian in texture. It would be surprising if Troilus and Cressida did not share some of this Apuleian quality itself. There is no surprise, but the amount of the Apuleian material is not quite so substantial as that in Hamlet.

Shakespeare would have recalled the conjunction of the names "Troilus," "Cressida," and "Apuleius" in Gascoigne's The Posies, a work already noted as influential upon Love's Labor's Lost. The poem "David saluteth Bersabe" which has a preface citing The Golden Asse, refers explicitly to Lucius' Fotis. The poem is preceded by a lyric in which Gascoigne argues that the depth of his pain was not surpassed by "The longing lust which Priames sonne of Troy,/Had for to see his Cresside come againe."[2] It is followed by a lament expressed in similar terms, "For Cresside faire did Troilus never love,/ More deare than I esteemde your freamed cheare."[3]

When in the play Shakespeare first came to draw upon The Golden Asse, he chose not the episode of the amorous Fotis but a conflation of diction from three disparate adventures. First, when Psyche is sent down into the underworld to fetch some of Proserpine's beauty for Venus, she is warned against the "marvailous dogge with three heads barking continually at the soules of such as enter in . . . before the gate of Proserpina" (126), and urged to gain "accesse to Proserpina" (127), receive "such beauty as she giveth" (127) and to "appease

97

the rage of the dogge" (127). Second, when the pre-metamorphosed Lucius listens to the story of Socrates and Aristomenus, he learns that Aristomenus was victimized by the witches in a particularly obscene manner. After Meroe and Panthia have cut the throat and withdrawn the heart of Socrates, "one of them moved and turned my bed (says Aristomenus), and then they strid over mee, and clapped their buttocks upon my face, and all bepissed mee till I was wringing wet" (28-9).[4] This use of Aristomenus as a jakes or toilet stool is only the grossest of his experiences this night, not the most dangerous, for he later believes that his state is so parlous that he says "I saw at hell gate the Dog Cerberus ready to devour mee" (30). Third, when Charite rides in triumph upon Lucius the "Asse" (145), she calls him her "Camell" (146) and promises to reward him, but as things turn out he falls into the hands of those who use him so badly that they make him carry burdens so heavy that they are better suited to "Elephants" (148) than to Lucius. The diction from these three episodes is reflected in the vitriolic indictment of Ajax by Thersites in II.i:

> Thou grumblest and railest every hour on Achilles, and art as full of envy at his greatness as Cerberus is at Proserpina's beauty, ay, that thou bark'st at him . . . Do! Do! thou stool for a witch! ay do! do! Thou sodden-witted lord . . . you scurvy valiant ass . . . Mars his idiot! Do, rudeness, do, camel, do, do.
> (II.i.32-5, 42-3, 44-5, 53-4)

and in Thersites' subsequent observation "Shall the elephant Ajax carry it thus" (II.iii.2-3). "Cerberus" in the mouth of Aristomenus links his experience with that of Psyche in the underworld and the three beasts of burden, ass, camel, and elephant associated with Lucius are easily applied to Ajax. The tracks of Thersites' train of thought are quite clear.

In between these two scenes of Thersites' abusive virtuosity there is the extraordinary debate among the Trojans on the theme of keeping or not keeping the abducted Helen. Paris, the sole beneficiary of this rape, argues that had he sufficient power alone, he would never retract what he has done. His father Priam points out the obvious self-interest on the part of Paris:

>   Paris, you speak
> Like one besotted on your sweet delights,
> You have the honey still, but these the gall;
> So to be valiant, is no praise at all.
>   (II.ii.142-45)

Paris replies that "The pleasures such a beauty brings with it" (II.ii.147) are shared! The diction here echoes that in the episode where Fotis as she stirs the pot and Lucius so arouses him that, after a disquisition on the particular beauty of women's hair, he kisses her. When he has analyzed the nature of feminine beauty, he concludes that "there is such a dignity in the haire . . . yet if her hair be not curiosly set forth shee cannot seem faire" (47). The diction of this analysis seems to have affected Hector's analysis of the current problem of keeping Helen and her beauty, "yet . . . our joint and several dignities" (II.ii.189, 193). Following this analysis and his subsequent kissing of Fotis, Lucius is told by Fotis, who has had her "beauty" increased by her unlacing, that perhaps what he is gaining will cost him, "O Scholler, thou hast tasted now both honey and gall, take heed that thy pleasure do not turn into repentance" (47). Lucius is unaffected by this argument and continues kissing her, finding "the liquor of her tongue was like unto sweet nectar, wherewith . . . my mind was greatly delighted" (47). Fotis then promises him satisfaction at a later time, a satisfaction described in military terms in which she herself will encounter him "valiantly and courageously" (47). The links between the passages in the novel and that in the play are the themes of passion and possible repentence of a young lover (Lucius and Paris), the analysis of a dignity centered upon a woman (Lucius of feminine beauty, Hector of keeping the beautiful woman Helen), and the imagery of warfare.

When Thersites analyses the stupidity of the Greeks in the opening of II.iii, he addresses the gods (after having referred to the "elephant Ajax") Jove and then "Mercury, lose all serpentine craft of thy caduceus" (II.iii.11-12). Frank Kermode in The Riverside edition glosses line 12 thus, "the caduceus was the wand bearing two intertwined serpents which was carried by Mercury, who was also associated with cunning and deception; (my italics) hence serpentine craft."[5] Both "serpentine" and "caduceus" are unique in the canon and each occurs in The Golden Asse. "Caduceus" occurs in the pageant of the Judgment of Paris, which also has a reference not only to Paris, naturally, but also to Ulysses and Ajax

-- "Ulisses being but of base condition, was preferred in Martiall prowesse above great Ajax," (226), seen by Lucius in Book X. A young man appears in the pageant so attired that "you might conjecture that he was Mercury, with his rod called Caduceus" (224). There are no serpents and consequent craftiness on the part of Mercury in this episode, but the crafty sisters of Psyche who tell her that her mysterious husband is a "Serpent" (111) are described as "breathing out their Serpentine poyson" (108). Psyche is in this predicament because of the jealousy of Venus, the sister of Mercury. Thersites may have used this diction because of the obvious relationship of the story of the Judgment of Paris to his own current environment, but it is also the case that Thersites is amazed at the absolute incongruity of having Ajax become such a success, and that the amazement has a parallel in the perceived incongruity of the asinine Lucius as an interpreter of life. Thersites asks "What, lost in the labyrinth of thy fury? Shall the elephant Ajax carry it thus" (II.iii.1-2). Lucius anticipates an obvious objection, "but to the end I may not be reproved of indignation by any one that might say: what, shall wee suffer an Asse to play the Philosopher? I shall returne to my further purpose" (226). The amazement and bestial incongruity have affected the diction of Thersites' rhetorical question.

The asinine Lucius' excursus on injustice (225-6) which starts from Paris' decision in favor of Venus and goes on to the preferring of Ulysses over Ajax may have prompted Ulysses' mock support of Ajax who will not be allowed to "assubjugate" (II.iii.192) himself by going to Achilles.

There are phrases in the play which appear to be some of the tesserae which went into the design of the tale of Cupid and Psyche. Among these are Helen as "the mortal Venus" and "love's invisible soul" (III.i. 32-3), where the parallels are with Psyche as mortal Venus and as, etymologically, the soul married to an invisible love. In addition, there is Helen's triple invocation of "Cupid" (III.i.111). There are several other references to Cupid in the play by Troilus at III. ii.75, Pandarus at III.ii.210, and Patroclus at III.iii. 222, but the most interesting piece from the mosaic of the story of Cupid and Psyche is one which comes from the end of the tale, and part of which Thersites used when he spoke of Cerberus and Proserpina's beauty in II.i. This is Troilus' astonishing evocation of romantic/sexual expectation.

Troilus is about to be joined with Cressida. Their
relationship is scarcely so symbolically potent or morally significant as the ultimate joining of Cupid and
Psyche, but some of the diction describing Psyche's last
experiences in hell and in the palace of heaven has been
influential. It will be remembered that Psyche (the
soul) must bring back water from the "Stix" (125) --
with help she does so quite "joyfull" (125) -- and after
being called an "enchauntresse" then by Venus must descend into hell and return with a box of Proserpina's
beauty. She must wait for "Charon . . . (who) will carry the soules over the river" (126) and following certain instructions return with the box. Of course, she
is "too curious about the treasure of divine beauty"
(127), is indeed "ravished with great desire" (127) to
open the box, does open it, and swoons into a "deadly
sleepe." "Cupid" rescues her after "receiving his
wings," (127) berates her for her "overmuch curiositie"
(128) but "fearing the displeasure of his Mother" (128)
asks Jupiter to make Psyche immortal. Jupiter does so
and there follows a banquet at which the "drinke was
Nectar" (129) and the atmosphere was marked by "sweet
harmony, Apollo tuned pleasantly to the Harpe, (and)
Venus danced finely" (129). Troilus, playing the role
of the exclusus amator, brilliantly and painfully gives
expression to his desire, a desire so intense that he
almost swoons in its intensity:

> No Pandarus, I stalk about her door,
> Like to a strange soul upon the Stygian banks
> Staying for waftage. O, be thou my Charon
> . . . .
> . . . . O gentle Pandar,
> From Cupid's shoulder pluck his painted wings,
> . . . .
> I am giddy; expectation whirls me round;
> Th' imaginary relish is so sweet
> That it enchants my sense; what will it be,
> When that the wat'ry palates taste indeed
> Love's thrice repured nectar? Death, I fear
>   me,
> Sounding destruction, or some joy too fine,
> Too subtle, potent, tun'd too sharp in sweet-
>   ness
> For the capacity of my ruder power.
> I fear it much . . .
>
>   (III.ii.8-10, 13-14,
>   18-26)

What is particularly striking in this passage (which is reflected in the "Ode on Melancholy" by Keats, author also of the "Ode to Psyche"), paralleling the swooning and ultimate satisfaction of Psyche after her trial, is that the echoed diction follows the order of the appearance of the words in The Golden Asse. Shakespeare seems to have taken the idea of ravishment, the hope of amorous union, and the hellish pain and expected heavenly rewards of desire from the tale and compressed and heightened the mood into the almost unbearable condition of Troilus, the Psyche figure in the parallel, a reversal of gender by now frequent in the canon.

Troilus and Cressida in other ways may be the result of a "palimpsest of conflicting and incompatible texts possible to Shakespeare through remembrance, allusion, and revision of earlier sources,"[6] but a layer nearest the surface, that of The Golden Asse, reveals in its themes of both asinine stupidity and amorous trials of the most extreme kind a compatibility that provides matter for Thersites, Paris, Hector, Helen, and Troilus.

All's Well That Ends Well is based on Boccaccio (the ninth novella of the third day), Boccaccio the translator of Apuleius and the artist who incorporated episodes from the Metamorphoses into The Decameron. The ninth story of the third day is not obviously Apuleian in origin, but scholars and critics are agreed in finding behind Helena's efforts the trials of Psyche. For example, Peter Ure wrote of "Helena's fable of impossible tasks triumphantly accomplished in the manner of Psyche,"[7] and Anne Barton described the play itself as "a tissue of traditional folk motifs. The story of the abandoned wife who performs a seemingly impossible series of tasks in order to regain her husband and is at least as old as the myth of Eros and Psyche."[8]

Of particular interest in terms of the idea that Helena is a Psyche figure are 1) her social inferiority in comparison with her husband, 2) the initial sexual union as one whereby only one partner is known for certain in the darkness that surrounds the act (the Apuleian tale involves something of a "bed-trick" as well, for the god of love is substituted for the dire Serpent predicted as the spouse of Psyche), and 3) Helena's pregnancy matches that of the condition of Psyche.

As if to underscore the Helena-Psyche parallel, Shakespeare has presented Bertram most often as "a 'boy' -- a 'rude boy,' a 'proud scornful boy,' a 'lascivious boy,' a 'rash and unbridled boy,'"[9] the first image that we have of Cupid. In Adlington's version Venus calls her "winged sonne Cupid, rash and hardy" (99), and addresses him in indignation with "thou trifling boy" (117) immediately after the gull tells Venus that Cupid is just like his Mother who "lasciviously use to ryot in the sea" (116). At the end of the tale Jupiter tells the other deities that he has chosen to "bridle and restraine (the) raging flames of his first youth" (128). Indeed, the raising by Jupiter, the King of the gods, of Psyche to equality of rank with Cupid exactly anticipates the French King's raising of Helena to equality with the ever-so-reluctant (and therefore un-Cupidean) Bertram.

There are references to Cupid on the part of Helena (I.i.175) and the Clown (III.ii.15), and to the ass by Lafew (II.iii.100) and Parolles (IV.iii.337), and there is the unique "fistula" (I.i.34), the ulcer-like sickness from which the King of France is suffering and which may have been prompted not only by its clear presence in Painter's version of the story in The Palace of Pleasure but also by Shakespeare's recent reading of Apuleius' Latin description of the end of the tale of Cupid and Psyche where at the celebration of the marriage of the lovers "Satyrus et Paniscus ad fistulam dicerent" (6.24.13). "Fistulam" and "fistula," pipe and ulcer are related by shape (cf. OED) as well as by sound -- and with Helena as Psyche and Bertram as reluctant Cupid there is a fittingness that the fistula of the king should bring them together.

However, the most interesting borrowing from the novel exists in the most moving interview between the Countess of Rossillion and Helena in I.iii. Here the influence is less a matter of diction and more of scenic structure. The Countess is a creation by Shakespeare not found in either Boccaccio or Painter. She is not only mother to Bertram but "mother" or voluntary stepmother to Helena, the physician's daughter soon to be physician to the king. The opening of the play reveals how auto-plagiaristic Shakespeare can be, with the Countess and Lafew playing Gertrude and Claudius on the theme of excessive grief as suffered by the absent Helena and Lafew playing Polonius to the departing Bertram. The interview between Helena and the Countess is somewhat analogous in its themes of the painful discovery of true feelings and implicit incest ("He must not be my brother," I.iii.160) to the interview between Hamlet and Gertrude, with a reversal of focus from the

guilt of the mature woman (Gertrude) in the tragedy to
the anxiety of the young woman at the analysis by the
mature woman (Countess) in the comedy. The hostility
and direct sexual tension between speakers of the scene
in Hamlet are absent from All's Well That Ends Well,
I.iii, but, as in the case of Hamlet III.iv, the scene
between Helena and the Countess derives ultimately from
the frequently used episode in Book X of The Golden Asse
in which a wise Physician resolves a plot begun with an
interview between a stepmother and her shy stepson.

   Some indication that the Apuleian story has given
the scenic structure for the Helena-Countess interview
is provided by the jokes made by Lavatch before the actual meeting between the two women. Lavatch talks of
the "cuckold" (I.iii.45) and the puritan and papist who
are united in their cuckoldry "like any deer i' th'
herd" (I.iii.54-5). It will be remembered that the
stepmother-physician story is told by Lucius as the
last in a sequence of tales on the theme of cuckoldry.

   The diction in both the novel and play gives further weight to the scene's having been influenced by the
episode. Indeed, in the opening of the play the Countess gives her blessing to her son and wishes that he
may "succeed (his) father/In manners as in shape" (I.i.
61-2). The words here echo the stepmother's first words
to her stepson, when she began "in this manner . . .
thou dost resemble thy fathers shape in every point"
(207). In the scene itself the parallel diction includes "mother" (I.iii.138, and elsewhere), "brother"
(I.iii.155), "humble" (I.iii.156), "master" (I.iii.158),
"servant" (I.iii.159), "daughter-in-law" (I.iii.167),
"pale" (I.iii.169), "asham'd" (I.iii.173), "eyes" (I.
iii.177), "son" (I.iii.186), "hate" (I.iii.208), "love"
(I.iii.208 and earlier), "virtuous" (I.iii.210), "flame"
(I.iii.211), "intent" (I.iii.219), and "medicine" (I.
iii.233). In the Apuleian story Lucius is given to one
of the "servants" (205), learns of a "master" (206) widowed with a son of "vertuous manners" (206) who marries
again. The stepmother, sometimes called the "mother"
of the boy (207), conceives an incestuous passion for
the boy, her "sonne in law" (206), a passion she struggles to conceal for a time with the result that she appears afflicted with a disease. She suffers "shame"
(206) lest her "intent" (206) be known. But she yields
to the flame of Cupid (206), signs of which appear in
her "pale" (206) countenance and sorrowfull "eyes"
(206). The boy in his innocence maintains a "humble
courtesie" (206) before the "mother of his brother"

(206) and when he realizes the nature of her desire he withdraws by many excuses. "Then she by how much she <u>loved</u> him before, by so much and more she <u>hated</u> him now" (207). She arranges the poisoning of the <u>son-in-law</u> but suffers confusion, for the physician from whom the poison is to be bought, on the grounds that it was "for one that was sicke of an incurable disease" (210), substitutes a sleeping potion for the poison, as he sought not death but the saving of "sicke persons by <u>medicines</u>" (212).

Thematically considered, the parallels treat of the disclosure of a guilty love (socially based in Helena's case), the shyness of a humble offspring before a stepmother's affection (benign and solicitous on the part of the Countess, aggressive and soliciting on the part of the Apuleian matron), and the dread of incest (with Helena's anxiety that she as "daughter" to the Countess will be the "sister" of her love Bertram), appearing as a dread of the lateral version of the vertical incest suggested by the Apuleian stepmother. That Helena should join the roles of male stepson and secretive lover is not surprising given what we already know of Shakespeare's willingness to change the genders of his source material and invert the passions of lover and loved, but this interview in the comedy adds also from the Apuleian source the role of the curing physician. For at the end of the interview Helena has as her "<u>intent</u>" the saving with her father's "<u>medicine</u>" the seemingly incurable king.

Shakespeare, already impressed by the value of this episode, especially in <u>Hamlet</u>, a play written only slightly earlier than <u>All's Well That Ends Well</u>, seems to have focused on the unnaturalness of the affections, keeping some of the tension between stepmother and son/daughter-in-law -- "shee caused her sonne to be called for (which word son she would faine put away if it were not for shame," 206) and "when I said 'a mother,'/Methought you saw a serpent. What's in 'mother,' That you start at it?" (I.iii.140-42) -- but transferring the sexual tension itself to the relationship between Helena and the son of the stepmother in the play. Shakespeare seems to have followed the larger rhythm of the Apuleian plot: first, tension between offspring and stepmother, then disclosure of the love, then the ultimate salvation by the medicine of a physician. Indeed, the king's disease is thought to be incurable (I.iii.237-39), a "<u>malady</u>" (II.i.121) past cure (note that "<u>malady</u>" appears in Adlington's version, 206).

There is near certitude that Helena derives the essence of her career from the trials of Psyche, but she also owes something of the versatility of her enterprising character to both the stepson and the physician of Book X of The Golden Asse.

Measure for Measure lacks the considerable weight of Apuleian influence carried by its companion bed-trick play All's Well That Ends Well, but it does have two passages which have been affected in terms of theme and diction by two different episodes in The Golden Asse.

The first of these passages is that of Elbow (II.i) as he appears before the bar of Justice to complain of the injury done to his wife. Elbow is a constable of limited imagination, indeed he seems to have graduated from the police academy in the same class as Dogberry. Like Dogberry, Elbow shows a passion for exactitude (seven and a half years on the force, II.i.260) and a clear indifference to embarrassment. Dogberry wants to be written down an ass and Elbow wants it known that Mrs. Elbow has been affronted in a bawdy house. And like Dogberry, Elbow has had his scene affected by the Risus-festival episode in the Apuleian novel.

He is not so skilled an arithmetician as Dogberry in terms of digit span as is clear from his "First . . . next . . ." (II.i.162-3) and subsequent abandonment of his series, but the brevity of his series allows him to avoid Dogberry's confusion in ordering of "secondarily . . . sixt and lastly . . . thirdly (Much Ado About Nothing V.i.215ff.). Both lists derive from Lucius' defense of himself at the Risus tribunal, "first . . . secondly . . . thirdly . . . last of all" (66-7). Elbow suffers the same ignorance of the meaning of "malefactors" as does Dogberry (and these are the only two instances of "malefactors" in the canon). The prosecution at the Risus tribunal describes Lucius as a "malefactor" (68), and both the prosecution and Lucius refer to the dignity and power of the "Commonweale" (64,67). Elbow's second line includes a reference to the "commonweal" (II.i.42).

Shakespeare was intrigued by trial scenes[10] and Apuleius has several, so that Shakespeare seems at times to have conflated more than one. It will be recalled that the Physician in the step-mother episode untangles matters before the Judges and Magistrates of Athenian law. In the course of his explanation the Physician refers to the agent of the step-mother as both "varlet"

(211) and "caytiffe" (211). Elbow seems to have recalled this part of the Physician's testimony immediately after his abbreviated series of reasons in his abuse of Pompey, "O thou caitiff! O thou varlet" (II.i.174, with repetition).

Two added elements which suggest that Shakespeare was recalling the Risus episode when he brought in Elbow and his attendant laughter are the introductory material preparatory to Elbow's arrival on the scene and his misuse of "cardinally" for "carnally" at II.i.80.

When Angelo and Escalus discuss the fate of Claudio, the themes include the need to set an example of punishment, the dignity of the criminal's lineage, and the paradoxical fact that the best intentions lead to disastrous consequences ("Some rise by sinne, and some by vertue fall").[11] The diction includes "thief" (II.i.20), even though there is no issue of theft in Claudio's crime,[12] "justice" (II.i.21), "executed" (II.i.34), and "condemned" (II.i.40) -- as well as the "ice" in the notorious crux at II.i.39-40, "Some run from brakes of ice and answer none,/And some condemned for a fault alone." In the Risus episode Lucius, according to the prosecution, must suffer "punishment . . . (as) a right good example to others" (64); he is praised at the end of the trial for his "dignity, and . . . the genealogie of your antient linage" (69); and Lucius is in his current predicament because with the best will in the world he tried to protect the property of his host Milo, "behold, I am condemned to die as a murtherer, for the safeguard of myne Host Milo" (67). Lucius is called a "Theefe," (68), is to have the Judges "execute . . . justice" (68) upon him when he is "condemned" (65, 66, 67).

Lucius is one of those "some (who) by virtue fall" (II.i.38), and one "condemned for a fault alone" (II.i.40). Whether he is one of those some who "run from brakes of ice and answer none" (II.i.39) depends upon the interpretation one gives to "brakes," What is clear is that Escalus is dealing with the theme of "the inequalities of temporal justice,"[13] that Lucius suffers from that kind of unequal justice, and that at the moment when he discovers that he is not to be executed, for it has all been a joke, he "stood stil as cold as ice" (69).

The "ice" of the Risus episode may or may not help to resolve the crux at II.i.39, but it, along with other elements of diction and the sequence of themes present in the episode, has affected Shakespeare's associative imagination as he constructed the opening of the scene, as well as Elbow's subsequent appearance.

As for Elbow's malapropism "<u>cardinally</u>" for "<u>carnally</u>," we laugh harder when we hear the words as the Elizabethans did as homonyms.[14] What the stimulus was for the joke in the first place remains a matter of speculation. Yet, we may suggest that in the midst of a scene echoing elements of diction from Adlington's version of the Risus episode, the malapropism is also derived from the Risus story, but from the original Latin. Elbow is speaking of his wife's experience in a bawdy <u>house</u>. Lucius tells of his discovering the thieves at the <u>house</u> of Milo (within which bawdy, if not financial acts take place) where they try to lift off doors by the hinges -- "<u>cardinibus</u>" (<u>Met</u>. 3.5.6). Elbow speaks of a "house . . . pluck'd down in the suburbs" (II.i.64-5), while Lucius tells of a house plucked open. The singular instance of a pun on "cardinal" may have been prompted by Shakespeare's "small Latin" which was quite easily enough to recognize etymological significance -- Mrs. Elbow is not really (1) carnally given, nor is she (2) so readily open as the swinging door of a bawdy house.

The asinine Lucius has affected <u>Measure for Measure</u> as well as his pre-translated self, but only once. J.W. Lever correctly noted that in terms of the lines,

> For like an ass, whose back with ingots bows,
> Thou bear'st thy heavy riches but a journey,
> And death unloads thee
>
> (III.i.26-8)

> the association of "ass" with "death" may have been suggested by an episode in <u>The Golden Asse</u> (tr. Adlington) 'then they broke open a great chest . . . wherin was layd all the treasure of Milo . . . and laded us . . . Later when the other ass was exhausted, they tooke his burthen . . . and cut off his legs, and threw his body from the point of an hill downe into a great valley' (<u>Tudor Transl</u>., IV.78-9, 86).[15]

Thus in <u>Measure for Measure</u> Lucius' adventures in protecting <u>the treasure of Milo</u> and its consequences and his adventure in carrying that same treasure have both become part of the texture of the comedy.

Timon of Athens has a character named Lucius, a mask of Cupid, and such phrases as "if thou wert an ass" (IV.iii.323), and "seest not thy loss in transformation" (IV.iii.345), diction evocative of the "ass" and "transformation" of the protagonist in The Golden Asse. However, it is a single scene that is quintessentially Apuleian.

The most memorable scene in Timon of Athens is the third scene of the fourth act where Timon delivers his most impassioned and King Lear-like invectives. Perhaps the most striking passage in that scene is Timon's preparation for death with the apostrophe to destructive gold (IV.iii.374ff). Part of the success of the passage derives not only from its tonal intensity, but from its familiarity, its echoing of Othello's address to the lamp as he prepares to kill Desdemona (Othello V.ii. 1-22), itself a heightened version of Tyrrel's description of the killing of the Yorkist princes in Richard III (IV.iii.1-22), where, as we have seen above, both the Othello and Richard III passages are derived from that episode in The Golden Asse in which Apuleius describes Psyche's attempted killing of Cupid.

Shakespeare's practice of auto-plagiarism, his polishing of his scenic art, is sufficiently familiar to us that re-use in Timon of Athens of a passage in Othello, itself a reworking of a passage in Richard III, occasions no surprise. What is interesting is that when Shakespeare reworked the passage from Richard III, IV. iii, he also looked again at the Cupid and Psyche passage which underlies the description of the death of the little princes, the pair of innocent Cupids. In so doing, he rediscovered not only the theme of violated innocence, but also the truth which Psyche painfully discovers and the Moor tragically discerns, that love is blind. In the composition of Timon of Athens Shakespeare refreshed his artistry yet again by returning to his prime source so that beneath the layers of this address to gold we find the ur-text, the Apuleian description of the innocent and sleeping Cupid, upon which has been modelled the description of the innocent and sleeping princes and the innocent and sleeping Venetian bride.

We begin by noting that the gold, like Cupid in the Apuleian scene,is asleep: "Here is no use for gold./ The best and truest;/For here it sleeps, and does no hired harm" (IV.iii.289-91). In the ensuing debate between Apemantus, the cynical philosopher, and Timon there appear words and phrases parallel to those in The Golden Asse and clearly indicative of the dramatist's use of the Apuleian material. Among these are "remain a beast with the beasts" (IV.iii.325) -- compare Cupid as "the sweetest beast of all beasts" (112) -- and "delicate wooer" (IV.iii.384) and "visible god" (IV.iii.386) -- compare Cupid, a wooer, who loves Psyche only in the dark, an invisible god, whose agents are "invisible" (104), and who is a god with "cheeks delicate" (109).

Some of the virulent vocabulary early in the scene may have been prompted by Apuleius' description of the attitude and circumstance of Psyche's evil sisters. We note "this is it/That makes the wappened widow wed again" (IV.iii.38-9), "ulcerous sores" (IV.iii.40), and "gouty keepers" (IV.iii.47), and the greed of Psyche's sisters into whose laps gold has been poured. They are anxious to be rid of their sexually inactive spouses:

> And in faith I am married to a husband that hath the gout, bent crooked, not courageous in paying the debt of love; I am fain to rub and mollify his crabbed and stony fingers, and I soil my white and dainty hands with stinking plasters and rank-smelling salves and the corruption of filthy clouts, so that he uses me not like a wife but more like a surgeon's servant (107).

In addition, Timon moves towards his own death, "then Timon presently prepare thy grave" (IV.iii.377), as Psyche later, a would-be suicide, moves towards the killing of the sleeping Cupid after hearing the advice given by her sisters, "presently (111) . . . she prepared her wicked intent" (112).

The location of the grave of Timon is "where the light foam of the sea may beat" (IV.iii.378). Psyche's mind just prior to her attempt on the life of Cupid is tossing "like the waves of the sea" (112), and she herself is compared to Venus who had been nourished by the "froth of the waves" (98).

The address to the "bright" (IV.iii.382) gold, "O thou . . ." (IV.iii.381,389) recalls Psyche's apostrophe to the lamp, "O rash and bold lampe . . . how darest thou . . ." (113), a lamp darkened by the "brightnesse" (113) of Cupid's "haires of gold" (113).

The phrase "natural son and sire" (IV.iii.382) is a more profound and emblematic version of the "natural sisters" (111) who set about to establish a divorce between Cupid and Psyche. Indeed, Psyche tells her sisters that Cupid has divorced her, "toro meo divorte" (Met. 5.26.25), echoed in "dear divorce" (IV.iii.361), her sisters who recall their visits to the palace of Cupid, "what gold we trod on" (106), and who have been dismissed by Psyche with "a little gold into our laps" (107). The repetition of "gold" and the pouring of some of it into their laps may have led to "Dian's lap" (IV.iii.386), from gold as simple bribe to its special power to melt even the chastity of Diana.

The reference to "Hymen's purest bed" (IV.iii.383) was easily derived from his lamp which shines at the bedside of Cupid, and Psyche herself began her marriage preparations hearing the melody of "Hymeneus" (101).

Further, the arrival of the banditti following the exit of Apemantus (IV.iii.397) is in keeping with the framework surrounding the story of Cupid and Psyche. The story is told by an old crone (who acts as housekeeper to a band of thieves who have their headquarters in a cave) to the captured maiden Charite who was about to be married. Indeed, so close to the wedding moment was she that "torches were set in every place as they chanted in honour of Hymeneus" (97).

The association of gold with Cupid, the mysterious husband of Psyche, casts the shadow of ambiguity over the gold of Timon. Timon thinks that gold is evil; Psyche in this scene in Apuleius from which Shakespeare drew for his description of gold, thinks that Cupid is evil, and if not a "king-killer" (IV.iii.381), at least a king's daughter-killer (Psyche is the daughter of "a certaine King, inhabiting in the West parts," 98). Psyche is wrong; Cupid is not a killer but a god of love. If we can believe that when Shakespeare borrowed words and phrases he also borrowed the theme of his source, then the assumption Timon makes is wrong and his very error is further evidence of his extreme and unjustifiable misanthropy. In his two earlier borrowings from this Apuleian passage in Richard III and Othello, Shakespeare focused on the innocence of the victims, as Apuleius had done in his description of Cupid. By parity of reasoning, we may assume that Timon, like Tyrrel and Othello, is dealing with innocence -- or in the case of the non-human entity, gold, with a thing indifferent, a thing made guilty only by the transference from the human agent.

Perhaps no member of the audience in the theatre or in the study believes that Timon is anything other than an extreme misanthropist given to categorical judgments radically mistaken, but certainly supportive of this critical view of Timon is his description of the gold, a description drawn from Psyche's mistaken view of innocent love.

Shakespeare may have recalled this passage in Apuleius not only for its beauty and proven malleability, but also because in Timon of Athens he remembered Apuleius' proud boast that "Hymethus, Athens, Isthmia, Ephyrus, Taenaros, and Sparta . . . be places where mine antient progeny and lineage did sometime flourish: there I say in Athens, when I was young, I went first to school" (15). Further, Shakespeare may have associated Apuleius the author of the Metamorphoses, this novel of a man transformed into an ass, with Lucian of Samosata, a Syrian contemporary of Apuleius, much admired by Erasmus and his circle, who also wrote, at least in the view of the sixteenth century, a story of asinine metamorphosis. Lucian's satirical dialogues included one on Timon, and although "no English translation of this dialogue in Tudor times is known . . . the dramatist may have read it in Erasmus' Latin version, in Italian or in French."[16] Certain it is that when Shakespeare wrote such a morally complex work as Timon of Athens, with appearance seldom reality, with much of the world as morally indifferent, made good or bad only by a man, he recalled the scene in Apuleius in which Psyche discovers that the golden-haired Cupid is not a sweet king's daughter-killer.

There are some few other echoes of the novel in the tragedy, including Apemantus' "the heels of an ass" (I.i.272) and his epithet for the servants of Timon, "asses" (II.ii.62), Flavius' verb for the revelry at Timon's parties where the evening "bray'd with minstrelsy," (II.ii.161), and Alcibiades' analogy in illustration of the unnaturalness of patience in contrast to aggression, "And the ass more captain than the lion" (III.v.49). Finally, Timon's remark to the whores Phrynia and Timandra, "Paint till a horse mire upon your face" (IV.iii.148) recalls the miring of Panthia and Meroe upon the face of Aristomenus, "then they strid over mee, and clapped their buttocks upon my face, and all bepissed mee till I was wringing wet" (28-9) -- see "mire" in Partridge's Shakespeare's Bawdy, "To befoul, to urinate, or to defecate upon."[17]

These scattered echoes indicate that Shakespeare had *The Golden Asse* in mind during the writing of the play, but the extended address to the gold in IV.iii. shows that "when he came to plan Timon, Shakespeare's own gradually accumulated vocabulary of scenic forms helped to furnish not only structure but matter for this part of the play."[18]

The befouling of the faces of whores recalls Ajax as a stool for a witch in *Troilus and Cressida*, with both passages having their ultimate source in the obscene experience of Aristomenus in Book I of *The Golden Asse*. The recollection suggests that even within the group of Problem Plays Shakespeare was becoming still more economical in the use of his source material, and that each of the plays makes use of previously worked Apuleian material. Troilus' ecstasy in anticipation of his union with Cressida derives much of its diction from the frequently used trials of Psyche as she moves on her way to union with Cupid. Helena is perfectly Psyche-like in her career, while her interview with the Countess her "stepmother" reworks the stepmother scene only recently absorbed into *Hamlet*. In *Measure for Measure* Elbow shows the same kind of Risus festival indebtedness as his elder colleague Dogberry. Timon's address is a reshaping of materials already used in *Richard III* and *Othello*. This artistic economy may be appropriate to Shakespeare as bourgeois artist and man, but its true significance lies in the clarity with which it reveals his basic interests in error and ironic misjudgment, desire satisfied and desire frustrated, trial, tribulation, and reward, and self-knowledge comically achieved and tragically lost.

CHAPTER FIVE

[1] Peter Ure, Shakespeare: The Problem Plays (London: Longman, 1964), 4.

[2] George Gascoigne, The Posies ed., John W. Cunliffe (Cambridge: Cambridge University Press, 1907), 462.

[3] Ibid., 464.

[4] William Theobald, using the Bohn translation, noted this parallel in his The Classical Element in the Shakespeare Plays (London: Robert Banks & Son, 1909), 76-77. Theobald was a Baconian who noted, correctly, the Apuleian elements in Cymbeline, 76, and The Winter's Tale, 78.

[5] The Riverside Shakespeare, 463.

[6] Bruce Erlich, "Structure, Inversion, and Game in Shakespeare's Classical World," Shakespeare Survey, XXXI (Cambridge: Cambridge University Press), 53.

[7] Ure, op. cit., 9.

[8] The Riverside Shakespeare, 499.

[9] Noted by G.K. Hunter, Jr., ed., All's Well That Ends Well (London: Methuen, 1962), xlvi.

[10] See the observations on this Shakespearean enthusiasm by Leo Salingar in his Shakespeare and the Traditions of Comedy (Cambridge: Cambridge University Press, 1974), esp., 298ff.

[11] See the note on this phrase in Mark Eccles, ed., A New Variorum edition of Shakespeare Measure for Measure (New York: The Modern Language Association of America, 1980), 60-61.

[12] The Riverside Shakespeare, 556.

[13] Ibid.

[14] According to Helge Kökeritz, as noted in Eccles ed., Measure for Measure, 64.

[15] J.W. Lever, ed., Measure for Measure (London: Methuen, 1965), 68.

[16] Geoffrey Bullough, ed., *Narrative and Dramatic Sources of Shakespeare* (London: Routledge & Kegan Paul, 1957-75) VI, 239.

[17] Eric Partridge, *Shakespeare's Bawdy, A Literary & Psychological Essay and a Comprehensive Glossary* (London: Routledge & Kegan Paul, 1955), 154.

[18] Emrys Jones, writing of *1 Henry VI* and *Timon of Athens* in his *Scenic Form in Shakespeare* (Oxford: Clarendon Press, 1971), 96.

CHAPTER SIX

THE GREAT TRAGEDIES (2)

The majesty alone of King Lear would seem proof that this tragedy at least is free of any influence from the sportive and grotesque Apuleian novel. Yet there are obvious elements common to both works, sufficiently common for Shakespeare to have consciously or subconsciously recalled diction from The Golden Asse as he wrote the most moving of passages, Lear's tortured final question and expression of belief that the dead Cordelia still lives.

The central episode of The Golden Asse is truly the fairy tale of Cupid and Psyche, a type of the Cinderella Märchen in which there are three sisters, one of whom, the youngest and the best is tormented by her less well-favored elders. It is well known that this motif is present in King Lear and its previously acknowledged sources, with Goneril and Regan as the evil sisters and Cordelia as the Cinderella figure. Shakespeare's recognition of the parallel between the family structures of Cordelia and Psyche included that of the martial hostility of each pair of elder sisters against the younger girl. In Lear Goneril and Regan prepare to take the field against Cordelia, while in The Golden Asse Cupid warns his bride:

> Behold the last day, the extreme case, and the enemies of thy blood, hath armed themselves against us, pitched their campe, set their host in array, and are marching towards us, for now thy two sisters have drawn their swords, and are ready to slay thee. O with what force are we assailed this day (108).

In addition to the identical Cinderella motif in the tale of Cupid and Psyche there is a passage in the following Book VII which describes a disguised man looking like a beggar as does Edgar in the guise of Tom o' Bedlam. Indeed, "hee was poorely apparelled, insomuch that you might see all his belly naked" (140). In the known sources for Tom there is no mention of nakedness. Yet Shakespeare describes Edgar's deciding

> To take the basest and poorest shape
> That ever penury, in contempt of man,

> Brought near to beast, My face I'll grime with filth,
> Blanket my loins, elf all my hairs in knots,
> And with presented nakedness outface
> The winds and persecutions of the sky
> (II.iii.7-12)

As the story continues, the disguised man in beggar's garb adds the interesting fact, "I am inheritour and follower of all my father's virtues, yet I lost in a short time all my company and all my riches, by one assault" (140). Admittedly, there are many elements in the story of this disguised man which are not operative in the Edgar plot of King Lear, yet the nakedness of the beggar and his filial loyalty are striking parallels, as is the curious collocation of the two words "pomp" and "delicacy" which occur some ninety words later in the story told by the disguised protagonist of this episode: "despised all wordly Pompe and delicacy" (141). The contiguity of the two terms led Shakespeare to recall them both in some of Lear's most celebrated lines:

> Thou'dst meet the bear i' th' mouth. When the mind's free,
> The body's delicate; this tempest in my mind
> Doth from my senses take all feeling else,
> Save what beats there -- filial ingratitude!
> . . . .
> Prithee go in thyself, seek thine own ease.
> This tempest will not give me leave to ponder
> On things would hurt me more. But I'll go in.
> . . . . O, I have ta'en
> Too little care of this! Take physic, pomp,
> Expose thyself to feel what wretches feel,
> That thou mayst shake the superflux to them,
> And show the heavens more just.
> (III.iv.11-14, 24-6, 33-6)

To reinforce the likelihood that Shakespeare had recalled this passage, it is important to note that the entire story is told by Lucius the ass who presents the narrative, "while I pondered with my selfe all these things, a great care came into remembrance" (139). "Ponder" is unique in Shakespeare. We know that Shakespeare read both Adlington's translation and the Latin original, and consequently he found in the original what Adlington who had relied upon a French version[1] missed, the vividness of "Talibus cogitationibus fluctuantem subit me illa cura potior" (Met. 7.4.1,2). The effect of "fluctuantem" is preserved in the Loeb translation: "While I pondered tempestuously."

Further, there is, apropos of meeting "the bear i' th' mouth," Lucius himself, also in Book VII, who is threatened by both castration and "a marvelous great Beare" (152). He runs away "to the intent I would escape from the terrible Beare, but especially from the boy that was worse than the Beare" (152). Here we have two dangers, one relatively worse than the other and in both cases the ursine threat is the lesser.

For the death of Cordelia and Lear's response to it Shakespeare did not go to the tale of Cupid and Psyche, but rather he took matter from the frame of that tale, the story of the capture and escapes of Charite to whom the story of Cupid and Psyche is told, particularly to that part which is recounted in Book VII.

Some supportive indication that the dramatist was aware of Apuleius at the end of the tragedy of King Lear (apart from Shakespeare's known modus operandi in death scenes) exists in the use in Timon of Athens, something of a companion play to Lear, of the arrival of the banditti who have their origin in the outlaws who capture Charite in the frame to the Cupid and Psyche story.[2] Further, in the opening of this final scene (V.iii.3-7) Cordelia with her "tougher stoicism" speaks as the Silvia of The Two Gentlemen of Verona (V.iii. 1-4) who provides "an exemplification of the uses of adversity"[3] as she is captured by the forest outlaws, who are (as we have noted above) Apuleian by birth and have their origin in the band of thieves of the frame tale to the story of Cupid and Psyche.

Shakespeare has followed the intertwined careers of Charite and Lucius to the point where Charite's fate is discussed by her captors in terms of many gruesome forms of death, including that of hanging. That Shakespeare elsewhere in this scene held this material in mind is reflected in the Captain's odd image, exactly fitting the laboring and asinine Lucius, "I cannot draw a cart nor eat dried oats" (V.iii.29) and the echoic noun in the line "Let's exchange charity" (V.iii.165). Earlier in the play the Fool had asked, "May not an ass know when a cart draws a horse" (I.iv.221) and had told Lear "thou bor'st thy ass on thy back o'er the dirt" (I.iv. 161-62).

Shakespeare has noted that Charite, the young bride, was carried from her prison in the cave by Lucius (on his back) while Cordelia, the young bride, is carried from the prison by Lear (in his arms), and that the diction of the description of Lucius in his frustration at an injustice made a parallel to Lear's tortured query. Lucius, reflecting upon both the blindness and the injustice of Fortune, goes on to describe his imperfect defense of his innocence in words which closely parallel those of Lear in his last lines:

> Yet might not I defend mine owne cause or denie the fact any way, by reason I could not speake; howbeit least my conscience should seeme to accuse me by reason of silence, and againe being enforced by impatience I endevoured to speake, and faine would have said, <u>never</u> did I that fact, and verely the first <u>word</u>, <u>never</u>, I cried out once or twise, somewhat <u>handsome</u>, but the residue I could in no wise pronounce, but still remaining in one voice, cried, <u>never</u>, <u>never</u>, <u>never</u>. Howbeit I settled my <u>hanging lips</u> as round as I could to speake the <u>residue</u>: but <u>why should</u> I further complaine of the cruelties <u>of my</u> fortune, since I was not much ashamed, by reason that my servant and my <u>horse</u>, was likewise accused with me of the <u>robbery</u>. . . . while I pondered . . . I thought of <u>my</u> <u>poore</u> gentlewoman that should be closed <u>within</u> me (139).

At the conclusion of the tragedy the tormented Lear speaks his moving lines:

> And <u>my</u> <u>poor</u> fool is <u>hang'd</u>! No, no, no life!
> <u>Why</u> <u>should</u> a dog, a <u>horse</u>, a rat, have life,
> And thou no breath <u>at all</u>? Thou'lt come no more,
> <u>Never</u>, <u>never</u>, <u>never</u>, <u>never</u>, <u>never</u>.
> Pray you undo <u>this</u> button. Thank you, sir.
> Do you see this? Look on her! Look her <u>lips</u>,
> Look there, look there!
> (V.iii.306-12)

The echoing of the phrase "<u>my</u> <u>poor</u>," the repetition of "never" for the same total <u>of</u> <u>five</u> instances, the rhetorical question "<u>why</u> <u>should</u>," the comparable and contrasting animal, "<u>horse</u>," the idea of <u>hanging</u> and the focus on "<u>lips</u>" all together suggest that Shakespeare had this passage from <u>The Golden Asse</u> in mind at Lear's final entry and particularly his final words. We note that Lucius complains that his was a condition "worthily to be lamented and pittied of the most hard and <u>stonie</u>

hearts" (139) while Lear had entered howling, "O, you are men of <u>stones</u>" (V.iii.258). Further, the theme of the passage, silence in the face of unjust accusation, recalls the origin of the problem between Cordelia and Lear. Indeed, the Cupid and Psyche episode revolved around Psyche's responsibility to keep a seal upon her lips. The themes of silence broken and inarticulateness may have led Shakespeare to be particularly attentive to those passages of <u>The Golden Asse</u> which he held in his memory as he wrote <u>King Lear</u>, a tale of an impatient father and his laconic daughter.

Yet why else might have Shakespeare thought of this episode in the most moving of all his death scenes? We may consider the fact that Lucius is a man punished for his transgression of curiosity and sexual license, but the punishment (until his ultimate regeneration) is far in excess of his crimes -- he is a man more sinned against than sinning. We note that although Lucius' difficulties are usually thought of as the result of his being <u>covered</u> with a bestial form, it is the simultaneous <u>stripping</u> of any recognition of his human dignity that is so striking -- indeed he is an ambulatory exemplum of how man's life can be as cheap as beast's. Lucius has been excluded from his familiar world, and while his moral fault has contributed to his predicaments, it is Fortune which has buffeted him. Finally, the very rhythm of Lucius' adventures proved attractive to Shakespeare for Lucius seems several times on the verge of escape to freedom and humanity, only in the event to be recaptured and denied his restoration. In <u>Lear</u> the pain of the audience comes in large part from the frustration of legitimate expectations that with the forces of good on the rise Lear and Cordelia will be saved. In all but the final episode of the novel we see an "ironic turn in events, this constant intensifying of disaster at the moment when disaster seems to be over."[4]

While an image of a comic donkey braying for justice may undercut the picture of Lear in his final agony, it is important to remember that Shakespeare was looking for aid in his diction and imagery, and if the theme was appropriate and the words of force, then he was content to leave behind the precise figure and to shift the tone so that the donkey and comedy disappear: only the diction, the pain, and the injustice remain.

Although each of the tragedies has Apuleian material, <u>King Lear</u> may have been especially influenced by

The Golden Asse by way of the judgment of Sir Philip
Sidney. Sidney's Arcadia contributed to the Gloucester
plot with its episode of the Paphlagonian king and his
sons and in his Defense of Poetry, as noted above, he
writes of a play structurally not unlike Lear, counting
the Fool as a clown:

> But besides these gross absurdities, how all
> their plays be neither right tragedies, nor
> right comedies, mingling kings and clowns,
> not because the matter so carrieth it, but
> thrust in the clown by head and shoulders
> to play a part in majestical matters with
> neither decency nor discretion, so as
> neither the admiration and communication,
> nor the right sportfulness, is by their
> mongrel tragi-comedy obtained. I know
> Apuleius did somewhat so, but that is a
> thing recounted with space of time, not
> represented in one moment . . .[5]

Shakespeare, of course, was not so narrowly educated in
the neo-classical fashion as to accept this stricture on
the difference between the narrative and dramatic modes,
but he did remember the reference to Apuleian tragi-
comedy and found a place for some of that material in
the conclusion of his most painful tragedy.

In addition to the critical Sidney, the censorious
Samuel Harsnett would have reminded Shakespeare during
his composition of King Lear of The Golden Asse. Shakespeare read carefully Harsnett's A Declaration of Egre-
gious Popish Impostures (London: James Roberts, 1603),
and discovered there not only the names of the devils
cited by Edgar in IV.i., but also diction which appears
in the central storm scenes. Of particular interest to
students of Shakespeare's use of Apuleius are two references to asinine metamorphosis. In the beginning of his
book Harsnett addresses the "seduced Catholiques of England," A2(v), and writes of the power of Catholicism
"to metamorphose men into asses, bayards, & swine. Is
not their owne brand they have stamped on your foreheads,
that England hath beene alwayes good asse to the Pope."

Later in the volume during a discussion of holy
water (and the Fool's unique reference to "holy-water,"
III.ii.10, suggests that Shakespeare had read this very
page in Harsnett), the then Chaplain to the Bishop of
London makes an explicit comparison between holy-water
and the ointment used by Lucius in The Golden Asse,

although he makes the frequent Renaissance error of confusing Lucius Apuleius with Lucian:

> Lucian's oyntment I confesse (that he got a little of by peeping at a crevice, and spying the Witch annoynt her body withall), came neere the force of this forcible water of Rome. For Lucian tels us himselfe, that by that time hee had annointed himselfe all over with that enchanted oyle, he was turned into an Asse, and that he so lived by the space of six, or seven yeeres in the shape of an Asse, under very cruell maisters that whipped him sore, as under a Gardiner a tyle man, a Corier, and such like: and that at last he was metamorphosed into the shape of a man by eating of Roses. What would a little of that Asse-making oyle doe, if it had the good hap to be blessed, and supercharmed by his Blessedness at Rome? Well, this holy water of Rome had as fayre a descent as that Lucian oyle . . . (102).

Harsnett read a great many plays in his capacity as a licenser of books and his references to plays and stage practices suggest that he was a great frequenter of playhouses as well. In either role he would have seen just how right Gosson's observation on the ransacking of The Golden Asse still was. His own explicit references to the novel in a work which Shakespeare carefully mined for diction in King Lear (and later, according to Kenneth Muir, in Pericles and The Tempest, plays also Apuleianly influenced) provided yet further stimuli for the composition of the tragedy.

Buchanan in his Rerum Scoticarum Historia was a scholar skeptical of much received material. In describing Macbeth's defeat by Malcolm he wrote:

> Makbeth being terrified at the Confidence of his enemy, immediately fled; and his Soldiers, forsaken by their Leader, surrendered themselves up to Malcolm; Some of our writers do here Record many Fables, which are like Milesian Tales, and fitter for the Stage, than an History.[6]

Now whether or not Shakespeare took the hint from this probable source of Macbeth, the dramatist in writing for the stage rather than for a history text, did indeed have Apuleius' Milesian tale in mind when he wrote of the witches and the moment of the ultimate defeat of Macbeth.

Starnes argued that the witches of IV.i. are scarcely the same figures as those derived from Holinshed with whom Shakespeare confronts Macbeth originally. Instead, they are more closely related to the Medea of Ovid and the Pamphile of Apuleius who have the most specifically described demonic practices in classical literature. And of the two it is Pamphile, with her confections which result in the conjuring up of her three men/bladders, who more closely resembles the creatures of IV.i. of the tragedy. Starnes pointed out that the pattern in each action has three strands which are parallel. First, the result of the conjuring in both works is the same: "in each scene the broth and enchantment result in the coming of three apparitions which deceive the hero."[7] Second, the compact account of Pamphile provides several details closely or exactly reproduced in Macbeth: "poisoned entrails" (IV.i.5), "Nose of Turk and Tartar's lips/Finger of birth-strangled babe" (IV.i.29-30), "pilot's thumb/Wrack'd as homeward he did come" (I.iii.28-29), and "Grease that's sweaten/From the murderer's gibbet throw/Into the flame" (IV.i.65-67), recall from the novel the "fibris spirantibus" (Met.3.18.1) translated in the Loeb edition as "entrails still warm and breathing," "the members of dead men, as the nosethrils and fingers" (73), "and the toes and fingers of such as are slaine" (53), "she prepared the bones of such as were drowned by tempest in the seas" (73), and "shee set out the limbs of flesh of such as were hanged . . . she threw the hair into the hot fire to burn" (73). Third, "Pamphile's scene of enchantment brings together, in almost the same order of appearance, many of the larger elements as well as the details which reappear in the incantations of Macbeth: the darkness, the witch (witches), the cauldron (by implication in Apuleius), the bizarre ingredients, the chanting of the charms, and, more important, the appearance and activity of the apparitions."[8] These three strands along with our knowledge of Shakespeare's earlier familiarity with this episode in the novel, suggest that the witches of IV.i. are, at least in large part, own sisters to Pamphile.

The description of the defeat of Macbeth stems both from Holinshed and Apuleius. Specifically, Shakespeare recalled the episode in Book IV of The Golden Asse in which the cornered thief Thrasileon is disguised as a bear. Simple elements common to Macbeth and Thrasileon

include the epithet for their courage, their title, and
their moral nature. They are both called "valiant,"
Macbeth at I.ii.40., and again at I.iii.47 (and his
fury is thought by some to be "valiant," V.ii.14); in
The Golden Asse Thrasileon is "that one of us being
more valiant than the rest" (91). They are both captains; Macbeth as one of two "captains" (I.ii.34) and
Thrasileon belongs to a group of "Theeves . . . who
. . . came to their den" (85). There is no theme of
thieving attached to Duncan in the Scottish sources,
yet the imagery of the murder scene (II.iii) includes
that of theft in lines spoken by both Macduff and Malcolm:

> Most sacrilegious murther hath broke ope
> The Lord's annointed temple, and stole thence
> The life o' th' building
> (II.iii.67-69)

and

> There's warrant in that theft
> Which steals itself, when there's no mercy
>   left
> (II.iii.145-46)

Macbeth is called a "hell-hound" to his face by Macduff
(V.viii.3), an epithet usually accepted as an echo of
that other and earlier villain protagonist, Richard
III, who is described by Queen Margaret in his absence
as a "hell-hound" (IV.iv.48). Yet notice also Thrasileon's fight:

> And although I might perceive that he was
> well-nigh dead, yet remembered he his own
> faithfulness and ours, and valiantly re-
> sisted the gaping and ravenous mouths of
> the hell-hounds (93).

Both Macbeth and Thrasileon are "bear-like."
Thrasileon is covered with a bear skin, "feigning that
hee were a Beare" (91) and to the last pretends to be a
bear. Macbeth identifies himself in a simile as bear-
like, but significantly falls short of Gloucester's
more metamorphic identification in King Lear, "I am
tied to th' stake, and I must stand the course" (III.
vii.54). The simile in "They have tied me to a stake;
I cannot fly,/But bear-like I must fight the course"
(V.vii.1-2), suggests that there is still distance between person and beast. Just as Thrasileon is only

disguised as a bear, so Macbeth, however bestial he in part has become, is still a human being.

In this play, particularly flattering to King James, Shakespeare seems to have looked deliberately for a reference to hunting and the chase, James' well-known enthusiasms. Accordingly, he found the cornered Thrasileon in the episode of Demochares who "greatly delighted in hunting and chasing" (90). We note the further bear image, "baited with the rabble's curse" at V.viii.29.

There is in addition to these parallels a number of words in this episode of The Golden Asse whose resonance seems to have echoed in the mind of Shakespeare as he wrote Macbeth. Among these are "seam," "porter," "compassed with," and "butcher."

First, in The Golden Asse there is a description of the taxidermy necessary to cloak Thrasileon in the guise of a bear:

> Then we put him into the Beares skin, which fitted him finely in every point, wee buckled it fast under his belly, and covered the seam with the haire, that it might not be seen (91).

It is well known that tailoring images are frequent in Macbeth, including "buckle" (V.ii.15), but the first such image in the play belongs to Macbeth's killing of Macdonwald, a figure whose career anticipates Macbeth's own:

> nor bade farewell to him,
> Till he unseam'd him from the nave to th' chops,
> And fix'd his head upon our battlements.
> (I.ii.21-3)

"Unseam'd" is unique in Shakespeare and there is as well no use of "seam" in the sense of a garment-working in the canon. Shakespeare may well have had in mind the seamed Thrasileon who, when killed, was "slit" open.

Second, the celebrated Porter scene (II.iii) is not accounted for by any of the known Scottish sources, though it does have a probable origin in the Mystery plays.[10] There is no Porter scene in the Thrasileon episode, but there is a concatenation of sleep, a porter, and murder:

> When we thought that every one was asleepe,
> we went with our weapons and beseiged the
> house of Demochares round about. Then
> Thrasileon was ready at hand, and leaped
> out of the caverne, and went to kill all
> such as he found asleepe: but when he came
> to the Porter, he opened the gates and let
> us all in (92).

If Shakespeare had been impressed first by Macbeth as bear-like, working back through the career of Thrasileon, he may well have noted this gate-opening episode. Particularly, he would have seen that the thieves, just before their arrival at the gates, opened "a great sepulchre . . . covered with the corruption of man" (92). Such phrases might have led him to recall Mystery plays with their comic gate-keepers.

Third, "compass'd with" is unique in Shakespeare.[11] Macduff, returning with the severed head of Macbeth, addresses Malcolm as king with the added observation, "I see thee compass'd with thy kingdom's pearl" (V.ix.22). Thirty lines earlier Macbeth had said to Macduff:

> I will not yield,
> To kiss the ground before young Malcom's feet,
> And to be baited with the rabble's curse.
> (V.viii.27-9)

The Thrasileon episode seems to have provided both "rabble" and "compass'd with":

> but when he was at liberty abroad yet could
> he not save himselfe, for all the dogs of
> the Streete (=rabble, cf. O.E.D., A1) joyned
> themselves to the greyhounds and mastifes of
> the house, and came upon him.
>   Alas, what a pitiful sight it was to
> see our poore Thrasileon thus environed and
> compassed with so many dogs that tare and
> rent him miserably (93).

Fourth, Malcolm, thirteen lines after Macduff's observation, calls Macbeth "this dead butcher" (V.ix.35). "Butcher," though frequent enough in the canon, is used only this once in this play. Following closely upon the instance of the street dogs who tore Thrasileon when he was compassed as well with mastiffs is the passage:

>   no person was so hardy untill it was day, as
>   to touch him, though he were starke <u>dead</u>:
>   but at last there came a <u>Butcher</u> more valiant
>   than the rest, who opening the panch of the
>   beast, slit out an hardy and ventrous theefe
>   (94).

Macbeth is both bear and butcher, victim and knife, inasmuch as Shakespeare has the tyrant refer to himself as bear and has Malcolm call him butcher.

Finally, there is the element of play-acting common to both texts. Macbeth informs us of the nihilistic nature of life with the poor player who struts and frets, and Thrasileon is praised for playing his part to the very end: "so tooke hee in gree the pagiant which willingly he tooke in hand himself" (93).

Shakespeare's habit of amalgamating disparate source materials has partly obscured the origin of bear-like Macbeth. But an examination of diction and theme suggests that Shakespeare did take Buchanan's unintentional hint about a Milesian tale and turned for the conclusion of his drama of witches to the great novel about a man bewitched,[12] even to the point of calling his protagonist "<u>Bellona</u>'s bridegroom" (I.ii.54), "Bellona," twice referred to in the novel (<u>Met</u>.8.25.12 and 11.4.30).

A number of scholars have commented on the Apuleian element in <u>Antony and Cleopatra</u>. Several years ago Michael Lloyd demonstrated that Shakespeare used certain aspects of the Egyptian goddess Isis as described by Plutarch and Apuleius for the development of the personality and character of Cleopatra.[13] He argued cogently that Shakespeare had incorporated in his Egyptian queen the role of Isis as maternal and procreative force from Book XI of <u>The Golden Asse</u> and even more so from Plutarch's "De Iside et Osiride" in the <u>Moralia</u> (Philemon Holland translation). Lloyd concluded that Shakespeare had avoided the use of any Osiris references to Antony, thereby denying "to Antony that quality of devoted love which would have been associated with Osiris, and which he chose to keep as the peculiar attribute of Cleopatra-Isis."[14]

Earlier D.T. Starnes had determined that both the hair-haling episode of II.v and the description of Cleopatra on her barge (II.ii) are influenced by the novel in Adlington's translation. He noted the similarity between Cleopatra's treatment of the messenger from Rome with the abuse and especial hair-pulling and Venus' treatment (and, of course, Cleopatra is in some degree a Venus figure) in her jealousy of Psyche who is abused to the point where Venus "tooke her by the haire and dashed her head upon the ground" (122). Starnes noted also that the description in Plutarch's Life of Marcus Antonius (North's translation) of Cleopatra on the Cydnus, clearly the chief basis for Enorbabus' description at II.ii.190ff., is paralleled by a description of Venus in Apuleius' Book X of the novel, and that Shakespeare seems to have borrowed some few details of the latter as well as the many from the former. Most importantly, Shakespeare saw in Adlington's version not only the plural "cupidoes" (225) who accompany Venus and in Apuleius' Latin the "delicatis . . . gestibus" (10.32.19) which phrase has affected the "delicate cheeks" (II.ii. 204) of Venus, but he found in the behavior of the Venus in Book X a hint for the phrasing in the notorius crux:

> Her gentlewomen, like the Nereides,
> So many mermaids, tended her i' th' eyes,
> And made their bends adornings.
> (II.ii.206-8)

Apuleius describes the Graces and Hours who tend upon the wishes of Venus who "mooved forward more and more, and shaking her head answered by her motion and gesture" (225). The Loeb version, but not Adlington's, has Venus "gently bending her body and moving her head." Starnes found that the bending movement of Venus herself has been transferred by Shakespeare to the motion of her handmaidens and that their response to her eyes derives from the fact that Venus, as source for Cleopatra, used her eyes to indicate her desire and the bribe she was willing to give in order to gain that desire:

> For sometimes she would winke gently, sometimes threaten and looke aspishly and sometimes dance onely with her eyes: As soone as she was come before the Judge, she made a signe and token to give him the most fairest spouse of all the world (225).

Starnes stated that "it is not too much to suppose that Shakespeare endowed his Cleopatra-Venus with similar eyes; and, if so, her gentlewomen would have watched her eyes for their cues. They "tended her i' the eyes."[15]

The Isiac quality of Cleopatra is of great importance in the play according to Harold Fisch in the most ambitious interpretation of the tragedy in the light of Apuleius. Fisch argued that in Shakespeare's stress upon both death and fertility he made Cleopatra the point at which both principles unite: "she represents the Liebestod, the downward drag of nature into unconsciousness and death. And this is entirely in keeping with her archetypal character . . ."[16] Insofar as Cleopatra is Isis, she is also the various aspects of Isis and "we recall that among the other personae of Isis (according to Apuleius) is the goddess Proserpine, and she is the bride of death ruling with him in the underworld."[17] Having established the Liebestod theme as Apuleian, Fisch went on to point out in the final act of the play that Shakespeare gives us the obverse of the coin of death, the dying into immortality, in "a ritual of apotheosis."[18] However, the apotheosis of the lovers must be qualified against the play's backdrop of universal history which deals with time and eternity. Nevertheless, on the plane of private, not public significance Cleopatra's death, the most memorable episode in the tragedy, has at least three facets, and at least two of them are clearly Apuleian: "in one sense (her death is) a ritual apotheosis; in another sense it is a deserved punishment for a sinful life (this is the motif stressed in the conversation with the Clown); and in a third sense it is a marriage ceremony . . ."[19] Indeed, as Fisch properly concluded, "the final speeches of Cleopatra suggest not the meeting of Mars and Venus, nor of Isis and Osiris, but rather of Cupid and Psyche . . ."[20]

I suggest that other elements from The Golden Asse deserve attention in any interpretation of Antony and Cleopatra. There are three passages in The Golden Asse which shed light on Antony's irascible and concupiscible weaknesses. Moreover, in sum they provide a more likely interpretation of the celebrated reference to the "terrene moon" (III.xiii.153) than those readings hitherto accepted.

"Terrene" is unique in the canon until The Two Noble Kinsmen (at I.iii.14, in a scene usually attributed to Shakespeare). In The Golden Asse, Venus in her anger and indignation, Cupid in his voluptuousness, and the followers of Isis in their radiant subservience, all present the term "terrene" in passages the themes of which parallel those inherent in the character of Antony.

Venus is angered because her ceremonies have been neglected in favor of admiration for the beautiful and younger Psyche:

> This sudden change and alteration of celestiall honour, did greatly inflame and kindle the love of very Venus, who unable to temper her selfe from indignation, shaking her head in raging sort, reasoned with her selfe in this manner, Behold the originall parent of all these elements, behold the Lady Venus renowned throughout all the world, with whome a mortall maiden is joyned now partaker of honour: my name registred in the city of heaven, is prophaned and made vile by <u>terrene</u> absurdities (99).

Indeed, she is so angered to discover that her former superiority has been eclipsed by a younger rival, just as Antony is frustrated over his eclipse by the younger Caesar, that she has her rival scourged, even as Antony has Caesar's representative Thidias whipped.

Further evidence of Antony's reflecting the intemperate nature of Venus is provided by Caesar's ironic description of Antony's drinking:

> Let's grant it is not
> Amiss to tumble on the bed of Ptolomy,
> To give a kingdom for a mirth, to sit
> And keep the turn of <u>tippling</u> with a slave,
> To reel the streets at noon, and stand the buffet
> With knaves that <u>smells</u> of sweat:
> (I.iv.16-21)

"<u>Tippling</u>" is unique in the canon and it recalls Venus' excessive celebrating after the capture of Psyche. "When night came, Venus returned home from the banket wel <u>tippled</u> with wine, <u>smelling</u> of balme . . ." (123).

The attitude of Antony toward the theme of Pleasure versus Honor is paralleled by that of Cupid. Jupiter criticizes the god of love who has asked for permission for a more than "mortall marriage" between himself and Psyche:

> O my well beloved sonne, although thou haste not given due reverence and honour unto me as thou oughtest to doe, but haste

> rather spoiled and wounded this my brest
> (whereby the laws and order of the Elements
> and Planets be disposed) with continuall
> assaults, of Terren luxury and against all
> laws, and the discipline of Julia, and the
> utility of the publicke weale, in trans-
> forming my divine beauty into serpents,
> fire, savage beasts, birds, and into Bulles
> . . . (128).

Antony, against a backdrop of planetary imagery, has offended the public weal by his luxuriousness and, technically, the only reason that he has not broken the Julian law (so humorously operative on Mt. Olympus) is that it was not passed on earth until a dozen years after his death.

In Book XI the male followers of the goddess Isis have "had their crownes shaven, which were the terrene stars of the goddesse, holding in their hands instruments of brasse, silver and gold, which rendered a pleasant sound" (236). Antony follows too close in the train of the Isiac Cleopatra.

All three passages from The Golden Asse have bearing upon the position and attitude of Antony when he utters the moving lines:

> Alack, our terrene moon
> Is now eclips'd, and it portends alone
> The fall of Antony!
> (III.xiii.153-55)

Most critics[21] have seen the phrase "terrene moon" as a reference to Cleopatra who herself recognizes a previous lunar fickleness in her nature near the end of the drama: "I am marble-constant; now the fleeting moon/No planet is of mine" (V.ii.240-41). There is no doubt that the possibility exists that Cleopatra in all her fickleness is the moon to which Antony refers. Yet it is important to note that the eight references to the moon in Antony and Cleopatra, all clustered in the last half of the play (III.xii.6; III.xiii.95; III.xiii. 153; IV.ix.7; IV.xii.45; IV.xv.68; V.ii.80; V.ii.240) are by no means associated primarily with Cleopatra. Dolabella, Enobarbus, and Antony all make such references without observable allusion to her, and Antony himself is associated with the moon by the queen with no link to herself at V.ii.80.

But inasmuch as he has been reflecting upon his own subservient relationship with her and the attendant, if not indeed consequent loss of respect, it seems more likely (given the themes of the immediate context and the uniqueness of the adjective recalled from The Golden Asse) that the "<u>terrene moon</u>" is Antony himself. His eclipse logically precedes his fall; first loss of power, then loss of position.

If the three passages can be used to reinforce the current critical view of Antony, namely that Shakespeare has deliberately limited his attractiveness while enhancing that of Cleopatra, I suggest a fourth passage which supports the ultimate stress upon their immortal unity and equality. To avoid an otherwise morganatic marriage Jupiter transforms Psyche: ". . . he tooke a pot of immortality, and said, Hold Psyches, and drinke, to the end thou maist be <u>immortall</u>, and that Cupid may be thine everlasting <u>husband</u>" (129). The diction of this passage suggests Cleopatra's celebrated "immortal longings" speech in which, for the first and only time, she calls Antony her husband:

> Give me my robe, put on my crown, I have
> <u>Immortal</u> longings in me. Now no more
> The juice of Egypt's grape shall moist this
>   lip.
> . . . .
> . . . . <u>Husband</u>, I come!
> Now to that name my courage prove my title!
> I am fire and air; my other elements
> I give to baser life.
>   (V.ii.280ff.)

Indeed, Cleopatra's subsequent image of herself as nursing mother may derive as much from the pregnant Psyche as the procreative Isis:

> Peace, peace!
> Dost thou not see my baby at my breast,
> That sucks the nurse asleep?
>   (V.ii.308-10)

For aspects of Antony, of Cleopatra, and of their supraelemental unity, Shakespeare recalled elements of <u>The Golden Asse</u>. These reminiscences of Apuleius are easily explained apart from Shakespeare's natural fondness for and familiarity with the text. Plutarch is Shakespeare's prime source for <u>Antony and Cleopatra</u>, and the dramatist who had made use of <u>The Golden Asse</u>

in so many earlier plays would have recalled Apuleius' proud boast at the opening of the novel:

> . . . (for there myne auncestry by my mothers side inhabiteth, descended on the line of that most excellent person Plutarch, and of Sextus the Philosopher his Nephew, which is to us a great honour) . . .(19).

Equally he would have noted the passage in Book VII where Lepolemus, disguised as the thief Haemus, invents an adventure which is received as proof of his own prowess:

> . . . God speed yee souldiers of Mars and my faithful companions, I pray you make me one of your band . . . I have been a Captaine of a great company . . . But when they were arrived on the sea coast of Actium . . . this most holy woman, faithful and true to her husband . . . returned to Caesar . . . when all my band was lost, and taken by search of the Emperours army . . . I onely stole away . . . for I clothed my selfe in a womans attire . . . I escaped away, because every one deemed that I was a woman by reason I lacked a beard (140-41).

The reference to Actium, Caesar, and women's attire could scarcely have escaped Shakespeare as he was writing about the battle of Actium, won by Octavius Caesar over men who were women's men. Indeed, Antony himself is actually dressed as a woman by Cleopatra:

> I drunk him to his bed;
> Then put my tires and mantles on him, whilst
> I wore his sword Philippan.
> (II.v.21-23)

In addition, Shakespeare returned again to his near favorite episode of the adulterous stepmother and the saving physician for some of the diction in Cleopatra's lament at the absence of Antony near the end of the opening act with its "<u>drink</u>" of "<u>mandragora</u>" (I.v.4), "<u>sleep</u>" (I.v.5), "<u>treason</u>" (I.v.6), and "<u>poison</u>" (I.v.27), echoing the already familiar diction of the ancient physician, "<u>medicines</u> . . . <u>poyson</u> . . . <u>drinke</u> of <u>mandragora</u> . . . <u>sleepe</u> . . ." (212).

There is much that is brave and noble, done in the high Roman fashion in <u>Antony and Cleopatra</u>, but in its sources the tragedy is at times not so much Roman as Milesian.²²

There are several instances of Apuleianly derived material in <u>Coriolanus</u>. Menenius by implication first lends approval to those interpretations of significantly ambiguous pronunciation in the plays, (as we have noted above, for example, in the case of <u>Othello</u>). The operative expressions are to the tribunes, "(I cannot call you Lycur<u>guses</u>)" and "I cannot say your worships have deliver'd the matter well, when I find the <u>ass in com</u>pound with the major part of your syllables" (II.i.55, 58-9). The gloss in <u>The Riverside</u> edition on the second expression, "an <u>element of the</u> fool in all you say (with play in <u>ass in compound</u> on the grammatical sense 'words compoun<u>ded with -as</u>, e.g. 'whereas') is quite correct but does not add that the second expression is a particular gloss upon the first expression with its "Lycur<u>gasses</u>." Menenius returns to the theme of asininity in his caustic observation that the beards of Sicinius and Brutus, the Tribunes, are not worth the stuffing of "an <u>ass's</u> pack-saddle" (II.i.89).

In turn the Tribunes in their plot against the newly honored Coriolanus recall diction used by Lucius when he thought he was to be perpetually honored for his role in the saving of Charite. Sicinius speaks of Coriolanus' "<u>honors</u>" (II.i.229), of the insolent "<u>fire</u>" (II.i.257) that will kindle the "<u>dry stubble</u>" (II.i.258) of the citizenry as easily as one sets "<u>dogs</u> on sheep" (II.i.257), while Brutus' version of Coriolanus will have him turn the people into "<u>mules</u>" (II.i.247), "<u>camels</u>" . . . "who have their <u>provand</u>" (II.i.251), and who are good enough only for bearing "<u>burthens</u>" (II.i.252). Lucius tells of how Charite calls him "her little <u>Camell</u>" (146), of how her parents promise him to reward him "with great <u>honours</u>" (146), of how he looked forward to a liber<u>tine</u> existence in the fields where he would find mares upon whom to beget "<u>mules</u>" (146) and of how he would no longer have to carry "<u>fardels</u> (see discussion of <u>Hamlet</u> above) nor <u>burthens</u>" (146). He did envy the "<u>dogges</u>" (146) initially, for they were already fed and in the event he is deprived of honors, mares, and proper "<u>provender</u>" (147). So badly do things turn out that he is placed in the custody of a vicious boy who torments him to the point of tying "<u>rub</u><u>ble</u>"/"<u>rubbell</u>" (149) which is very "<u>dry</u>" (149) to his back and then lighting it into a "<u>fire</u>" (149). The theme of expected honors frustrated and proper reward denied is common to both episode and tragedy. Shakespeare may have been thinking of Coriolanus here in terms of Lucius not only because of the similarity of theme but also because in the Apuleian-influenced Titus Andronicus he had joined at least their names:

> They hither march amain, under conduct
> Of Lucius, son to old Andronicus,
> Who threats, in course of this revenge, to do
> As much as ever Coriolanus did.
> (IV.iv.65-68)

In Act II, scene iii, there are two possible Apuleian echoes. First, when the Third Citizen speaks of having Coriolanus show his wounds, he tells of the necessity of avoiding ingratitude, else the multitude would be "monstrous members" (II.iii.12-13). Coriolanus is a play generally free from "objectionable" material,[23] but it is also a play marked by analogies to the human body. If "monstrous members" is a double entendre, its source may be the description of Lucius at the moment of transformation, "my face became monstrous . . . my members increased likewise" (77). Second, when Coriolanus thinks of letting "the high office and honor go" (II.iii.122) to somebody willing to humble himself, he speaks also of the force of custom and the "unswept" (II.iii.119) dust of time. Venus, of course, as we have observed above in our discussion of Sonnet 55, suffers neglect with her "altars unswept" (99) and is absolutely indignant that anyone receive what is rightly hers; indeed, she is "unable to temper her selfe from indignation" (99) at the change in her "celestiall honour" (99). Shakespeare's protagonist suffers from just such a pride that will not allow easily for indignities and made natural a recollection of terms associated with the proud and indignant Venus. It will be remembered also that when Venus finally captures Psyche she has her "scourged . . . with rods . . . ." (122), while Coriolanus is described by the Fourth Citizen as "a scourge" to his country's enemies (II.iii.91) and "a rod to her friends" (II.iii.92).

If we pass over the unique "cymbals" (V.iv.50) which with "trumpets" (V.iv.49) and other instruments herald the arrival in the city of the good news of the salvation of Rome as only possibly derived from Shakespeare's recollection of the "Cymbals" (175) and other instruments which accompany Lucius and the effeminate priests and "all their trumpery" (175) into "a noble City" (175), there is but one other instance of

Apuleian influence in the tragedy. Within seventeen lines Menenius describes Coriolanus' lack of subtlety in terms of mixed fodder, "meal and bran/He throws without distinction" (III.i.320-21) and Coriolanus stresses his self-consistency in the face of any threat, "Let them pull all about mine ears, present me/Death on the wheel, or at wild horses' heels" (III.ii.1-2). These words echo those at the end of the episode already borrowed from in this tragedy, in which Lucius was frustrated of the honors he had earned. He is forced to eat "filthy branne" (147) and is attacked by the "hinder heels" (147) of one of several horses [another of which "dressed his eares" (147) before biting Lucius], who are likened to the "wild Horses" (147) of the King of Thrace.

The themes of injustice, frustration of earned honors, and proud indignation, which appear in the lives of both Lucius and Venus are so obviously parallel to themes in Coriolanus that Shakespeare incorporated pieces of diction from the novel in these few apposite passages in the tragedy. When the Third Servant of Aufidius says of the disguised Coriolanus "what an ass it is" (IV.iv.43-44), he speaks to the students of Shakespeare's source work far better than he knows.

In these last tragedies Shakespeare has done what he had practiced in the earlier plays, although with, if anything, a still greater ease in adaptation. The injustice suffered by Lucius and his consequent inarticulateness has affected the response of the royal protagonist to the cosmic injustice dealt to him at the conclusion of King Lear -- and it is important to note that in these plays it is the protagonist who exhibits the chief Apuleian influence(s); the theatrical and ursine-imaged last moments of the brave thief Thrasileon have become part of Macbeth's last words and deeds in his tragedy; the apotheosis of Psyche has affected the ritual death of Cleopatra and the frequent use of the adjective "terrene" casts new light on the proper application of that word to Antony in the tragedy; and finally, the frustration of expected rewards due earned honor, and the bestial appetite and behavior of Lucius and his hostile fellows have become part of the texture of Coriolanus. As Lucius proceeds along his career towards self-knowledge, the various Shakespearean protagonists who have only sometimes, if ever, but slenderly known themselves acquire words and images which make more vivid their own thematically parallel experiences on their several paths to perception.

CHAPTER SIX

[1] See Charles Whibley's analysis of Adlington's use of an intermediary French text in the Introduction to The Tudor Translation, IV, xxv-xxviii.

[2] See reference to these Apuleian banditti in Timon of Athens, supra.

[3] Emrys Jones, Shakespeare's Scenic Art, 174.

[4] John Holloway, quoted by Nicholas Brooke in his "The Ending of King Lear," in Edward Bloom, ed., Shakespeare 1564-1964 (Providence: Brown University Press, 1964), 76.

[5] Sir Philip Sidney, An Apology for Poetry, ed., Geoffrey Shepherd (Manchester: Manchester University Press), 135.

[6] Quoted in Bullough, Narrative and Dramatic Sources VII, 516-17. Shakespeare would have had to use the original Latin.

[7] Starnes, "Shakespeare and Apuleius," 1035.

[8] Ibid., 1036

[9] It must be admitted that Holinshed described Macbeth as both "a valiant gentleman" and "as excellent capteine."

[10] See Bullough, Narrative and Dramatic Sources VII, 461.

[11] There are several instances of "compass'd" in the canon but no immediately contiguous "compass'd" and "with" appears but for this example.

[12] For Francis Douce's argument that the witches imitate the greasy practices of Milo's wife in The Golden Asse, see his 1839 Illustrations of Shakespeare (New York: Burt Franklin, rprt, 1968), 245.

[13] Michael Lloyd, "Cleopatra as Isis," Shakespeare Survey, XII (Cambridge: Cambridge University Press, 1959), 88-94.

[14] Ibid., 94.

[15] Starnes, "Shakespeare and Apuleius," 1024.

[16] Harold Fisch, "Antony and Cleopatra: the Limits of Mythology," Shakespeare Survey, XXIII (Cambridge University Press, 1970), 62.

[17] Ibid.

[18] Ibid., 63.

[19] Ibid., 66.

[20] Ibid., 67.

[21] An outstanding exception is J.L. Hotson who argued that the phrase refers to the Egyptian fleet. See Shakespeare's Sonnets Dated (New York: Oxford University Press, 1949), 10.

[22] For a criticism of Lloyd's view, see John Adlard, "Cleopatra as Isis," Archiv für das Studium der neueren Sprachen und Literaturen, cxii (1975), 324-28.

[23] Eric Partridge, Shakespeare's Bawdy, 54.

CHAPTER SEVEN

THE ROMANCES

    The Romances of Shakespeare, those special comedies of the miraculously unexpected and so satisfying reconciliations, are by kind the most likely to have been influenced by The Golden Asse, itself a descendant of the Greek romance.[1] Each of the four Romances, Pericles, Prince of Tyre, Cymbeline, The Winter's Tale, and The Tempest reveals Apuleian material in either structure or texture, or in some cases both.

    The heroines of these plays in particular share a common ancestry in the figure of the vulnerable Psyche whose much tried sweet innocence is finally rewarded with the right husband and an everlastingly blissful marriage. These young women of the last plays with their gentle natures acquire character through their experiences with demanding Fortune with the result that they are more interesting people when they are joined with their husbands than they were before their time of testing. So too, of course, is the archetypal tested innocent Psyche whose restoration to Cupid is as a true person with genuine moral experience.

    Pericles is a play which gives new meaning to the word improbable, but the final three acts provide some of Shakespeare's most affecting expression, and some of this language derives from The Golden Asse. Most critics deny Shakespeare any hand in the first two acts and in so doing they may find support in the absence of almost any Apuleian elements. The single exception, one which might help the case of those who like Philip Edwards find the entire play Shakespearean, but by memorial reconstruction with the reporter of the first two acts inferior to his partner,[2] occurs in Pericles'

> Thou speak'st like a physician, Helicanus,
> That ministers a potion unto me
> That thou wouldst tremble to receive thyself
>   (I.ii.67-69)

This passage echoes the diction in the episode of the murderous woman who is to be Lucius' sexual partner in Book X. She had hired a "traiterous Physitian" (220) to kill her husband. The physician pretends to mix a sacred Potion" (221) but substitutes a poison; he in turn is embarrassed into drinking the poison and dies before he can obtain an antidote. The murderous wife confronts him with "I pray you master Physitian, minister not this drinke unto my deare Husband, untill such time as you have drunke some part therof your selfe" (221). The faithful Helicanus shares none of the characteristics of the physician himself, but the idea and the diction of the lines stem from the ambiguous act of the episode in Book X of the novel.

However, it is in the manifestly Shakespearean acts that some still clearer Apuleian elements appear, although not so many as may seem likely given the lineage of both play and novel, the latter indeed is called by its author "a pleasant Grecian jeast" (16). Such elements as do appear occur mainly in the brothel scenes and derive chiefly from the adventures of Psyche and of Charite to whom the story of Psyche is told.

When Pericles appeals to "Lucina" (III.i.10) it may be that Shakespeare was partly recalling the name of the wife of Prince Apollonius in one of his recognized sources, Laurence Twine's The Patterne of Painfull Adventures, but as the context indicates Juno in her capacity as protectress of women in the throes of childbirth he may have recalled Psyche's similar appeal in The Golden Asse:

> O deere spouse and sister of the great God
> Jupiter . . . goddesse of goddesses . . .
> all the world calleth thee Lucina . . .
> deliver me . . . (120)

Pericles' invocation is to "Lucina, O!/Divinest patroness" (III.i.10-11).

When Marina finds herself in the brothel discussing her condition with the Bawd and Boult, she responds to the Bawd's question, "Why lament you, pretty one" (IV.ii.68), with the poignant observation "That I am pretty" (IV.ii.69). This exchange reflects that between the parents of Psyche and Psyche herself when she has been committed not to a brothel but to a marriage with a dire serpent. "They began to lament . . . Psyches spake unto them . . . Now you see the reward of my excellent beauty . . ." (101). Ironically, when Psyche is wafted to the palace of Cupid, she finds that with the doors unlocked, there is "no . . . bolt" (103). "Boult" is not in Shakespeare's acknowledged sources for Pericles. The name has obvious phallic appropriateness and may have as much to do with sifting, with examining the would-be patrons of the brothel, as it does to the locks and bolts of doorkeeping. In either case, the word appears frequently in the novel, not only "bolt" as here in Psyche's adventure, but also in the tale of Philesitherus and Myrmex who combine to cuckold Barbarus in Book IX, where Myrmex is to "boult out the matter" (190). This tale is told by a "bawd" (191) to the Baker's wife whose husband unexpectedly returns home as she is feeding her lover who has scarcely "eaten the first morsell" when he is "thrust . . . into the bin where she bolted her flower" (191). We recall that the Bawd promises Boult that he may metaphorically "cut a morsel off the spit himself" (IV.ii.131).

It may be that Marina's desire to be metamorphosed into a bird is so natural a wish that she is not to be thought of as echoing Lucius' desire that "I may bee turned into a bird" (75),

>That the gods
>Would set me free from this unhallowed place
>Though they did change me to the meanest bird
>That flies i' th' purer air!
>(IV.vi.99-102)

but the brothel in which she finds herself is itself Apuleian. We know that while Gower is a greater influence upon the play than is Twine, "only in a few instances does the play follow Gower's wording closely."[3] Neither Twine nor Gower refers to a "brothel," although Gower comes close with the word "bordel." Gower tells us that Leonine places Thaise (our Marina) "ad lupanar."[4] "Lupanar" (brothel or bordello) occurs also in Apuleius where Charite, like Marina, an innocent and virtuous maiden, is threatened with life in a bawdy house. Lepolemus, disguised as the thief Haemus, convinces the band of thieves that they should not sew Charite in the hide of the ass but rather bind her in slavery to a brothel "lupanari" (Met. 7.9.30). Lucius, ignorant of the fact that Charite recognizes the disguised Lepolemus, wonders that a virtuous maiden can rejoice in conversation about a brothel "lupanaris" (7.10.11).

Lysimachus, at first a would-be user of Marina, ultimately befriends her. He is a shadow version of Lepolemus, who at first would have Charite in a brothel but ultimately secures her escape. Gower in the play (but not in Confessio Amantis) tells us that Marina has escaped "the brothel" (V.i.1). Adlington has Lucius comment on Haemus' plan and Charite's response with reference to "brothels" and "a wicked brothel house" (143). Lysimachus in the play (the Lepolemus figure) gives "gold" (IV.vi.113), curses any violator of Marina so that he will die "like a thief" (IV.vi.114), and tells Boult that but for "this virgin" (IV.vi.119) his bawdy "house" (IV.vi.119) would collapse around him. Lepolemus promises the "theeves" (142) that he will turn their "house . . . into gold" (142) and that "this virgin" (142) will be best sold to "bawdy Merchants" for "gold" (143).

The improbable escape of Marina has much in common with that of Charite, and something in common with that of Psyche, whose exemplary tribulations are narrated the better to calm the initially distraught Charite. We recall that Lysimachus is said by Boult to have enough money to line Marina's "apron with gold" (IV.vi.58-9). Charite hears of the trial of Psyche which involves her gathering the "golden Fleeces" (124) of certain great sheep. Following helpful counsel, Psyche "gathered up such lockes as shee found and put them in her apron" (124). "Apron" is a rare word in the canon, occurring only here and as a missing garment for the carpenter in the opening of Julius Caesar. Its presence here adds to the constellation of injured innocence, gold, brothels, and the most improbable adventures of Psyche, Charite, and Marina.

There are two chief Apuleian elements and fragments of lesser significance in Cymbeline. The most obvious link between the novel and the play is that of the poisoning stepmother motif. This episode in Book X of the novel fascinated Shakespeare, as we have seen above, especially in our discussions of Hamlet, Othello, and All's Well That Ends Well, and the particular motif of poison/sleeping potion fascinated dramatists of the period, as we know from the case of Dekker and his Satiromastix. D.T. Starnes supplied a table of correspondence between characters and roles, one which is quite accurate:

> 1) In Cymbeline as in The Golden Ass a stepmother procures from a physician what she supposes to be poison to administer to a stepchild. In Cymbeline the queen has Cornelius prepare a draught for Imogen; in the story the stepmother, though a servant, procures a potion for her stepson.

2) In the play and in the story the stepchild in trouble seeks counsel of a trusted older person, and is advised to go away. Imogen in distress is advised by Pisanio to leave (III. iv.145ff.) The stepson in the story consults a sage old man, a tutor, and is counselled to absent himself (X, 235-36).

3) In both pieces the stepmother employs a servant to secure the poison. Pisanio, in Cymbeline, is her evil intent (V.v.237ff.). The servant in The Golden Ass is an accomplice.

4) In play and story a court doctor, suspecting the purchaser, provides a sleeping potion instead of poison. Cornelius, the court physician, furnishes the draught for the queen-stepmother (I.v.6-10). In The Golden Ass a "sage and ancient Physitian" testifies that he sold the potion (instead of poison) to the stepmother's servant (X, 239).

5) In each instance the child partaking of the potion sleeps and is saved from death. Imogen is thus preserved in Cymbeline; the stepmother's son, in the story.

6) In the play as in the story the child, supposedly dead from the poison, makes a dramatic reappearance at the end of the episode and is restored to his parents.

7) An incidental correspondence of play and story is the restoration at the end, of two sons to their father. In Cymbeline the kidnapped sons are brought back; in the novel, the son saved from poisoning, and the stepson from false accusations of his murder are returned whole to their father.[5]

Starnes went on to point out some general similarities in diction, and concluded by noting that the King's rejoicing at the recovery of Imogen and his two sons parallels that of the troubled father in the stepmother episode:

O, what, am I
A mother to the birth of three? ne'er mother
Rejoic'd deliverance more.   (V.v.368-70)

and

> Behold how the fortune of the old man was changed, who thinking to be deprived of all his race and posterity, was in one moment made the Father of two Children (212).

He rightly observed that "in the stepmother-poison-plot narrative of The Golden Asse we have the real source of the 'queen and her plots' in Cymbeline."

Iachimo's description of the apartment of Imogen with its reference to the carving of Diana at the bath as so exquisite that the art was equal to nature (II.iv. 80ff.) parallels Lucius' experience on his way to the house of Byrrhena where there is exquisite statuary illustrating the fable of Diana and Actaeon "wherein Art (was) envying Nature" (43). Fotis' explanation that the bladder-men slain by Lucius were the result of Pamphile's "confections" (73) uses a word rare in the canon, one which appears in the speech of the wicked Queen and by its echoing presence reminds us both of her power and her evil intent, "my confections" (I.v.15), and her cordial given to Pisanio, "that confection" (V.v. 246).

The Roman General Caius Lucius reluctantly tells Cymbeline that "I am to pronounce Augustus Caesar" (III.i.62) an enemy to the British king who has protested at having been put under the yoke. The newly metamorphosed Lucius, burdened by a heavy load, tries to appeal for relief, but his attempt to call out the name of Caesar fails, "but Caesar I could in no wise pronounce" (79). These echoes of phrasing are of minor importance and possibly subconscious. Of considerably greater interest is the instance of the lovely lyric sung by Guiderius and Arviragus over the body of Imogen/Fidele.

The matter surrounding this song is suggestively Apuleian, so much so that we can hardly do other than acknowledge the likelihood that the song itself is equally derivative from the novel, especially from the tale of Cupid and Psyche, the central episode of The Golden Asse. We note first that Belarius describes their condition (that of himself, Guiderius, Arviragus and Imogen/Fidele) as one of "outlaws" (IV.iii.138) who live, as we know, in a "cave" (IV.ii.138) and that Charite to whom the story of Cupid and Psyche is told is brought by the now familiar thievish outlaws to a "cave" (95). Imogen awakes and, seeing the body of

Cloten, is dismayed for she had thought that she had been a "cave-keeper/And cook to honest creatures" (IV. ii.298-99), not in the midst of those motivated by "malice and <u>lucre</u>" (IV.ii.324). Imogen had the role of the old woman <u>who</u> kept the cave and cooked for the outlaws, the outlaws who so "preferre their owne <u>lucre</u>" (142) that they will rather sell Charite than <u>kill</u> her, and she reacts as did Charite when she believes that the dead Cloten is her husband Posthumus -- Imogen falls upon the body of her "<u>husband</u>," just as Charite did upon that of her husband Lepolemus (162). "<u>Lucre</u>" is rare in the canon[6] and "<u>Zephyrs</u>" (IV.ii.172) is <u>unique</u>. In the story of Cupid and Psyche told to Charite after she has been brought to the cave and before she can escape with her husband-to-be Lepolemus, Charite learns of Psyche's being wafted to the palace of her husband. The description of this bridal flight has affected the texture of Belarius' praise of Arviragus and Guiderius,

> They are as <u>gentle</u>
> As <u>Zephyrs</u> <u>blowing</u> the <u>violet</u>,
> Not wagging his <u>sweet</u> head; . . . .
> . . . . as the rud'st <u>wind</u>
> That by <u>the</u> <u>top</u> doth take the mountain pine
> And make <u>him</u> stoop to th' <u>vale</u>. 'Tis wonder
> That an <u>invisible</u> instinct should frame them.
>   (IV.ii.171-77)

In Adlington's version we read that

> Thus poore Psyches being left alone . . . on the <u>toppe</u> of the rocke, was <u>blowne</u> by the <u>gentle</u> aire and of shrilling <u>Zephyrus</u> . . . brought her downe into a deep <u>valley</u>. where she was laid in a bed of most <u>sweet</u> and fragrant flowers . . . (102) . . . when Psyches was set downe . . . as it were with a <u>winde</u> . . . one came in and sung <u>invisibly</u> . . . (103) . . . soone after came her <u>invisible</u> servants (104).

The outlaws in the cave, the cave-keeper who cooks, the lucre, and the grieving wife who throws herself upon the body of her husband, together with the image of gentle wafting by zephyrs combine to remind us of the world of Psyche and Charite, so that we discern more easily the same source for much of the texture of the opening of the lyric sung by Guiderius and Arviragus,

>   Fear no more the heat o' th' sun,
>   Nor the furious winter's rages,
>   Thou thy worldly task hast done,
>   Home art gone, and ta'en thy wages,
>   Golden lads and girls all must,
>   As chimney-sweepers, come to dust.
>   Fear no more the frown o' th' great
>   Thou art past the tyrant's stroke;
>   Care no more to clothe and eat,
>   To thee the reed is as the oak.
>   The sceptre, learning, physic, must
>   All follow this and come to dust.
>   (IV.ii.258-69)

The singular "the heat o' th' sun" recalls that episode in Psyche's adventures where at the command of the frowning and tyrannical Venus she must retrieve the golden fleece of great sheep. It is the second "taske" (123) and she accomplishes it with the aid of "the gentle and benign reed" (124), who urges her to wait until "the heat of the sunne be past" (124), when the sheep are less "furious" (124) in order to obtain the "lockes of their golden Fleeces" (124). Charite who has listened to this tale hears her rescuing lover address her captors as "lads" (139) tell them that they can "live like tyrants" (139), and gain "gold" (140) and that "as for death (which every man doth feare)" he considers it as nothing (140). The song goes on to mention "lovers young" (IV.ii.274) and concludes with "Quiet consummation have,/And renowned be thy grave" (IV.ii.280-81). Psyche and Cupid are young lovers (as are, presumably Imogen and Posthumus) and theirs was a "perfect consummation" (104).

It is important to observe the irony of the situation in Cymbeline, for not only is Fidele Imogen, but she is not dead; her tasks are not yet over; the song is premature for she will be rejoined with her husband, even as Psyche is rejoined with Cupid.

Some added evidence that Psyche's tasks were in the mind of Shakespeare in the latter part of the play exists in "Lucina" (V.iv.43), already noted above in the discussion of Pericles, but also in the "crystal"/ "crystalline" (V.iv.81,113), "Jupiter" (V.iv.77 and elsewhere), "eagle" (V.iv.113), "palace" (V.iv.113), "royal bird" (V.iv.117) and "immortal," (V.iv.118), all amid Jupiter's raising of Posthumus for his "trials well are spent" (V.iv.104). We recall that Psyche's task immediately after the garnering of the golden

Fleece is the bringing of the water from the Styx in a "Christall" bottle (124), a task met with the help of "the royall bird of great Jupiter, the Eagle" (125). Restored at the end of her trials to Cupid, Psyche is brought up to the "Pallace of heaven" (129) where Jupiter makes her "immortal" (129).

The tone and atmosphere of Cymbeline depend not only upon the stepmother-poison plot of The Golden Asse but also on the trials and tribulations of Psyche and Charite. Like the novel itself with its ultimate restoration of Lepolemus and Charite, and of the union, reunion, and glorification of Cupid and Psyche, the romance that is Cymbeline is as much a Milesian drama of reconciliation as British.

There are three Apuleian elements in The Winter's Tale, attached to Antigonus, Autolycus, and Julio Romano. As D.T. Starnes noted, the demise of Antigonus as satisfaction for the appetite of a bear is not found in Greene's Pandosto, the prime source of the romance. The relevant action in the play was correctly summarized by Starnes in the following way:

> The stage direction in The Winter's Tale (III.iii.58ff.) reads "Exit, pursued by a bear." The reference is to Antigonus, who has just exposed the infant Perdita. A shepherd appears, searching for two stray sheep, and finds the infant. Soon he hears from his clownish son, who is nearby, that the son has seen a bear dining on a man -- Antigonus. "The bear tore out his shoulder bone" (III.iii.95). Near the end of this scene, as the shepherd and his son part, the latter goes to see whether the hungry bear has finished his meal: "if there be any left of him, I'll bury it" (III.iii.131-32). Later (V.ii.63ff.) we hear inquiry as to Antigonus' fate, and the reply that "he was torn to pieces with a bear."[7]

In the novel Lucius breaks his halter when "a marvailous great Beare, holding out his mighty head" (152) surprises the wicked boy who has been leading the ass. As we noted in our discussion of King Lear, Lucius runs "to the intent I would escape from the terrible Beare, but especially from the boy that was worse than the Beare" (152). Starnes summarized the subsequent action:

> Shepherds, seeking a stray cow, find an ass,
> ridden by a stranger, and try to take the
> beast to the rightful owner -- the cruel boy.
> They find the boy's body "rent and torne in
> peeces and his members dispersed in divers
> places," which, Lucius says, "I well knew
> was done by the cruell Beare" (153) . . .
> "Then they gathered together the peeces of
> his body and buried them" (153).

Starnes then drew the conclusion:

> It will be observed that in both accounts are
> shepherds searching for stray sheep (cow);
> they are surprised by finding what they are
> not looking for (an infant, an ass); then they
> discover the mangled body of a man, partly
> eaten by a bear; and they resolve to bury
> what remained of the body. The similarities
> in characters, in incident, in the bizarre
> quality of the episode, in the order of de-
> tails, and in the feeling produced that Anti-
> gonus and the cruel boy met a deserved fate
> can hardly be explained as coincidence.[8]

This bear may have affected the subsequent observation of the shepherd's son when he and his father are frightened by the imagined punishments they face according to Autolycus whom they then wish to placate: "and though authority be a stubborn bear, yet he is oft led by the nose with gold" (IV.iv.801-02). These punishments are a more extended version of that meted out to Aaron in *Titus Andronicus*. Autolycus describes with great gusto the tortures to come from the spirit of vengeance:

> He has a son, who shall be flay'd alive; then
> 'nointed over with honey, set on the head of
> a wasp's nest; then stand till he be three
> quarters and a dram dead; then recover'd
> again with aqua-vitae or some other hot infu-
> sion; then raw as he is (and in the hottest
> day prognostication proclaims), shall he be
> set against a brick-wall, the sun looking
> with a southward eye upon him, where he is
> to behold him with flies blown to death.
> (IV.iv.783-91)

Geoffrey Bullough noted that this passage derives in part from the punishment of the lascivious servant in Book VIII:

> The Master . . . tooke his servant . . . and . . . <u>annointed</u> his body <u>with honey</u>, and then bound <u>him sure to a fig-tree</u>, <u>where</u> in a rotten stocke a great number of Pismares had builded their <u>neasts</u>; the Pismares after they had felt the <u>sweetness</u> of the honey came upon the body, and by little and little . . . devoured his flesh, in such sort that there remained on the tree but his bare bones (171).[9]

Starnes, however, had earlier noted that Autolycus' imagined torments are the result of a conflation of the fortunes suffered by the lascivious servant and those designed by the thieves for Charite and the asinine Lucius.[10] These latter include the fourth thief's judgment that "she should <u>be flead alive</u>" (133) and another of the brigand's plan <u>to kill Lucius</u>, eviscerate him, then sew up Charite in the hide, and

> Then let us lay this stuffed ass upon a great stone against the <u>broiling heate</u> of <u>the Sunne</u>, so they shall both sustaine all the punishments which you have ordained (134).

The description of the "statue" of Hermione in the final scene of the play is itself Apuleian and the attribution of it to Julio Romano additionally so. When the court moves to Paulina's house, passes through her gallery, sees the marvellously life-like "statue," and learns from Paulina that this achievement is not the result of witchcraft, the action of the scene is following that of Lucius' meeting with his aunt, Byrrhena, in Book II.

Lucius, newly arrived in Hipata, accidentally meets his aunt Byrrhena who invites him to her house where there is much sculpture so finely carved that "Art (is) envying Nature" (43). The chief works are statues of "the Goddesse of Victory" so well done that "you would verily have thought that she had flyed" (43), and of Diana (with Actaeon, and Actaeon's hounds), so carved that "she seemed as though the wind did blow up her garments, and that she did encounter with them that come into the house" (43). After a tour of the house, Byrrhena lectures Lucius on the dangers of witchcraft as practiced by Pamphile. In the play Leontes and his court visit Paulina's self-styled "poor house" (V.iii. 6) in order to see "the statue of (Perdita's) mother" (V.iii.14), find the "statue" astonishingly life-like, and hear Paulina assure her audience that she has not been "assisted/By wicked powers" (V.iii.90-91). Some of the diction in both novel and play reinforces the probability that Paulina's exhibit echoes that of Byrrhena. We note that when Lucius meets Byrrhena, he does not recognize her immediately, with the result that "halfe ashamed I drew towards her" (42), she recognizes him as the "naturall childe" (42) of her sister, they go to her "house," and see the wonderfully "carved statues and images" (43), "so lively and with such excellencie portrayed" (43), one of which is of "marble," (43) others of "stone" (43), ". . . (which was a greater marvel to behold) the excellent carver . . . had fashioned the Dogs to stand up fiercely" (43), "Diana was carved with the same stone, standing in the water" (43). The tour of the statuary finished, Byrrhena warns Lucius of the evil arts and wicked allurements" (44) of Pamphile, that "Magitian" (44).

The "statue" of Julio Romano "would beguile Nature of her custom" (V.ii.99). It draws even those who at the reunion of Leontes and Perdita were "most marble" (V.ii.90). They go to Paulina's "house" (V.iii.6), wonder at the "natural posture" (V.iii.23) of the "stone" (V.iii.24) worked upon by "our carver's excellence" (V.iii.30), and note that "Hermione" coldly "stands" (V.iii.36), and the sight makes Perdita "Standing like stone" (V.iii.42). Leontes confesses "I am asham'd" (V.iii.37), and speaks of the "magic" of the statue (V.iii.38, 110) and of his "evils" (V.iii. 39). Paulina denies the aid of "wicked powers" (V.iii. 91) as she has the "marvel" (V.iii.100) move.

The statue scene which concludes the play is only the most striking of a number of turns on the theme of art becoming nature and nature becoming art in The Winter's Tale. Shakespeare found the statuary in the house of Apuleius' Byrrhena a contributing source for this theme and Hermione's "statue" (and the presence of the Actaeon pieces at Byrrhena's fits the self-destructive thoughts of the sexually jealous Leontes). From Apuleius Shakespeare is likely to have found Julio Romano as the artist responsible for the "statue." The Julio or Giulio (as we know him) Romano was one of the great painters of the High Renaissance; a student of Raphael, he was praised by Aretino, Vasari and Titian, and influenced Poussin and Rubens as well.[11] Giulio

Romano's greatest work was done in Mantua for the Gonzaga family, especially the Palazzo del Te within which there are several rooms decorated with highly symbolic paintings. The loveliest room, and the one most interesting to us, is the Sala di Psiche in which "the fable of Cupid and Psyche is . . . divided into twenty-three scenes, consisting of eight octagons, twelve lunettes, the central marriage ceremony, and two wall frescoes of the wedding feast . . . and on the walls six scenes which have no direct connection with the Cupid and Psyche story."[12] The subject seems to have been chosen for its personal allegorical features whereby the irate Venus represents Isabella d'Este and Cupid her son Federigo. Psyche is Federigo's love Isabella Boschetta.[13] The New Arden editor of The Winter's Tale, J.H.P. Pafford, without reference to Apuleius or the Sala di Psiche, pointed out that "Shakespeare may have seen some of Julio's paintings, and Vasari's Lives in Italian."[14] We know that he was interested in the Gonzagas and Mantua, possibly in Measure for Measure and certainly in Hamlet where in the mousetrap play "Gonzago is the duke's name" (III.ii.239).[15]

The celebrity of the Gonzaga-patronized Julio Romano and his particular work on Apuleius' story of Cupid and Psyche from The Golden Asse made him more than any other Renaissance artist, the most appropriate creator of the "statue" of Hermione.

In Othello, Shakespeare's earlier study of unwarranted masculine sexual jealousy, several elements from Apuleius affected theme and diction. So it is hardly surprising that there are still other influential Apuleian elements in the texture of The Winter's Tale, in addition to those which have affected Autolycus and Julio Romano. Even as the play ends with Hermione restored to Leontes, the king echoes some diction of the story of Psyche when she moves toward restoration with Cupid. The last line is "We were dissever'd. Hastily lead away" (V.iii.155). Psyche's first task when "these two lovers were divided one from another" (123) was "to dissever" (123) a heap of mingled grain. Some helpful ants accomplish the task for Psyche, doing the "dissevering" (123) and then running "away againe in all haste" (123). Leontes' line is doubtless a subconscious echo of the tale of Cupid and Psyche, but with her arms about his neck Hermione is a mature and restored Psyche, no longer dissevered and better than a figure in "an old tale" (V.iii.117).

The Tempest is the crown of Shakespeare's career, a perfect play of thematic recapitulations, a richer, more mature work than its anticipation, A Midsummer Night's Dream. Yet, like A Midsummer Night's Dream, The Tempest is a play affected by The Golden Asse, if without the same degree of absolutely pervasive Apuleian influence as in the earlier comedy. Puck who is a rambunctious Cupid is succeeded by Ariel who, as D.T. Starnes observed,[16] functions as the airy agent of Cupid, the gentle Zephyrus, who moves people about with consummate efficiency. Ariel is invisible like Zephyrus, and so are the spirits attendant upon Psyche during her wedding night and subsequent life in Cupid's palace. When Ferdinand hears Ariel's song, he describes it as "no mortal business, nor no sound/That the earth owes" (I.ii.407-08) and repeats the experience of Psyche who "heard a voyce without any body" (103) which asks why she should marvel "at so great riches" (103). We recall that Ariel's song heard by Ferdinand is partly about the riches "coral" and "pearls" which combine into "something rich and strange" (I.ii.398, 399, 402). The incorporeal "voyces" (103) heard by Ferdinand are also heard by Caliban, so that Shakespeare is seen as reversing gender and then nature. Caliban's are the most affecting lines in the play,

> Be not afeard, the isle is full of noises,
> Sounds, and sweet airs, that give delight
>   and hurt not.
>
> Sometimes a thousand twangling instruments
> Will hum about mine ears; and sometime voices,
> That if I then had wak'd after a long sleep,
> Will make me sleep again, and then in dreaming,
> The clouds methought would open, and show
>   riches
> Ready to drop upon me, that when I wak'd
> I cried to dream again.
>   (III.ii.135-43)

Psyche is initially afraid, the palace is full of noises, she refreshes herself with "sleep" (102), hears "in her ears" (104) the "harmony of the instruments" (104) and "voyces" (103), sees the "great riches" (103), and learns to desire the repetition not only of lovemaking, "but specially the sound of the instruments" (104). Starnes pointed out that not only is there a parallel between the invisible voices and instruments of Cupid's palace and those of Prospero's island, but also, "giving point, by contrast, in each piece is that in the midst of the idealized surroundings is introduced the realistic and disturbing motif of the treachery and exposure of kinsmen."[17]

The tale of Cupid and Psyche is a story of love, trial, and marriage, as is <u>The Tempest</u>, a play clearly intended to compliment some pair of noble or royal newlyweds.[18] The wedding masque within the play, ordered by Prospero for the marriage of Ferdinand and Miranda, features divinities also prominent in the adventures of Psyche. Ceres and Juno are naturally present, protectresses of fertility generally and human childbirth specifically. Venus by virtue of her infidelity and her son Cupid in his role of trouble-maker are naturally absent (we recall that in the opening of the tale Venus views her son as a vengeful trouble-maker, only later discovering his unsuspected maturity).

In her quest for her husband, the pregnant Psyche seeks help first from Ceres and then from Juno. In the play Ceres appears first and is joined by Juno. The attributes of Ceres in the masque recall both those of the goddess in the tale and certain elements in Psyche's first task. Iris, the messenger of Juno, addresses Ceres by name,

> Ceres, most bouteous lady, thy rich leas
> Of <u>wheat</u>, rye, <u>barley</u>, fetches, oats and
> <u>pease</u>;
>
> (IV.i.60-61)

Ceres responds by saying that she will not "disobey the wife of Jupiter" but wonders if at this celebration of this contract of true love Venus and Cupid will be attending Juno. Iris assures her that those two who had thought "to have done/Some wanton charm upon this man and maid" (IV.i.94-5) have instead flown "towards <u>Paphos</u>" (IV.i.93), Cupid with broken "<u>arrows</u>" (IV.i.98). Juno arrives, and Iris calls forth the nymphs who perform a dance. In the novel Ceres is reluctant to disobey Venus who is in pursuit of Psyche. Her attributes in the story are those of the play. She has a temple surrounded by "sheffes of corn lying on a heap, blades withered with garlands, and reeds of <u>barley</u> . . . <u>sickles</u> and other instruments" (119) -- we recall the nymphs who arrive in the masque as "sunburn'd <u>sicklemen</u>" (IV.i.134). Ceres in the play has had her grain added to by the heap of confused seeds set as a task for Psyche, following the denial of help by Ceres and

Juno, "then she tooke a great quantity of wheat, of barley, poppy seede, peason, lintles, and beanes, and mingled them together on a heape" (123). Ceres in the novel is appealed to by Psyche "by thy plenteous and liberall right hand" (119). Juno calls Ceres her "bounteous sister" and goes on to bless the marriage with wishes for "issue" and "increasing" (IV.i.105, 107).

In the novel Juno is no more helpful than Ceres, even though she is particularly appealed to as "Lucina" (120). In the play Juno like her sister Ceres acts beneficiently, a reversal of source material completely characteristic of Shakespeare. She joins in dance with Ceres and the nymphs, rather as all Olympus finally did at the wedding feast of Cupid and Psyche.

Considerable supporting evidence for the view that Shakespeare had the Apuleian story in mind during the composition of The Tempest is provided by the number of identical attributes associated with Venus and Cupid in both the short passage of the play describing their absence, and those in the novel. Among the terms associated with the two are "Dis" (IV.i.89), "clouds" (IV.i.93), "Paphos" (IV.i.93), "Dove-drawn" (IV.i.94), "Hymen's torch" (IV.i.97), "lighted" (IV.i.97), "arrows" (IV.i.99), and "sparrows" (IV.i.100). "Dis" occurs in the canon only here and later in The Two Noble Kinsmen -- it occurs in the last of the tasks set by Venus for Psyche in the genitive "Ditis" (Met.6.18.4, 17).[19] Venus first learned of Psyche and her striking beauty when no one visited "Paphos" (99). She set her son "armed with fire and arrows" (99) against Psyche who is forced to marry with "black torches lighted" (101), and an interrupted "melody of Hymeneus." Later, in her continuing quest for Psyche, Venus flies to Heaven, as the "clouds gave place" (121), doves guided the chariot, "pigeons" in Adlington, but "columbae" in Apuleius (Met.6.6.8), and "sparrowes" (121) flew about. These attributes are so common to Venus and Cupid that doves, sparrows, Paphos, and arrows may be overlooked as Apuleian derived, but their presence together with the rare "Dis" and the torch of Hymen combine to make such a collocation hardly fortuitous.

The wedding masque is one of the central episodes of The Tempest, one with "the simple theme of immortality through generation."[20] Shakespeare found in the tale of Cupid and Psyche the identical theme and did not hesitate to borrow circumstantial details which, while underscoring the themes of the play, add to its fairy tale atmosphere.

All four of the Romances have been affected by *The Golden Asse*. Each has some part of its texture influenced by the story of Cupid and Psyche, and all but *The Tempest* have had incorporated elements from other episodes as well. The stepmother-poison episode and its analogous story of the poisoning-poisoned physician have been used again in *Pericles* for a vivid analogy and in *Cymbeline* as a structural device. The adventures of Charite who listens to the tale of Cupid and Psyche have affected the presentation of character and description of setting in both *Pericles* and *Cymbeline*. Indeed, the common nature of the heroines of these last plays owes much to their belonging to the same sisterhood as their source models, Psyche and Charite. *The Winter's Tale*, a serious work which plays with the theme of art and nature, has been influenced by Apuleius' set piece on the same theme, to the point where Shakespeare has attributed the most natural piece of art work to the Apuleianly motivated painter-architect Julio Romano. The very natural bear in the play is one from the several who dwell in the novel, the same creature whose fearsomeness influenced the speech of Lear, while his cousins affected the characteristics of Macbeth.

The Tempest is Apuleian solely in terms of Cupid and Psyche where reversal of gender and nature have allowed Psyche's wonderment at the palace of Cupid to become part of the experience of both Ferdinand and Caliban, and Psyche's experience with the goddesses Ceres, Juno, and Venus have been folded into the wedding masque of the play with intensification of theme and atmosphere.

Although the variety of episodes in *The Golden Asse* allowed Shakespeare to draw on all sorts of material, the general improbability of adventures in the novel and its heavily tragi-comic plotting made the work itself especially appropriate for use in these last lyrical but ever so improbable romances. The lyricism of their fairy tale mood is particularly derived from the central fairy tale of Cupid and Psyche whose hero and heroine prefigure the separated and rejoined lovers within these last works and perhaps those out in the audience, like Elizabeth and Frederick, Elector Palatine.

CHAPTER SEVEN

[1] See P.G. Walsh, The Roman Novel (Cambridge: Cambridge University Press, 1970), 144ff.

[2] See Philip Edwards, "An Approach to the Problem of Pericles," Shakespeare Survey 5 (Cambridge: Cambridge University Press, 1952), 25-49.

[3] F.D. Hoeniger, ed., Pericles (London: Methuen, 1963), xv.

[4] Geoffrey Bullough, ed., Narrative and Dramatic Sources of Shakespeare (London: Routledge & Kegan Paul, 1957-75) VI, 407.

[5] Starnes, op. cit., 1043.

[6] Elsewhere in the canon only in 1 Henry VI, V.iv. 141.

[7] Starnes, 1045.

[8] Ibid.

[9] Bullough, Narrative and Dramatic Sources, VIII, 16.

[10] Starnes, 1046.

[11] Frederick Hartt, Giulio Romano (New Haven: Yale University Press) I, xvi.

[12] Hartt, op. cit., 130.

[13] Hartt, 139.

[14] J.H.P. Pafford, ed., The Winter's Tale (London: Methuen, 1963), 150.

[15] See Bullough, Narrative and Dramatic Sources, VII, 38-44.

[16] Starnes, 1046-47.

[17] Starnes, 1047.

[18] The masque is believed an addition for the wedding of the Princess Elizabeth and Frederick, Elector Palatine in 1613.

[19] Although in at least one modern edition, that of Helm, "*Ditis*" is emended to "*Dis*."

[20] Don Cameron Allen, *Image and Meaning* (Baltimore: The Johns Hopkins Press, 1960), 60.

CONCLUSION

The first and irreducible fact in the life of a professional Elizabethan dramatist was the need to provide sufficient material often enough to satisfy his employer or employing colleagues. The voraciousness of the medium devoured plots derived from ancient and modern history, novellas, romances, current pamphlets, classical and medieval poetry, indeed from any source not nailed shut by exotic language or domestic authority. Shakespeare as just such a professional dramatist was not an exception to this pressure, even if he was able by his so early proven excellence to avoid the output of clearly hasty and slapdash performances by some of his contemporaries. Those contemporaries continued in their ransacking of all available material including The Golden Asse with its treasury replete with colorful episodes.

However, none of his contemporaries shows Shakespeare's complete familiarity with the text to the point where he could select details from several discrete episodes for use in one play or scene, or even passage, without taking along with those details any of the non-usable material with which the episode had begun and had ended. Shakespeare's great power to associate seemingly disparate materials and to experiment in the twisting and reversing of them, coupled with his great familiarity with the novel led to his use of The Golden Asse in more than thirty of his works.

The Golden Asse provided not only stories with appropriate themes and memorable diction, but also some of the techniques already favored by Shakespeare for the moving forward of story lines. We know how important for his drama are such devices as disguise and mistaken identity, eavesdropping, and evil intrigue. Apuleius had used the same tactics in his novel. What is supposed to be a dire serpent turns out to be the god of love; a handsome thief is really the fiancé of a kidnapped damsel; three murder victims are only magically inflated animal bladders; a menacing bear is a brave robber; and the protagonist himself is not truly an ass, but a thinking human being in an ass's form. Most of Lucius' narrative is based upon events he quite innocently observes and/or overhears as the more obviously human beings confidently and obliviously love, lie, poison, and deceive in his asinine presence. As for evil intrigue, there are the envious sisters of

Psyche, several adulterous wives (one a poisoning stepmother to boot), inveigling priests, and conspiring thieves, to mention only the most obvious.

Apuleius also supplied an atmosphere of magic and witchcraft which Shakespeare translated into several of his plays from such an early comedy as The Comedy of Errors to a mature tragedy like Macbeth. In addition, the great amount of circumstantial detail, the specificity with which Apuleius narrated the adventures of Lucius allowed Shakespeare ready access to words and phrases sufficiently vivid to be reused, sometimes in contexts far different from those of their Apuleian original. Pismires tasting the sweetness of honey, unswept altars, the heat of the sun, a truckle-bed, an unlucky inheritrix, a princely factor, terrene stars, Verges personified, a duplicitous fishmonger, a flaxen-haired lover, Charon and other band-dogs, Bellona, fardels, Zephyr, and contumely, and much, much more diction, all of which is unique in the canon and Apuleianly derived.

The folk elements too which Shakespeare drew upon from his other sources have parallels in The Golden Asse. Among the many folk motifs noted by Geoffrey Bullough as having been incorporated by Shakespeare into the heart of his plays, we may point out that the "faithless-friend" motif of The Two Gentlemen of Verona "the impossible task" element of All's Well That Ends Well, and the motif of "the incestuous parent" in Hamlet, and the "Cinderella theme" of King Lear, all derive, in large part at least, from episodes in The Golden Asse.

Shakespeare's prudent recidivism, his repeated reworking of proven material, reveals an economy of energy quintessentially professional. The same elements in the novel recur in various guises in the plays. For one example, Psyche is wafted to the palace of Cupid with musical accompaniment. Music and Psyche appear along with and behind the Psyche-like Ophelia in both her St. Valentine's Day Song and her elegiac ditties in the fatal brook; they appear in the seemingly funereal song of Arviragus and Guiderius with part of its lyric drawn from the description of Psyche's subsequent adventures; and they appear in the poignant longing of Caliban to hear the music again on the Ariel-controlled island, so like the Zephyrus-ordered world of Cupid. For another, the bears who inhabit the novel can have one of their number become an aphorism in King Lear, another turn into a metaphor in Macbeth, and the first reappear in actuality in The Winter's Tale.

Certain scenes from the novel recur in the plays, most especially the bed-chamber near-murder of Cupid by Psyche, and the stepmother poison plot episode. The description of the murder of the innocent Yorkist princes, Othello's flaming minister speech at the bedside of the innocent Desdemona, and Timon's address to the innocuous, or at least morally indifferent gold, all derive much of their diction and theme from Psyche's attempt upon the sleeping god of love. From the poison plot episode itself Shakespeare derived his confection-working queen in Cymbeline, and from the action of the good physician he found material for several plays, including the tragedies, Romeo and Juliet, Hamlet, and Othello, but within the episode itself the interview between stepmother and stepson with its theme of incestuous love served as a model for both the interview between Gertrude and Hamlet and that of the Countess and Helena in All's Well That Ends Well.

All four of the central Bradleian tragedies show significant aspects of theme, plot, and diction derived from The Golden Asse. Indeed, many of these aspects from Apuleius occur at extremely important moments within the plays, including Hamlet's most famous soliloquy, the madness of Ophelia, Iago's haunting prophecy of the Moor's anxiety, Othello's flaming minister speech, Lear's terrible final question, and Macbeth's bestial defiance and death.

Other of the plays of Shakespeare both early and later are heavily influenced by The Golden Asse, but it is especially noteworthy that Shakespeare at the time of what is arguably the height of his powers recalled a fundamentally comedic story whose episodes of magic, adultery, and bestial metamorphoses were transmuted by his creative imagination into the pure gold of the central tragedies.

Not only are the most famous of Shakespearean characters from the Bradleian tragedies, The Prince of Denmark, Ophelia, The Moor of Venice, Iago, King Lear, and Macbeth in part Apuleian in diction, parallel experience, or both diction and experience, but so too are the most celebrated figures pre- and post-Bradleian tragedies, Falstaff and Cleopatra. And as in the case of the other characters, the cheerfully imaginative Vice and the Egyptian queen have their especially

Apuleian qualities or experiences at some of the most important moments in their careers. Falstaff, not just in his description of his rag-tag company on march to Shrewsbury, or in his dealings with Mistress Quickly and Doll Tearsheet at the Boar's Head, and Mistress Ford at Windsor, but in his most notorious counterfeiting on the battlefield at Shrewsbury, is composed in part of acts and agents seen or heard by Lucius in the novel. Cleopatra, as Isis, in part of her descent down the Cydnus, in her hair-pulling episode with the messenger, but chiefly in her final ritualized apotheosis, is especially Apuleian.

And it is not just Falstaff and the tragic protagonists of the greatest celebrity who derive facets of their nature from The Golden Asse, but so too do, among still others, the clowns Dogberry and Elbow, about their policing rounds, the lover Troilus in the midst of ecstatic anticipation, difficult sons, Hotspur and Hal, in dialogue with difficult fathers, villain Aaron and villainess Tamora in their deaths, rebel Cade in his last metamorphosis, Autolycus at his threatening best, Antony at his most politically brutal, Valentine in the forest, greasy Joan at the pot, and, of course, bully Bottom in the arms of Titania.

Of special interest is the fact that several of the heroines of Shakespeare, in addition to the obviously analogous young girls of the Romances, share qualities of tenderness, passivity or subservience, sweetness, and vulnerability. Although they appear on a spectrum moving from near complete passivity to enterprising activity, Ophelia in her social inequality, abandonment, and suicidal drowning, Juliet with her mortal paramour, Cordelia with her evil sisters, Helena with her trials, and even the "lass unparalleled" in her immortal longings owe something of their natures to the heroine of Apuleius' central fairy tale. That no one confuses any one of these women with one another is the result not only of Shakespeare's unequalled powers of individualizing typical figures, not only of Shakespeare's having chosen different facets of the career of Psyche for each of his heroines, but also of the basic truth that the attitude of the author towards his source material determines its nature in the new text. Tone makes even the same source materials essentially different.

The eleventh book of the novel is not a part of the pervasive borrowings of Shakespeare, with the single exception of the "terrene stars of the goddesse," a phrase which had its affect upon Antony and Cleopatra and Antony as "terrene moon." It may well be that Shakespeare perceived that this final book was too serious in tone, that its narrative of religious conversion was not the same kind of material which he had been able to rework from the rest of the novel. But the reasons for his having omitted material are harder to discover than those we may cite for his having used certain incidents and episodes. For we are hard pressed to see why it is that Apuleian material does not appear in 1 and 3 Henry VI, The Taming of the Shrew, The Rape of Lucrece, King John, Richard II, The Merchant of Venice, As You Like It, Twelfth Night, Henry VIII, and The Two Noble Kinsmen. There was of course, no compulsion upon Shakespeare always to use elements from The Golden Asse in his work, and in the midst of so much borrowing from the novel in narrative poetry, in lyrical poetry, and in plays comic, historical, tragical, and tragical-historical-comical to the number of twenty-eight, he may have needed a therapeutic holiday from time to time. And ultimately, it may be that these works, too, have Apuleian features hitherto unnoticed by scholars so intent upon subtleties that they have missed the obvious. If so, then the future may bring forth a Shakespearean Golden Asse still greater in dimension than the rough, if quite friendly beast who has moved in oddly purposeful ways throughout the rest of the canon.

We have found that both Shakespeare's hard-boiled sophistication with its emotional detachment, coupled with the neutrality of feeling derived from the grotesque's simultaneously produced laughter and revulsion, and his generous and delicate sympathy with vulnerable human beings are found in The Golden Asse and in its central fairy tale. The overriding Shakespearean theme of self-knowledge acquired especially through the trial of changing rôle and identity is at the heart of the novel, and so too is the complete gamut of the emotions, lust, anger, jealousy, greed, fear, hope, despair, and love, human and divine, sighted and blind.

I suggest that The Golden Asse was one of Shakespeare's early reading experiences for the imprint of it upon his memory was so deep that at times he evoked its diction and cadences with seemingly little surface provocation from plot or character. In those instances where he recalled obviously parallel elements he was often careful to suppress both Apuleius' comic conclusions of otherwise tragic episodes, and the tragic resolutions themselves when his context required a comic turn.

Further, perhaps helped by Adlington's own lack of perception about the exact nature of his original, Shakespeare omits the constant and sophisticated play of wit and humor which Apuleius provides the reader in the midst of his grotesque and violent stories. Shakespeare doubtless enjoyed the novel for its own compelling vivacity, but as a craftsman about his business, he saw The Golden Asse as a mine of short narratives, each one of which was of potential thematic or situational interest and value.

The Renaissance emblem of an ass carrying a statue, presumably that of the goddess Isis, before a crowd of worshippers was used to signify the sin of vanity. The ignorant ass believes that the attention which is directed at his burden is really intended for him. There is some danger that such a misplaced focus belongs also to the student of Shakespeare's use of sources as he stresses the sources at the expense of the plays and the poems. The Golden Asse carries the burden of much of the most precious of Shakespearean works, but even the staunchest enthusiast of Apuleius and his rôle does not confuse source and work, ass and icons. Even though he may be pleased to see that the versatile and only sometimes rough beast has had his hour of recognition come round at last.

APPENDIX A

CHAPTER HEADINGS OF THE GOLDEN ASSE

PAGE

THE FIRST CHAPTER — 19

How Apuleius riding in Thessaly, fortuned to fall into company with two strangers, that reasoned together of the mighty power of Witches.

THE SECOND CHAPTER — 21

How Apuleius told to the strangers, what he saw a Iugler do in Athens.

THE THIRD CHAPTER — 23

How Socrates in his returne from Macedony to Larissa, was spoyled and robbed, and how he fell acquainted with one Meroe a Witch.

THE FOURTH CHAPTER — 25

How Meroe the Witch turned divers persons into miserable beasts.

THE FIFTH CHAPTER — 27

How Socrates and Aristomenus slept together in one Chamber, and how they were handled by Witches.

THE SIXTH CHAPTER — 33

How Apuleius came to a city named Hipate, and was lodged in one Milos house, and brought him letters from Demea of Corinth.

THE SEVENTH CHAPTER — 35

How Apuleius going to buy fish, met with his companion Pythias.

THE EIGHTH CHAPTER — 41

How Apuleius fortuned to meet with his Cousin Byrrhena.

THE NINTH CHAPTER   45

How Apuleius fell in love with Fotis.

                 THE TENTH CHAPTER   48

How Byrrhena sent victuals unto Apuleius, and
how hee talked with Milo of Diophanes, and
how he lay with Fotis.

                 THE ELEVENTH CHAPTER   52

How Apuleius supped with Byrrhena, and what a
strange tale Bellephoron told at the table.

                 THE TWELFTH CHAPTER   63

How Apuleius was taken and put in prison for
murther.

                 THE THIRTEENTH CHAPTER   64

How Apuleius was accused by an old man, and
how hee answered for himselfe.

                 THE FOURTEENTH CHAPTER   67

How Apuleius was accused by two women, and
how the slaine bodies were found blowne
bladders.

                 THE FIFTEENTH CHAPTER   70

How Fotis told to Apuleius, what witchcraft
her mistresse did use.

                 THE SIXTEENTH CHAPTER   74

How Fotis brought Apuleius to see her Mistresse
enchant.

                 THE SEVENTEENTH CHAPTER   76

How Apuleius thinking to be turned into a Bird,
was turned into an Asse, and how hee was led
away by Theeves.

                 THE EIGHTEENTH CHAPTER   83

How Apuleius thinking to eat Roses, was cruelly
beaten by a Gardner, and chased by dogs.

THE NINETEENTH CHAPTER 85

How Apuleius was prevented of his purpose, and how the Theeves came to their den.

THE TWENTIETH CHAPTER 91

How Trasileon was disguised in a Beares skin, and how he was handled.

THE TWENTY-FIRST CHAPTER 95

How the Theeves stole away a Gentlewoman, and brought her to their den.

THE TWENTY-SECOND CHAPTER 98

The most pleasant and delectable tale of the Marriage of Cupid and Psyches.

THE TWENTY-THIRD CHAPTER 130

How Apuleius carried away the Gentlewoman, and how they were taken againe by the theeves, and what a kind of death was invented for them.

THE TWENTY-FOURTH CHAPTER 137

How hee that was left behinde at Hippata did bring newes concerning the robbery of Miloes house, came home and declared to his Company, that all the fault was laid to one Apuleius his charge.

THE TWENTY-FIFTH CHAPTER 142

How the death of the Asse, and the Gentlewoman was stayed.

THE TWENTY-SIXTH CHAPTER 143

How all the Theeves were brought asleepe by their new companion.

THE TWENTY-SEVENTH CHAPTER 145

How the Gentlewoman was carried home by her husband while the theeves were asleepe, and how much Apuleius was made of.

THE TWENTY-EIGHTH CHAPTER   148

How Apuleius was made a common Asse to fetch
home wood, and how he was handled by a boy.

THE TWENTY-NINTH CHAPTER   150

How Apuleius was accused of Lechery by the boy.

THE THIRTIETH CHAPTER   152

How the boy that lead Apuleius to the field,
was slaine in the wood.

THE THIRTY-FIRST CHAPTER   154

How Apuleius was cruelly beaten by the Mother
of the boy that was slaine.

THE THIRTY-SECOND CHAPTER   159

How a young man came and declared the miserable
death of Lepolemus and his wife Charites.

THE THIRTY-THIRD CHAPTER   166

How Apuleius was lead away by the Horsekeeper:
and what danger he was in.

THE THIRTY-FOURTH CHAPTER   169

How the shepheards determined to abide in a
certaine wood to cure their wounds.

THE THIRTY-FIFTH CHAPTER   170

How a woman killed her selfe and her child, because her husband haunted harlots.

THE THIRTY-SIXTH CHAPTER   171

How Apuleius was cheapned by divers persons,
and how they looked in his mouth to know his age.

THE THIRTY-SEVENTH CHAPTER   179

How Apuleius saved himselfe from the Cooke,
breaking his halter, and of other things that
happened.

THE THIRTY-EIGHTH CHAPTER   181

Of the deceipt of a Woman which made her husband Cuckold.

THE THIRTY-NINTH CHAPTER   183

How the Priests of the goddesse Siria were taken and put in prison, and how Apuleius was sold to a Baker.

THE FORTIETH CHAPTER   186

How Apuleius was handled by the Bakers wife, which was a harlot.

THE FORTY-FIRST CHAPTER   188

How Barbarus being jealous over his wife, commanded that shee should be kept close in his house, and what happened.

THE FORTY-SECOND CHAPTER   190

How Apuleius after the Baker was hanged, was sold to a Gardener, and what dreadfull things happened.

THE FORTY-THIRD CHAPTER   200

How Apuleius was found by his shadow.

THE FORTY-FOURTH CHAPTER   205

How the souldier drave Apuleius away, and how he came to a Captaines house, and what happened there.

THE FORTY-FIFTH CHAPTER   213

How Apuleius was sold to two bretheren, whereof one was a Baker, and the other a Cooke, and how finely and daintily he fared.

THE FORTY-SIXTH CHAPTER   217

How a certaine Matron fell in love with Apuleius, how hee had his pleasure with her, and what other things happened.

THE FORTY-SEVENTH CHAPTER   231

How Apuleius by Roses and prayer returned to his humane shape.

THE FORTY-EIGHTH CHAPTER   241-49

How the parents and friends of Apuleius heard news that he was alive and in health.

FINIS

APPENDIX B

OTHELLO AND THE APOLOGIA OF APULEIUS

Othello's defence of himself against the charge of witchcraft (I.3.76ff.)[1] is one of the most memorable passages in the tragedy and one that does much to establish the audience's high opinion of the Moor. Scholars have established that for Othello's apologia Shakespeare borrowed, as was his custom, from more than a single source. With his enthusiasm for trial scenes Shakespeare recalled the defence of C. Furius Cresinus in Pliny's Natural History (Philemon Holland, trans.) against the accusation that he had acquired a great deal of property by means of sorcery.[2] Some of the diction, including the address, "My maisters," and the use of traveller's tales later in the translation are particularly compelling. The dramatist also made use of certain phrases and ideas of travel and hardship from the address to the reader by Sir Lewes Lewkenor in his translation of Cardinal Contareno's The Commonwealth and Government of Venice. Of course, neither Lewkenor nor Pliny offers a defence against the charge of using witchcraft for the procuring of a bride. For that Shakespeare used the Apologia of Apuleius, one of the works recommended by Humanist educators of the Renaissance for grammar school study.[3]

Shakespeare made considerable use in Othello of Apuleius' Metamorphoses both in William Adlington's translation and in the original Latin.[4] He might have been led easily to the Apologia with its central accusation of witchcraft, if he did not know it already, by Venus' argument in the Metamorphoses that the marriage of Cupid and Psyche is shameful and illegal because it had been conducted in private and without witnesses (Bk IV, ch. 9). The similar view that something is wrong with the marriage of Apuleius and Aemilia Pudentilla is made by the accusers of Apuleius in the Apologia (ch. 88). Whatever the link that led Shakespeare to the second of the works of Apuleius which he could mine, and whatever the difficulties presented to him by Apuleius' baroque, indeed Euphuistic Latin,[5] the elements in the Apologia found also in Othello are too numerous and suggestive to be coincidental.

The Apologia is Apuleius' rather confident defence of himself against the charge that he had gained the love of his wife by the use of charms, drugs, and magic. Material common to both Othello and the Apologia include: 1) the charge of witchcraft made for the purpose of annulling a marriage (the pervasive concern with magic and witchcraft present in the Metamorphoses, Apologia and Othello is absent from Shakespeare's prime source of plot in Gli Hecatommithi, III.7);   2) the central concern with reputation;   3) a magical handkerchief;   4) a marriage of persons disproportionate in age and country;   5) a marriage which begins in a kind of elopement (in Cinthio Desdemona's relatives grudgingly consent to the wedding);   6) the presence of an epileptic and a drunkard;   7) the theme of subornation; and finally,   8) diction unique in the Shakespearian canon, and derived from words present in the Apologia.

    The defence begins with Apuleius explaining to the judges how he came to be accused by the old man Sicinius Aemilianus of magical practices. In this attitude of elderly accuser Sicinius is a forerunner of Brabantio. In brief, the circumstances were these: Apuleius had been urged to marry the widow Aemilia Pudentilla (one notes both the Folio spelling of the name of Iago's wife and the intimate of Desdemona, a name not given in Cinthio, and the significant meaning of her second name which links her with the modest Desdemona). The chief advocate of this marriage, Aemilia's son Pontianus, reversed his position under the envy-ridden influence of his uncle, Sicinius Pontianus ("disappointment and envy are the sole causes that have involved me in this trial," 66.8-9).[6] Pontianus died, but his brother, Pudens, at the urging of Sicinius, placed a charge of witchcraft against Apuleius, accusing him of arts inhibited ("magicorum maleficorum"), and of having forced Pudentilla into marriage ("that Pudentilla had never thought of marriage until I compelled her to be mine by my exercise of the black art; that I alone had been found to outrage as it were the virgin purity of her widowhood by incantations and love philtres," 69.15-16).[7] In addition to playing a Brabantio-like role, Sicinius Pontianus displays some of the tactics of Iago as slanderer:

> he persistently shirks the perilous task of a direct attack, and perseveres in his assumption of the safe role of the accuser's legal representative . . . Just as a good man studiously avoids the repetition of a sin once committed, so men of depraved character repeat their past offence with increased confidence, and, I may add, the more often they do so, the more openly they display their impudence. For honour is like

a garment; the older it gets, the more carelessly it is worn (2.15-16, 2.7-9).[8]

Apuleius' defence is made "pro integritate pudoris mei," and it is presented "lest by passing over some of their more ridiculous charges, to have tacitly admitted their truth" (3.10, 22-3).[9] The theme of reputation is at the heart of the Apologia, as it is in Othello,[10] with its defence of Apuleius' existimatio against the invidia of Sicinius.

The prosecution seeks to use as evidence for the guilt of Apuleius a certain handkerchief which they say, although they have not seen it, is a token of magic. This handerkerchief is made of linen, not of silk as in Othello, but as in Othello is associated with Egypt (". . . that handkerchief/ Did an Egyptian to my mother give," III.4.55-6), and "the purest of all growths and among the best of all the fruits of the earth, is used by the holy priests of Egypt, not only for clothing and raiment but as a veil for sacred things," 56.8-9).[11] As in Othello much is made of the whereabouts of the "magical" handkerchief ("although I might deny that I had deposited any handkerchief of mine in Pontianus' library," 55.7-8).[12] Apuleius mockingly tells Pontianus who had not actually seen the handkerchief: "and yet you assert that it was some instrument of magic," (53.5-6).[13] In words with which Thomas Rymer might have been pleased Apuleius punningly states: "how much perspiration this one handkerchief would cause the innocent," (55.2-3).[14] This punning on the similar terms for sweat and handkerchief (sudores/sudariolo) reminds one of the great trouble caused by the missing handkerchief in Othello, and of the sweat referred to in Act III, scene 4, the scene of the description of the Egyptian origin of the handkerchief which has magic in the web of it[15] at line forty-two.[16] Apuleius concludes by arguing that the handkerchief is not what they think it is; it is a religious article and not a magical instrument. If Brabantio had known of the allegedly magical handkerchief of Othello, it would have been the "evidence" he could have used very well in his prosecution of Othello. However, Shakespeare was more interested in the Othello-Iago-Desdemona complex than he was in that of Othello-Brabantio-Desdemona, and accordingly, kept the handkerchief for an emotional trial greater than any legal confrontation.

Othello is considerably older than Desdemona, a factor which Shakespeare added to the description of Cinthio's Moor who is handsome. In the Apologia there is a difference in the couple's ages. The woman is older, but, as in Othello, the senior partner is loved for virtue rather than beauty ("I saw Othello's visage in his mind," I.3.252, and, "I had had ample opportunity for observing Pudentilla's character, for I had lived for a whole year in her company and realized how rich was her endowment of good qualities," 73.21-3).[17] This reversal of the couple's ages in the movement from the Apologia to Othello is a parallel to the reversal of gender in the flaming minister speech of V.2.1-22 where Othello is in the role of the would-be murderer, Psyche, and Desdemona is in the position of the sleeping and innocent Cupid.[18]

Othello is a Moor in Venice; less unusual but nevertheless analogous is Apuleius' being a Numidian stranger in Oea. Although both defendants, Othello and Apuleius, are Africans, only Othello is black. Yet the issue of blackness and the theme of racism occur in the Apologia when Apuleius attempts to insult Sicinius Pontianus with the expression of mock puzzlement: "I am not naturally of a quarrelsome disposition, and secondly, I am glad to say that until quite recently you might have been white or black for all I knew. Even now my knowledge of you is inadequate" (16.24-6).[16]

In both defences the narrative of travel plays an important part in making the woman interested in the man, directly in the case of Othello and Desdemona and indirectly in the relationship of Apuleius and Pudentilla.

Othello and Desdemona elope, an act which is an addition by Shakespeare to the materials in his known sources. Apuleius and Pudentilla, instead of marrying as expected in the city, escape to the country for a private service.

Apuleius is accused of working his witchcraft upon a boy who is so overcome that he falls down. In his defence Apuleius distinguishes epilepsy from witchcraft.[20] In the tragedy Iago specifically explains the Moor's collapse at IV.1.50 as epilepsy. In the Apologia Apuleius adds a particular piece of medical information about epilepsy which is of interest in any evaluation of the alertness of Othello. He points out that the poisonous humours rise to "that royal part of a man's spirit which is endowed with the power of reason and is enthroned in the head of man, that is, its citadel and palace" (50.13-15).[21] The Greeks call it the divine disease, for this sickness does outrage to the rational part of the soul, which is by far the most holy" (50. 23-4).[22]

The drunkard in the Apologia, Junius Crassus, is not so important a character as is Cassio in the drama, but inasmuch as there is no warrant for Cassio's drunkenness in the known sources, it is of interest to note that this weakness in Crassus is a part of his general lack of moral and physical propriety. Crassus has spent his inheritance, is willing to bear false witness, and, among other things, lacks his beard even though he is a physically mature young man (59.21).[23] Shakespeare who had shifted genders and ages in his borrowing from Apuleius for his treatment of the married couple may have divided the weaknesses of Crassus, an agent of the invidious Sicinius Pontianus, giving the inebriation to Cassio, and the lying, spending, and beardlessness to Roderigo (a character not found in Cinthio), who it will be remembered was urged by Iago at the end of the trial scene to "defeat thy favour with an usurp'd beard" (I.3.340-1).[24]

In both Othello and the Apologia there is the issue of the manipulation of witnesses. Desdemona, of all people to invoke such a technical term, tells of her misinterpretation of Othello's hostile attitude, "But now I find I had suborn'd the witness,/ And he's indicted falsely" (III.4.151-2). The subornation of witnesses is a theme in the defence as Apuleius ironically tells the court: "Maximus, and you, gentlemen, his assessors, I fear you may think that I have suborned my accusers to bring these charges" (67.19-20).[25]

There are several words unique in the canon to Othello, or used uniquely in the play, which derive from Apuleius. Some of these terms come from the Metamorphoses and its translation by Adlington.[26] Others, the adjectives "acerb" (I.3.350) and "ocular" (III.3.360), and the phrase at the end of the trial scene, "led by the nose as asses are," (I.3.401-2), have been prompted by the diction of the Apologia.

The two terms "acerbe" and "ocular," each unique in the canon, are often cited by those who support the idea that Shakespeare read Cinthio in the Italian and not in a French translation. 'Acerbe' is thought to derive from Cinthio's "in acerbissimo odio." Perhaps, although it should be noted that there are many instances of 'acerbus' in Apuleius, both in the Metamorphoses and in the Apologia where "acerbissimas" appears in reference to the hostile letters of Pudens to his mother whom earlier he had loved. "Ocular" is sometimes thought to come from the Italian "occhi." Possibly, but one notes that "ocular" is neatly Latinate and that the Apologia has a large number of references to "oculos" and "oculis," to seeing and to spying.

Florio in his World of Words translated "menar per il naso" as "to lead by the nose, to make a fool of."[27] An ass is a metaphor for a fool clearly enough, but one notices how the young Pontianus under the influence of his wife is led by his father-in-law against his mother's remarriage. The operative words are: "To be brief, he so wrought upon the simple-minded young man, who was, moreover, a slave to the charms of his new bride, as to mould him to his will and move him from his purpose," (77.10-12).[28] "Obfrenatum" in a context of the newly wedded means literally "led by the nose."[29]

Not at all unique in the canon or the play is "purse." Indeed, the word appears a dozen times in Othello as part of the theme of economics and theft.[30] It has been argued that Roderigo is used by Iago in a manner analogous to that of Sir Andrew Aguecheek by Sir Toby Belch in Twelfth Night, holding out the promise of love while using the would-be lover's funds. Almost all of the references to "purse" in Othello are to filling it, but in the central scene we have Iago's "Who steals my purse steals trash," an aphorism parallelling an illustration in Wilson's Rhetorique.[31] Apuleius, however, in the course of his denial that any magical power is to be found in his handkerchief compares the prosecution's belief that something of importance lies within to that of the equally mistaken belief of the companions of Ulysses. They had made something of nothing when they imagined the contents of Ulysses' bag which contained only wind. Apuleius says that they were "busied about purses" ("manticularentur" from "manticula" meaning "a little purse").[32] The context of the Apologia stresses the making of something from nothing. Iago is busied about purses, both the liberal purse of Roderigo which he can use and the rhetorical stolen purse of III.3.157; in both cases he is attempting to make something of nothing.

The number of elements of circumstance, plot, theme, and diction common to the Apologia and Othello seems too large to be the result of coincidence. The Apologia begins with a statement of unsubstantiated charges by an older man who is related to the bride of magical practices used by a foreign husband in order to gain the woman. Heavy stress is put on the disproportionate age differential between husband and wife, admittedly in inverse relationship to that in Othello, and the whereabouts of an allegedly magical handkerchief. Apuleius, like Othello, is vitally concerned with his reputation. Like Othello he has passed the prime of physical energy. In his case his studious habits have dried the sap of his vital juices.[33] As in the tragedy, the couple in the defence was created by the mutual admiration of moral qualities. In both works there is an elopement, an epileptic, and an "Aemilia." It may well be that there existed a now lost English translation of the Apologia available to Shakespeare, or it may be that Shakespeare who had read the Latin of Apuleius' Metamorphoses had read the Latin of Apuleius' Apologia. At all events, the dramatist who had used in Othello Apuleius' novel for Iago's "mandragora" observation[34] and the Moor's flaming minister speech, borrowed for Othello's apologia, as well as for the incriminatory handkerchief, from Apuleius' splendidly ornate defence of himself against the charge of having gained a bride by means of witchcraft.

NOTES

1. Line references are to The Riverside Shakespeare, ed. G.B. Evans (Boston, 1974).

2. See Kenneth Muir, The Sources of Shakespeare's Plays (London, 1977), 186-7.

3. See T.W. Baldwin, William Shakespeare's Small Latine and Lesse Greeke (Urbana, 1944), I, 190; II, 26, 185, 247.

4. See above pages

5. See the note in H.E. Butler and A.S. Owen, ed., Apulei Apologia (Oxford, 1914), lv.

6. Chapter and line references as in Butler and Owen. Translation here and in the following citations are those of H.E. Butler (with some few adjustments) in his The Apologia and Florida of Apuleius (Oxford, 1909).

7. "Priusquam foret magicis maleficiis a me coacta, me solum repertum, qui viduitatis eius velut quondam virginitatem carminibus et venenis violarem." For Iago as dealer in evil potions, see Robert B. Heilman, "Dr. Iago and His Potions," VQR, XXVIII (1952), 568-584, and for the role of black magic in the entire tragedy see James A.S. McPeek, "The 'Arts Inhibited' and the Meaning of Othello," Boston University Studies in English, I (1955), 129-147.

8) "Ita totiens ab accusandi periculo profugus in assistendi venia perseveravit . . . ita qui ingenio malo est confidentius integrat ac iam de cetero quo saepius, eo apertius delinquit. pudor enim veluti vestis quanto obsoletior est, tanto incuriosus habetur."

9) "Quid maculae aut inhonestamenti in me admittam."

10) See especially Madeline Doran, "Good Name in Othello," SEL, VII (1967), 195-217.

11) "Sed enim mundissima lini seges inter optumas fruges terra exorta non modo indutui et amictui sanctissimis Aegyptiorum sacerdotibus, sed opertui quoque rebus sacris usurpatur."

12. "At ego quanquam omnino positum ullum sudarium eum in bibliotheca Pontiani possim negare."

13. "Tamen illa contendis instrumenta magiae fuisse."

14. "Quantique sudores innocentibus hoc uno sudariolo adferantur." This pun is pointed out in the anonymous Bohn translation in The Works of Apuleius (London, 1853), 303.

15. For the argument that the phrase, "prophetic fury" comes from Ariosto's description of Cassandra at the end of Orlando Furioso, see Muir, Sources (1977), 183.

16. See the argument that the handkerchief is a vehicle of black magic in McPeek, 144.

17. "Non quin ego Pudentillam iam anno perpeti adsiduo convictu probe spactassem et virtutium eius dotes explorassem."

18. Noted above on page

19. "Praeter quod non sum iurgiosus, etiam libenter te nuper usque albus an ater esses ignoravi et adhuc hercle non satis novi."

20. Butler and Owen, 144, cite as a gloss on "tu potius caducus," Julius Caesar I.2.254-5: "Brut.: ''Tis very like: he hath the falling sickness.' Cass.: 'No, Caesar hath it not; but you and I/ And honest Casca, we have the falling sickness.'"

21. "Regalem partem animi . . . quae ratione pollens verticem hominis velut arcem et regiam insedit."

22. "Quod animi partem rationalem quae longe sanctissimast."

23. "Caput invenis barba et capillo populatum."

24. For the argument that the relationship between Roderigo and Iago is based on that of Sir Andrew Aguecheek and Sir Toby Belch in Twelfth Night see Muir, Sources (1977), 191.

25. "Maxime quique in consilio estis, ne demissum et subornatum a me accusatorem putetis."

26. Noted on pages

27. Noted by M.R. Ridley in his New Arden edition of Othello.

28. "Invenem simplicem, praeterea novae nuptae illecebris obfrenatum suo arbitratu de via deflectit."

29. So glossed by Butler who notes the spelling 'offrenatum' in Metamorphoses 6.19 where Shakespeare may have also seen the word. For the 'overdetermination' of sources see the review of Emrys Jones, The Origins of Shakespeare by John Harvey, Essays in Criticism (July, 1977), 266.

30. See Muir, Sources (1957), 139, referring to the work of R.B. Heilman.

31. Noted by Ridley.

32. Butler and Owen, 118.

33. See Apologia, 4.24 "sucum exsorbet."

34. See Metamorphoses 10, 11, 12.

Index of Shakespearean Characters

Aaron, 14,16,17,19,20, 21,164
Adonis, 7-9,20
Adriana, 11
Aemilia, 13
Ajax, 98,100
Alcibiades, 112
Andronicus, Marcus, 15
Andronicus, Titus, 16, 17,21
Antigonus, 149
Antipholus of Ephesus, 11,12
Antipholus of Syracuse, 10,11
Antony, Mark, 71-73,128, 130,131,132,133,134, 137,165
Apemantus, 111,112
Ariel, 154,162
Armado, Don, 32
Arviragus, 146-148,162
Autolycus, 149,150,151, 153,164

Bardolph, 57,58,59,67
Bawd, 142-143
Belarius, 146,147
Berowne, 28
Bertram, 102,103,105
Bianca, 89
Borachio, 65
Bottom, xi,32,33,38,39, 40,90,164
Boult, 142-143,144
Boy, 74
Boyet, 27,28,31
Brabantio, 90,174,175
Brutus, 135

Cade, Jack, 1-3,20,73, 164
Caliban, 154,162
Captain, 119
Cassio, 177
Ceres, 155-156
Chiron, 14,18,19,23
Claudius, 85,86,103

Cleopatra, 73,128-130,132, 133,134,137,163,164
Cloten, 160
Conrade, 64
Cordelia, 117,119,121,164
Coriolanus, 135-137
Cornelius, 144-145
Cressida, 97,101,113

Demetrius, 14,18,19,23
Desdemona, 90,91,92,109,163, 174,175,176
Dogberry, 51,62-67,106,113, 164
Dromio of Ephesus, 11,12
Dromio of Syracuse, 10,11, 12,13

Edgar, 117-118
Elbow, 67,106-107,108,113, 164
Escalus, 42

Falstaff, 51,53-54,55-56, 57-62,67,68,69,163,164
Ferdinand, 154,155
Flavius, 112
Fool (Lear's), 119
Ford, 60,61
Ford, Mistress, 68,164
Forrest, 4

Gertrude, xxi,82-84, 103- 104,163
Goneril, 117
Guiderius, 146-148,162

Hal, 51-58,67,164
Hamlet, 75-76,78-81,84-86, 92,163
Helen, 98-99,100
Helena, 102-106,113,163,164
Hermione, 153
Hotspur, 51-53,57,67,164

Iachimo, 146
Iago, 87-88,89-91,163,174- 182

183

Imogen, 144-145,146, 147,148

Joan (greasy), 30-31, 164
Jourdain, Margery, 2
Julia, 27
Juliet, 41,164
Juno, 156

King Henry the Fourth, 52,55
King of Navarre, 28

Laertes, 80,81,82,85,86
Lafew, 103
Lavatch, 104
Lavinia, 16,17
Lawrence, Friar, 41-42, 84
Lear, 118-121,137,163
Leontes, 153
Lepidus, 71-73
Luciana, 11
Lucius, son of Titus, 19
Lucius, grandson of Titus, 19
Lucius, Caius, 146
Ludovico, 91
Lysimachus, 143-144

Macbeth, 73,124-128,137, 138,163
Macduff, 127
Malcolm, 141
Maria, 31
Marina, 142-144
Menenius, 135,137

Northumberland, 51

Oberon, 34,35,36,39
Octavius, 73
Ophelia, 76-81,82,83, 92,163,164
Othello, 87-92,109,111, 163,173-179

Page, 60

Paris (Trojan), 98-99
Paulina, 151-152
Pedro, Don, 66
Pericles, 142
Phrynia, 112
Pisanio, 145,146
Pistol, 58,67
Poins, 57
Polonius, 75-81,92,103
Porter, 126-127
Posthumus, 148
Proteus, 27
Puck, 35-36,154

Quickly, Mistress, 57-59, 67,68,164

Regan, 117
Roderigo, 89,177,178,181
Romeo, 41
Rosaline, 28
Rossillion, Countess, 103-105,113,163

Sicinius, 135
Silvia, 26,119
Slender, 60

Tamora, 14,16-20,164
Tearsheet, Doll, 58-59,67, 164
Thersites, 98-100
Timandra, 112
Timon, 109-113,163
Titania, 33-36,39-40,90,164
Troilus, 97,100-102,113,164
Tyrrel, 3-4,91,109,111

Ulysses, 100

Valentine, 25-27,164
Venus, 7-9
Verges, 64

Westmoreland, 54
Witches, 124,138

Yorkist Princes, 3-4,20,91, 109,111,163

Index of Apuleian Characters

Aristomenus, xiii,58,59, 60,67,68,69,98,112

baker's daughter, 59, 74,77-78
baker's wife, 57,77,86, 170
Byrrhena, xxii,9,30,61-62,146,151-152,167, 168

Captain of the Watch, 64
Charite, xiii,xvi,xx,7,8, 17,18,26,27,53,55,56, 98,111,119,135,143-144,147-148,149,151, 157,170
Corinthian matron, 33, 47,93,95,171
cowardly soldier, 55
Cupid, passim

evil servant, 91

fishmonger, 74-75
Fotis, 16,30-32,47,62, 97,99,146,168

Isis, 39,128,130,164

Jupiter, 101,103,133

lascivious servant, 14, 51-52,67,151
Lepolemus, 5,26-27,47, 53,55-56,67,134, 143-144,147,149,170
Lucius, passim

Meroe, xvi,xxi,xxii,2, 11,58-59,67,68,69, 98,112,167
Milo, 9,13,30,107-108, 138,168,169

Pamphile, xxii,2,9,11, 13,62,124,138,146

Panthia, 58,67,68,69,98,112
physician (ancient), 41-42, 47,84-86,87-89,91,93, 119-122,144-145,157
physician (evil), 141-142, 157
Pithias, 64, 74-75,86
priests, 136,162
Psyche, passim

Socrates, xvi,58-59,69,98
stepmother (adulterous) xiii,xviii,74,84-86, 93,104-106,113,144-145, 149,157,162

Thelyphron, 11
Thrasileon, 73,124-128,169
Thrasyllus, xx,5,27,47,55-57,67

Venus, vii,34-36,45-46,79-80,81,82,83,92,100,129, 130-131,136

Zephyrus, 36,41,162

Index of Names

Actaeon, 61-62,67,69, 146,152
Adlard, John, 139
Adlington, William, passim
Allen, Don Cameron, xxvi,159
Allot, R., xxiii
Althaea, 2,57-58
Andrews, Michael Cameron, 94-95
Aptekar, Jane, xxvi
Apuleius, passim
Aretino, Pietro, 152
Ariosto, 181
Aubrey, John 63,66
Augustine, St., Bishop of Hippo, xii
Ausonius, xii

Baldwin, T.W., xxv,23,180
Barton, Anne Righter, 94,102
Belleforest, F. de, 83, 84
Boccaccio, xii,xxiv,102, 103
Booth, Stephen, 50
Boschetta, Isabella, 153
Brooke, Nicholas, 138
Brooks, Harold F., xxv,23
Buchanan, George, 123,128
Bullough, Geoffrey, xi, xxv,xxvi,22,23,33, 66,69,94,115,138, 151,158
Bush, Douglas, 49
Butler, H.E., 180,181, 182

Chambers, E.K., xxvii
Chapman, George, xvii, xviii,xix,xx,xxvii,5
Chaucer, xii
Cicero, 72
Cinthio, Geraldi, 174,175, 177
Connell, Dorothy, xxvi

Creizenach, Wilhelm, xxvii
Chettle, Henry, xviii,xxiii
Comes, Natale, xv

Daniel, Samuel, 41
Davis, Walter R., 69
Day, John, xviii,xxiii
Dekker, Thomas, xiii,xviii, xix,xxiii,144
Dick, Oliver Lawson, 69
Doran, Madeline, 180
Douce, Francis, 138

Eccles, Mark, 114
Edwards, Philip, 141,158
Erasmus, xii,xiii,xxvi,86, 112
Erlich, Bruce, 114
d'Este, Isabella, 153
Evans, G.B., 22,68,69,180

Ferguson, W.K., xxvi
Fisch, Harold, 130,139
Florio, John, 178
Fulgentius, xii
Frye, Northrop, 37
Frye, Roland Mushat, xxv

Gascoigne, George, 31-32, 48,97,114
Gaselee, S., 22,35,94
Geckle, George, xix,xxvii
Generosa, Sister M., 34-35,48
Geoffrey of Monmouth, xii
Gerard, John, 27
Gibbons, Brian, 50
Golding, Arthur, 4,5,6,8, 43
Gonzaga, 153
Gosson, Stephen, xviii,123
Gower, John, 143
Grafton, R., 2
Greene, Robert, 149

Haight, Elizabeth H., xxv
Halstead, W.L., xxvii, xxviii

Hamilton, A.C., xv
Hammond, Antony, xxv
Harsnett, Samuel, 122-123
Hartt, Frederick, 158
Harvey, John, 182
Harvey, Gabriel, xix, 62-63,66,69
Hastings, W.T., 23
Heilman, R.B., 180,182
Hexter, J.H., xxvi
Heywood, Thomas, xviii, xxii-xxiii,xxvii
Hoeniger, F.D., 158
Holinshed, R., 124,138
Holland, Philemon, 128, 173
Holloway, John, 138
Horace, 44
Hosley, Richard, 68
Hotson, J.L., 139
Humphrys, A.R., 68
Hunter, George K., 114

Ingram, W.G., 46,50

Jenkins, Harold, 94,95
Jones, Emrys, 94,115, 138,182
Jones, Inigo, xxiii
Jonson, Ben, xviii, xxi-xxii,xxvii,10

Kafka, Franz, 21
Kaplan, Joel, xx,xxvii
Keats, John, 102
Kermode, Frank, 38-40, 49,99
Kökeritz, Helge, 114

Lactantius, xii
Lever, J.W., 108,114
Lewkenor, Sir Lewes, 173
Lloyd, Michael, 128,138,139
Lucian, 86,112

Maclure, Millar, xxvi

Marlowe, Christopher, xvii, xxvi
Marston, John, xviii,xix, xxi,xxvii,35
Martianus, Capella, xii
Martin, L.C., xxvi
Massey, Irving, 23
Maxwell, J.C., 23
McKerrow, R.B., 94
McManaway, J.G., 22
McPeek, James A.S., 37-38, 49,56,180,181
Meleager, 2,8,57
Meres, Francis, 16
Miller, Clarence H., xxvi
Milton, John, xvii,xxiv, xxvi,xxviii
Montemayor, J. de, 25
Montgomerie, William, 95
Moore, John R., 48
More, Sir Thomas, xiii, xxvi,86
Morris, Brian, 23
Muir, Kenneth, xi,xxv,22, 33,48,94,123,180,181, 182
Mynors, R.A.B., xxvi

Nashe, Thomas, xix,21,23, 24,51,62-63,84
North, Sir Thomas, 71,72, 129

Omerod, David, 38-39,49
Ovid, xi,4-8,19,43,44
Owen, A.S., 180,181,182

Pafford, J.H.P., 153,158
Painter, William, 103
Partridge, Eric, 31,48, 112,115, 139
Payne, F. Anne, xxv
Pearson, Jacqueline, 62,69
Petronius, xx
Plautus, 10,23
Pliny, elder, 173
Plutarch, xi,71,128,129, 133,134
Pope, Alexander, 81
Poussin, N., 152

Redpath, Theodore, 46,50
Reich, Hermann, 48
Rhodes, Neil, 21,23
Riche, Barnabe, 53
Ricks, Christopher, xxvi
Ridley, M.R., 182
Robertson, Jean, xxvi
Roche, Thomas P., xxvi
Romano, Giulio, 152-153
Rubens, P.P., 152
Rymer, Thomas, 175

Salingar, Leo, 114
Saxo Grammaticus, 83,84
Scot, Reginald, 32-33
Shady, Raymond C., xxviii
Shakespeare, passim
Shepherd, Geoffrey, xxvi
Sidney, Sir Philip, xiii, xix,xxvi,122,138
Spencer, T.J.B., 94
Spenser, Edmund, xiv,xxiv, xxvi
Starnes, D.T., 5,7,10,11, 22,25-27,33-34,35,48, 55,124,129,138,139, 144-146,149-151,154-155,158
Surtz, E.L., xxvi

Theobald, Lewis, 80,81,94
Theobald, William, 114
Thompson, Ann, xxv
Thomson, D.F.S., xxvi
Titian, 152
Twine, Laurence, 142-143

Ure, Peter, 102,114

Vasari, Giorgio, 152,153
Velz, John, xi,xxv,48
Virgil, 88
Vives, Juan, xii

Waddington, Raymond B., xxvii
Walsh, P.G., xxv,xxvii,23, 49,158
Watkins, W.B.C., 23
West, David, 49

Whibley, Charles, 4,22, 138
Wilkinson, L.P., 88,95
Wilson, Frank P., 69
Wilson, J. Dover, 22,35-37,49
Wilson, Thomas, 178
Wind, Edgar, 29,48,95
Woodman, Tony, 49